HITLER'S GHOST SHIPS

Graf Spee, Scharnhorst and Disguised German Raiders

BRITANNIA NAVAL HISTORIES OF WORLD WAR II

University of Plymouth Press

This edition first published in the United Kingdom in 2012 by
University of Plymouth Press, Formation Zone, Roland Levinsky
Building, Drake Circus, Plymouth, Devon, PL4 8AA, United Kingdom.

Paperback   ISBN 978-1-84102-308-3
Hardback   ISBN 978-1-84102-307-6

A CIP catalogue record of this book is available from the British Library

Publisher: Paul Honeywill
Commissioning Editor: Charlotte Carey
Publishing Assistants: Alex Hannon and Beth Skinner
Series Editors: G. H. Bennett, J. E. Harrold and R. Porter

Content courtesy of Britannia Museum, Britannia Royal Naval College,
Dartmouth, TQ6 0HJ

Cover image © Edward Stables 2012

Typeset by University of Plymouth Press in Janson 10/14pt
Printed and bound by Short Run Press, Bittern Road, Sowton Industrial
Estate, Exeter, EX2 7LW

The historical documents reproduced here appear as unedited text, apart
from minor changes made to date formats and corrections to typing errors
found in the original.

Britannia Royal Naval College

A majestic landmark, which towers above the harbour town of Dartmouth in Devon, Britannia Royal Naval College was designed by royal architect Sir Aston Webb to project an image of British sea power. A fine example of Edwardian architecture, the building has prepared future generations of officers for the challenges of service and leadership since 1905.

The Britannia Museum opened in 1999 to safeguard the College's rich collection of historic artefacts, art and archives and promote greater public understanding of Britain's naval and maritime heritage, as a key element in the development of British history and culture. It also aims to instil a sense of identity and ethos in the Officer Cadets that pass through the same walls as their forbears, from great admirals to national heroes to royalty.

Contents

Foreword

Admiral Sir Jonathon Band

The British military has been heavily involved in land campaigns: this, and a lack of recognition of the importance of the sea, has led to overlooking the United Kingdom as an island nation, dependent on trade and the safe and timely arrival of ships. Air travel and cargo has not changed this.

Throughout its history, the Royal Navy has protected the nation's merchant ships and engaged enemies that have threatened them. This is the strategic backdrop to *Hitler's Ghost Ships*, one title in the series BRITANNIA NAVAL HISTORIES OF WORLD WAR II. The relative strength of the *Kriegsmarine* vis-à-vis the Royal Navy clearly did not allow the former to deliberately engage in direct navy-to-navy operations. Apart from undertaking the roles of Homeland Defence and Support to the Army, the *Kriegsmarine* followed the asymmetric option of attacking Britain's maritime interests at their weakest points, and these were the independent sailings of British shipping. Apart from the obvious damage to trade, the campaign severely stretched the Royal Navy, which had not recovered from the lack of investment of the inter-war years. The Navy was not scaled to deal with the challenges of the North Atlantic and Mediterranean as well as a wide-ranging, deep-ocean search and destroy mission. Cruisers, in particular, were needed to search out the German auxiliaries and these were in short supply, due to the demands of, and losses in, the Mediterranean campaign.

While the Nazi major surface units, such as the *Graf Spee* and *Admiral Scheer*, conducted more well-known operations, it was the activities of the German auxiliary cruisers, such as *Atlantis* and *Kormoran*, that warrant most attention. These converted merchantmen were imaginatively commanded and conducted long arduous patrols about the trade routes, thousands of miles from home, with minimal support. Finding and destroying these ships required good and timely intelligence, expeditious localisation, accurate look-out and, ultimately, rapid and accurate gunnery. By the end of 1943, the campaign was effectively over. All but one of the auxiliaries was destroyed, but not before they had collectively sunk 129 vessels, a total of 800,611 tons – an impressive feat.

Hitler's Ghost Ships covers a relatively less well-known aspect of the Royal Navy's World War II endeavours, but is no less interesting for it. Indeed, patrolling and providing maritime security is the day-to-day business of the Navy today, as it was in both world wars and has been for 400 years. The Royal Navy has an illustrious history, which in large measure matches the fortunes and aspirations of the nation. Britannia Royal Naval College is to be congratulated on its endeavours in promoting this history.

Introduction

Dr G. H. Bennett

September 1939 caught the *Kriegsmarine* unprepared to wage war across the oceans. Until the very last moment, Hitler had hoped to avoid war with the United Kingdom; indeed, Hitler had been willing to compromise the development of the German Navy in the interests of the Anglo-German relationship. In signing the Anglo-German Naval Agreement of 1935, while Germany was discarding every other restriction on the development of her military, the Führer had voluntarily accepted a size of navy inferior to that of Britain. Hitler did not really understand the sea, nor the role navies could play as part of a wider strategy. However, he did appreciate the symbolic importance of major warships as the embodiment of German national power. He also appreciated the potential role of the Navy as a diplomatic weapon in his dealings with the British, and the necessity of not engaging in the kind of naval arms race which had marked the build up to World War I. While the German Army and Air Force were to be ready for war by the end of the 1930s, the Navy, in its planning, was asked to assume a readiness date of 1944 for a possible confrontation with Britain. Hitler hoped that, to Prime Minister Neville Chamberlain and other British statesmen, a weak German Navy would act as a kind of guarantee of his good faith towards Great Britain. Unfortunately for Hitler, that 'guarantee' did not prevent the British from declaring war on Germany on 3 September 1939.

While the German Navy was more than ready to undertake tasks in the Baltic in support of operations against Poland, a protracted war against Britain and France was an altogether more formidable task. The German Navy was in transition, and had only just begun the process of building the battleships of the *Bismarck* class which would form the first part of Plan Z: the plan which would create a surface fleet capable of defeating the Royal Navy on the high seas. The surface fleet at the disposal of Grand Admiral Raeder, the head of the German Navy, was inadequate in almost every respect. Beyond a modern destroyer fleet and a handful of modern cruisers, in 1939 Raeder was reliant on the ships built under the Weimar Government (1918–1933), obsolete units such as the battleship *Schleswig-Holstein*, and the hybrid modern battlecruiser design of the *Scharnhorst/ Gneisenau* class. The Weimar era pocket battleships (*Graf Spee*, *Admiral Scheer* and *Deutschland*), which combined heavy armament with a tonnage restricted by international treaties, were unknown quantities. As Koop and Schmolke have argued: "On the whole the *Panzerschiffe* were political ships. They were to bring Germany political respectability within international naval treaties and win allies. In war, their tasks would be to safeguard the security of East Prussia and protect the Baltic entrances and the North Sea approaches".[1] International reaction to them had ranged from "depreciation to admiration".[2] Just how effective they would be in battle would remain to be seen. Similarly, there were questions over the battlecruisers *Scharnhorst* and *Gneisenau:* both had been completed in the mid-1930s as a conscious response to the French *Dunkerque* class.[3] With the resources at his disposal in 1939 Raeder knew there was no question of engaging units of the Royal Navy in a Jutland style battle, at least until 1941–42 when *Bismarck* and her sister ship *Tirpitz* would be ready. The war mission of the German surface fleet would therefore be threefold:–

1. To defend the approaches to German-held territory and to keep the Royal Navy out of the Baltic.
2. To undertake limited operations in support of offensives by the German Army.
3. To attack Britain's maritime interests at their weakest points.

The latter mission offered considerable possibilities. War against Britain's commerce was the primary task of the German submarine arm. Britain's merchant fleet was the largest in the world and the United Kingdom relied on imports both to feed the population and to deliver vital materials for the British war economy. Admiral Dönitz, the head of the German submarine arm, was already envisaging a tonnage war whereby he hoped to strangle Britain's sea lines of communication. If his submarines could sink more ships than the British could replace, then Britain's importing capacity would decline. If that decline was maintained, then sooner or later the critical point would be reached whereby Britain could no longer remain an active participant in the war. If the major surface units could not engage the home fleet of the Royal Navy in a decisive battle, then they could usefully support the tonnage war. They could range into the grey wastes of the Atlantic and beyond, seeking out lone British merchant ships or overwhelming weakly defended convoys. Commerce raiding was a long established feature of war and some German units, particularly the cruiser *Emden*, had excelled at this kind of warfare during World War I.

In pursuing the war on commerce, the German Navy could also employ auxiliary cruisers to augment its strength. The auxiliary cruisers were ordinary merchant ships taken from trade and hastily converted into warships while retaining their outward appearance. Heavy guns would be hidden behind drop-down plates cut into the hull, or in special enclosures which had all the appearance of deck cargo. Mines could be stored in the hold to be sown in areas where shipping was known to concentrate.

With the appearance of an ordinary merchant ship, often flying the flag of a neutral nation, the auxiliary cruiser could close with a British merchant ship before revealing its true identity. A shot across the bow would usually compel the unfortunate British crew to stop their engines. Any attempt to radio for help would result in fire being brought to bear on the bridge and radio operator's cabin. A boarding party from the German cruiser would often board the British vessel to determine whether the nature of the prize, in terms of vessel and cargo, merited sinking the vessel as being of no immediate or long term use. Alternatively the vessel might be retained as a floating supply depot, or sent to a German-controlled port.

The life of an auxiliary cruiser was not very different to that of a pirate ship of the seventeenth century. They carried prize crews to man their conquests and sufficient timber, paint and other supplies to change the identity of their vessel radically and regularly. Without the watertight integrity, strengthening and damage control systems of purpose-built warships, disguise and subterfuge represented the most effective weapon available to the auxiliary cruisers. In any encounter with a regular British cruiser, the auxiliary cruiser would soon be battered into a flaming wreck unless it could strike a first and decisive blow.

Work on the auxiliary cruisers began immediately after the outbreak of war. Suitable ships were selected and work undertaken to equip them as makeshift men-of-war. Turning merchant ships into warships was no easy task. The vessels selected had to have weapons fitted and decks strengthened to cope with the recoil of the guns. Space had to be found to accommodate float planes that would act as spotters for the larger vessels. Three of the vessels selected would be equipped with large motor boats: two to act as minelayers and one (*Michel*) as a torpedo boat in its own right. In many cases, the equipment installed in the auxiliary cruisers was antiquated or deemed surplus to requirements by the *Kriegsmarine*. Crews also had to be found for vessels and in some cases personnel officers were eager to draft problem individuals to ships considered to be on a one-way ticket. The rush to complete the vessels was considerable, imposing heavy demands on the

German dockyards and on the crews of the raiders. Preparing for sea with journeys of many thousands of miles, all those onboard the raiders realised the extent to which they would have to operate in waters dominated by the Royal Navy.

The pursuit of a war on commerce using Germany's heavy ships and auxiliary cruisers would revolve around the strength of two networks. The primary network at issue was Britain's sea lines of communications that tied the British Empire together and which channelled vital imports from around the globe to the United Kingdom. That network was long-standing, considerable and vulnerable even though Royal Navy units would be deployed to protect convoys and to hunt down German commerce raiders. The second network was the product of improvisation and chance. While Britain had a network of bases around the globe the German Navy had no such convenient facilities on which to call. Instead an ever-changing network of supply ships, U-boats, blockade runners and other friendly surface units would do their best to support each other at sea. Meeting at remote rendezvous points, fuel and other supplies could be transferred to raiders enabling them to remain at sea, and prisoners could be trans-shipped to vessels returning to German-controlled ports. For the Royal Navy, destroying the German supply network was every bit as important as bringing to battle the surface units which relied on the network. Although later in the war allied maritime aviation and intelligence work (especially in the form of ULTRA decrypts) would play a vital role in allowing the Royal Navy to break up the German network, in the first months after September 1939 the British would have to rely on guesswork and good luck to find the supply runners.

In the lead up to the outbreak of war *Graf Spee* and *Deutschland* sailed into the Atlantic to launch immediate attacks on British merchant shipping. *Deutschland's* first war cruise was a failure: she sank just three ships in six weeks. *Graf Spee* meanwhile sank nine British merchant ships totalling 50,089 tons before she was found and engaged by three cruisers: HMS *Exeter*, HMS *Ajax* and HMNS *Achilles*.[4] After sustaining damage from the more lightly armed cruisers *Graf Spee* took refuge in the neutral harbour of Montivideo.[5] British efforts led Captain Langsdorff of *Graf Spee* to believe that when he put to sea again he would be met by superior British units. To save his crew, Langsdorff ordered the scuttling of *Graf Spee* which was carried out on 17 December 1939. The Battle of the River Plate and its unexpected ending caused a sensation in the United States.[6] The smouldering remains of the German vessel were left to settle into the mud of the River Plate, although parts of *Graf Spee*, including a stabilised 10 cm gun mounting, machine guns and armour plate, were subsequently removed by Admiralty officials and shipped to Milford Haven in 1940.[7] Within naval circles, Langsdorff's action was dismissed as the mistake of a man who had been wounded in the encounter with the cruisers.[8] Nevertheless Hitler was enraged, creating the first serious strain on the relationship between the *Kriegsmarine* and the Führer. It was not to be the last. The events of the war on commerce over the next three years would see repeated blows to Hitler's confidence in the surface fleet of the German Navy.

In the opening phases of the war on commerce, Hitler demonstrated a near-crippling fear of losing his few major surface units. In November 1939, the pocket battleship *Deutschland* was renamed *Lützow*. Hitler could not contemplate the potential loss of a vessel carrying the symbolic name of *Deutschland*. On 21 November, *Scharnhorst* and *Gneisenau* were sent into the North Atlantic to try to pull Royal Navy ships away from the South Atlantic where they were hunting *Graf Spee*. In the process, on 23 November, the German fleet encountered and sank the armed merchant cruiser *Rawalpindi*. Instead of taking the fight to the enemy and continuing their cruise, within four days both *Scharnhorst* and *Gneisenau* were back at Wilhelmsaven. The Norwegian operation in early 1940 prevented both ships from commerce raiding in the Atlantic, especially because of damage sustained on 8 June by *Scharnhorst* in sinking the aircraft carrier HMS *Glorious* and her escorting destroyers *Ardent* and *Acasta*.[9] It was not until January 1941 that *Scharnhorst* and *Gneisenau* would be ready to try to re-enter the North Atlantic.

This meant that during 1940 the commerce war above the waves would be carried by the auxiliary cruisers. They put to sea in two waves. The first wave, consisting of *Atlantis*, *Orion*, *Widder*, *Thor*, *Pinguin* and *Komet*, sailed between March and July 1940.[10] The second wave, consisting of *Kormoran*, *Thor*, *Michel*, *Stier* and *Komet*, commenced with the sailing of *Kormoran* in December 1941. They took a steady toll on lone-sailing British merchant ships in the remote waters of the South Atlantic and Indian Ocean. While the Germans referred to their raiders by number (*Pinguin* was Ship 33, for example), as evidenced in the Battle Summary the Royal Navy allocated particular letters to the raiders, blockade runners and supply ships. *Atlantis* was thus Ship 16 and raider C in the parlance of the two navies.

In February 1941, *Scharnhorst* and *Gneisenau*, and separately *Admiral Hipper*, entered the Atlantic in search of Allied merchant ships. *Hipper's* second war cruise lasted two weeks and was far more successful than her first in December, 1940, which had been dogged by poor luck and engine problems. In her two weeks at sea, *Hipper* attacked the convoy SLS-64, accounting for seven ships. She entered Brest Roads on 14 Feburary, and reached Kiel via the Denmark Strait on 28 November. *Scharnhorst* and *Gneisenau* meanwhile were even more successful. In the course of 60 days the two ships destroyed or captured 22 merchant ships, successfully avoiding engagements with convoys escorted by British capital ships. Operation 'Berlin' ended on 22 March, as both vessels entered the comparative safety of the port of Brest. Here, for the rest of the year, they became a regular target for the Royal Air Force. Sufficient damage was done to both vessels to convince the Naval High Command that sooner or later an attempt would have to be made to bring the ships out of the range of the Royal Air Force.

On 1 April 1941, just over a week after *Scharnhorst* and *Gneisenau* had entered Brest, the pocket battleship *Admiral Scheer* arrived in Kiel after a war cruise which had commenced on 14 October 1940. During her months at sea, *Admiral Scheer* had sunk 16 merchant vessels and had steamed 46,000 nautical miles. Her war cruise had carried her as far as the Indian Ocean demonstrating the vulnerability of Britain's sea lines of communication. Hitler was delighted at the successes of *Admiral Scheer*, which were reported at the regular Führer Conferences on Naval Affairs. The attack on a North Atlantic convoy on 5 November was especially pleasing, resulting in the loss of 85,000 tons of British shipping. Hitler commented: "This was an excellent achievement. Far reaching strategic effects are to be expected. An immediate reaction on the part of the enemy is evident; the Scapa Group has put out to sea and the Gibraltar Group is in a state of readiness. The enemy will be forced to provide greater protection of convoy traffic".[11] Events proved Hitler's assessment to be correct. Where possible, the Royal Navy would allocate one of its heavy ships as convoy escort across the Atlantic. The impact of the surface fleet in the war on commerce was having a significant strategic effect.

However, following the safe arrival of *Scharnhorst* and *Gneisenau* in Brest, Germany's luck in the surface campaign against British shipping seemed to change. On 27 May, the battleship *Bismarck* was sunk after a lengthy action with British surface units. The crews of those raiders still at sea recognised that the destruction of *Bismarck* impacted directly on their futures. Onboard *Atlantis*:

> "We observed a brief silence for her memory, gripped now by a heavy pessimism that weighed upon even the staunchest of us; stunning the crew, and making many of us consider the wisdom of her Captain's proceeding so far out into the Atlantic after his original action. *Bismarck's* sinking also meant much to us on a more selfish level. We had been on our way home... Now we knew that we should not be able to make it for the North Atlantic would be a hornet's nest... *Bismarck's* presence no longer tied down the other battleships and the accompanying paraphernalia of cruisers, destroyers etc".[12]

Pinguin had been lost on 8 May after an action with HMS *Cornwall*, the first of the raiders to be sunk by the British, and the net began to tighten around the other vessels still at sea. In November the raiders *Kormoran* and *Atlantis* were lost in action with the Royal Navy. During the sinking of *Kormoran* on 19 November the German raider inflicted fatal damage on the Royal Australian Navy cruiser HMAS *Sydney*. There were no survivors from *Sydney's* crew of 645 men. That fact, and the destruction of a purpose built cruiser by an auxiliary vessel, prompted a wave of suspicion about what had taken place, which would persist until the twenty-first century.[13] In 1997 the Australian Government released an extensive document on the sinking of HMAS *Sydney* which attempted to quash rumours that *Sydney* was torpedoed by a Japanese submarine and that her survivors had been machine-gunned in the water.[14] In 2008 an underwater survey team located the wrecks of both *Kormoran* and *Sydney*. Subsequent analysis of the *Sydney* wreck suggested that as many as 70 per cent of the crew may have become casualties before the vessel sank, and that the sinking itself was very rapid, possibly as a result of the failure of some of the warship's watertight bulkheads.

For the German Naval High Command the loss of *Kormoran* on 19 November was a severe blow. During her war cruise, *Kormoran* had captured one and had sunk 10 merchant ships. Worse still for the German Navy was the sinking of *Atlantis* on 22 November.[15] In the months that she had been at sea, *Atlantis* had captured or sunk 22 British merchant ships. She was the most successful German raider of World War II and her loss was a grave blow to the campaign against British commerce. The destruction of *Atlantis* under the guns of the cruiser HMS *Devonshire* was as a result of a signal detailing a rendezvous between *Atlantis* and U-126 being picked up and deciphered at Bletchley Park. On 1 December, HMS *Dorsetshire* intercepted and sank the supply ship *Python* carrying survivors from *Atlantis*. ULTRA decrypts would play an increasing role in allowing the Royal Navy to anticipate the moves of the German surface raiding fleet and the network of blockade runners and supply ships on which they depended.[16] In the face of losses the German Naval High Command could not believe that their codes had been broken and they were still ready to ascribe the losses to being "dogged by misfortune".[17]

Mid to late 1941 was to prove a pivotal period in the surface raiding campaign. Hitler became increasingly reluctant to risk the loss of his major surface vessel. With the failure of operation Barbarossa – the invasion of Russia in June 1941 – to deliver a knock-out blow against the Soviet Union, and the outbreak of war with the United States in December 1941, German strategy steadily shifted towards the defensive. This had profound repercussions for the heavy units of the German Navy. On 12 January 1942 the German Naval High Command concluded that the moment had arrived to move their heavy ships out of range of the RAF. Since the end of Operation Berlin in March 1941 *Scharnhorst* and *Gneisenau* in Brest had been subjected to constant watch by RAF photo-reconnaissance aircraft and ongoing aerial attack by Bomber Command.[18] The heavy cruiser *Prinz Eugen* had joined them on 1 June, making Brest an even more significant target for British bombers. At the meeting on 12 January, Hitler and the High Command concluded that passage through the English Channel represented the best chance of success in getting the three ships back to northern waters. No enemy fleet had forced the English Channel against the ships of the Royal Navy since the Spanish Armada in the sixteenth century. It was the last thing the British would expect, but given surprise and a solid escort of fighter aircraft, destroyers and motor torpedo boats it was believed that the operation could be successful. Operation 'Cerberus' was launched on 11 February. As the three ships left the safety of Brest, Propaganda Minister Joseph Goebbels noted Hitler's level of concern, "He is somewhat worried about our three men-of-war, the *Gneisenau*, *Scharnhorst*, and *Prinz Eugen*, which have left Brest to seek a safe harbour... We are all trembling lest something happen to them. It would be terrible if even one of these were to share the fate of the *Bismarck*".[19] Fortune, however, favoured the operation and the three ships had almost completed their transit of the English Channel before they were heavily engaged.[20] Despite determined efforts and 'suicidal bravery' on the British side the German fleet pressed on northwards towards safety.[21] *Scharnhorst* and *Gneisenau* were damaged by mines but overall the Naval High Command was well satisfied with the results of Operation 'Cerberus'. By 13 February all *Kriegsmarine* units involved in the operation had reached safety, and the inquest was already beginning within British political and military circles.[22]

While 'Cerberus' was a great triumph for the German Navy, the operation marked the beginning of the end for the commerce raiding operations of the major vessels of the German surface fleet. Even after the escape of *Scharnhorst*, *Gneisenau* and *Prinz Eugen* from Brest, the First Lord of the Admiralty could declare his satisfaction at the progress of the campaign against Germany's surface raiding fleet:

"I come now to commerce raiders. The past year has been better than we had at first expected. In the first few months converted merchantmen and the German battlecruisers had a period of fruitful activity. But after seeking refuge in Brest last March the battlecruisers, thanks to the sustained efforts of the RAF against one of the best defended bases in the world, remained immobile until their recent rush to their home ports. The German navy made a determined effort in May to send another force out on to the trade routes, but the Royal Navy and the Fleet Air Arm frustrated this attempt and sank the *Bismarck*, without any merchant ships being lost, though not without loss to themselves. For nearly a year, therefore, there were no mercantile losses at all from German warship raiders. The converted merchant raiders have continued to operate spasmodically but with little success. During 1941, 22 such raiders and their supply ships were put where they could do no more harm".[23]

From 1942 onwards, the German surface fleet, or at least those vessels not under repair, was largely confined to Norwegian and Baltic waters. The Norwegian fjords offered safe anchorages from which to menace the vital convoys going around the North Cape of Norway to the ports of North Russia. Following the German invasion of Russia in July 1941 the Anglo-American convoys represented a means to deliver material support to the Red Army in its desperate battle with German forces. The convoys also had a political significance. As Stalin demanded a second front in Western Europe to take the pressure off the Eastern Front, Churchill and Roosevelt could at least point to the convoys sailing to Russia, and to the Allied heavy bomber offensive, as important initiatives to try and relieve some of the pressure on the Red Army. The second front would come, but it would take time to build up the resources. Likewise, for Hitler, stopping the convoys to North Russia would relieve some of the pressure on his own forces on the Eastern Front. The potential political repercussions of stopping the convoys also appealed to Hitler. Thus Norwegian waters became the most important field of operations for Germany's remaining surface ships from 1942 to 1944.

During 1942, the luck of the German auxiliary cruisers appeared to run out. On 27 September 1942, *Stier* sustained fatal damage in action with Liberty ship SS *Stephen Hopkins*. Both ships sank, which was a remarkable outcome in a combat in which the German vessel heavily outgunned her American adversary. The following month, on 14 October 1942, *Komet* was sunk in the English Channel with the loss of her entire crew of 351 men, and on 30 November 1942, *Thor* was destroyed in harbour at Yokohama.[24]

The absolute nadir was reached on 31 December 1942 when *Lützow* and the heavy cruiser *Admiral Hipper* were in action against convoy JW51B off the north coast of Norway. In a confused action in the dead of the Arctic winter British destroyers, aided by the arrival later in the action of two cruisers, managed to drive off *Lützow* and *Admiral Hipper*. All 14 ships of the convoy succeeded in getting through to North Russia. Onboard the merchant ships were 202 tanks, 87 fighters and 33 bombers together with over 2,000 other vehicles, fuel and other supplies. Captain Robert St. Vincent Sherbrooke, who had commanded the destroyer HMS *Onslow* in the engagement, was awarded the Victoria Cross for his skilful defence and handling of both his ship and the convoy escort. On the German side there were no celebrations. The action against JW51B had thrown into sharp relief the problems of using heavy ships as commerce raiders. Under instructions not to risk their vessels, *Lützow* and *Hipper* had allowed themselves to be beaten off by a weaker force. In the Führer Conference on 6 January 1943, Hitler made clear his frustration with the *Kriegsmarine*. Grand Admiral Raeder was treated to a Hitler monologue, for 90 minutes, on the role played by the Prussian and German Navy since 1870.[25] Hitler then demanded the decommissioning of the remaining large vessels of the German Navy. Only Raeder's resignation, and the skilful diplomacy of Dönitz, Raeder's replacement as head of the German Navy, saved the heavy ships from decommissioning.

Following his appointment as head of the German Navy, Dönitz issued a directive to the commanding officers of the surface units in Norwegian waters. It contained a useful iteration of the kind of war on commerce that the surface ships were expected to engage in:

> "The conditions required for successful operations by surface ships against traffic in the Arctic will occur very seldom, since the enemy, to judge from past experience, will deploy for the protection – immediate and indirect – of his convoys, forces of such strength as will undoubtedly be superior to that of our own forces. Nevertheless there may occur opportunities for attacking unescorted or lightly escorted ships or small groups of ships sailing independently. Whenever such an opportunity occurs it must be seized with determination, but with due observance of tactical principles. It may also sometimes be considered necessary to attack heavily escorted convoys with all available forces; orders to deliver such an attack will be given if the convoy in question is deemed to be of such value that its destruction is of primary importance to the situation as a whole".[26]

Despite Dönitz's encouragement to the surface ships to be prepared to risk all, the days of them making a major contribution to the war on commerce were drawing to an end. Attacks by midget submarines on *Tirpitz* in September 1943 (covered elsewhere in this series) caused major damage to the vessel. On 17 October 1943, the raider *Michel* was torpedoed and sunk by American submarine USS *Tarpon*. Finally on 26 December 1943, *Scharnhorst* was hunted down off the north coast of Norway as she attempted to intercept convoy JW55B. A lengthy pursuit by British cruisers and the battleship HMS *Duke of York* resulted in the fiery death of the ship renowned as the luckiest in the *Kriegsmarine*. One of the vessel's forward magazines exploded. Just 36 men were plucked out of the water out of a total crew of 1,968.[27] As with the sinking of *Bismarck*, it had taken a monumental effort to stop the German vessel, with HMS *Duke of York* expending 446 rounds of main armament.[28] The *Daily Express* celebrated *Scharnhorst*'s sinking on 28 December under the title "*Scharnhorst*: We did not lose a single ship".[29] *War Illustrated* meanwhile remarked: "seldom has an enemy loss given greater satisfaction to the Royal Navy than the sinking of the *Scharnhorst*".[30] Hitler, angered by the sinking of *Scharnhorst*, was once again furious with the Navy. He believed that *Scharnhorst* had made the mistake of running away from the cruisers pursuing her instead of joining them in battle.[31]

During 1944 and 1945, Germany's remaining major surface vessels fought their last desperate battles. During 1944, *Tirpitz* was subjected to repeated bombing raids until she finally capsized after a raid in November 1944. *Lützow* and *Prinz Eugen* carried out bombardment operations in the Baltic in support of German ground forces. Badly damaged by aerial bombardment on 20 March *Lützow* was eventually scuttled by her crew on 4 May as the Russians neared the port of Swinemünde. The auxiliary cruiser *Orion* was sunk off the same port on the same day as a result of Russian bombs. In Kiel, *Admiral Scheer* had capsized after being struck by bombs on 9 April and *Admiral Hipper* was scuttled on 2 May.

The German Navy had entered World War II with a surface fleet which was inadequate to the task of either confronting the home fleet of the Royal Navy or of waging an effective war on commerce. The first warships of Plan Z had not yet reached operational status at the opening of hostilities in 1939, leaving the German Naval High Command to do the best it could with the pocket battleships, a handful of modern cruisers, and the intermediate battlecruiser types of the *Scharnhorst* and *Gneisenau*. To their number would be added the auxiliary cruisers: the bravery and ingenuity of their crews could not make up for the fact that they were simply converted merchant ships. While the auxiliary cruisers would prove remarkably effective (sinking 129 vessels totalling 800,611 tons) the major surface units were thrown into the commerce war amidst high expectations in 1939. In the event they proved largely inadequate to the task (sinking 59 ships totalling 232,633 tons). "Only *Admiral Scheer*, with an adroit commander, skilful handling by SKL (Naval Warfare Directorate) and a great deal of luck ... [reaped] a major dividend".[32]

However, the contribution of the surface raiders to *Kriegsmarine*'s war on British commerce cannot be assessed purely in terms of the number and tonnage of the ships they sank. The surface raiding fleet stretched the resources of the Royal Navy across the world's oceans from the Arctic to the Antarctic. The Royal Navy would not be free to concentrate its vessels in the Atlantic and against its principal opponent, the German submarine arm. In terms of morale, the German surface raiders were able to deal some major, if largely short term, blows to Britain's sense of herself as the pre-eminent maritime power. The sinking of HMS *Hood* in 1941 registered on British public opinion in ways which the destruction of *Bismarck*, *Scharnhorst* and other German surface vessels could not completely expunge. Despite the heroism of the men who launched desperate attacks to disable *Bismarck*, and the professionalism of the crews who stalked *Scharnhorst* off the North Cape of Norway, British naval power was steadily being eclipsed.

At war's end, only *Prinz Eugen* and the raider *Widder* (having been sent to Norway as a supply and repair ship following engine problems on her first and only war cruise) remained afloat from the fleet of ships which had sailed against Britain's sea lines of communication. In many ways, the commitment of the German heavy units to the commerce war was an act of desperation: the *Kriegsmarine*'s surface fleet was not capable of wresting the initiative from the Royal Navy. However, the *Kriegsmarine*'s assessment, and decision to allow its units to operate largely independently, was in some ways perhaps a mistake. If in April 1941 *Bismarck* had sailed with *Scharnhorst* and *Gneisenau* in company, or still better the operation had been postponed until *Tirpitz* was ready for sea, then narrow victory for the Royal Navy might have been transformed into a shattering triumph for the *Kriegsmarine*.

The battle summaries which follow chart some of the Royal Navy's operations to deal with the threat of Germany's commerce raiders of World War II (operations against *Bismarck* and *Tirpitz* will be dealt with by other volumes in this series). The war on commerce represented Germany's best hope to bring the British war economy to its knees. The U-boat would be the primary weapon in this war, but it was realised that surface units (even converted merchant ships) could play a support role to the submarine offensive. The three Battle Summaries contained in this volume show the desperate attempts of the Royal Navy to track down and neutralise these units, together with the network of supply ships and blockade runners which could allow their resupply at sea. There was much that the writers of the summaries could not know. The summaries were pulled together in some haste as the officers of the Royal Navy struggled to learn lessons for the future from recently concluded operations. The German perspective on these operations would not emerge until after 1945, and the ULTRA secret which allowed British code breakers a remarkable insight into the life of Nazi Germany's biggest battleship would remain out of the public domain until the 1970s. In some cases it was only the discovery of the wrecks of some of these vessels that would finally clear up the story of their sinking. Seventy years on from the events which they analyse, the Battle Summaries make interesting reading. They constitute the first draft of the history of the war at sea.

References

1. Koop, G. & Schmolke, K. P. (2000), *Pocket Battleships of the Deutschland Class*, Greenhill Books, London, p.220.
2. Koop, G. & Schmolke, K. P. (2000), *Pocket Battleships of the Deutschland Class*, Greenhill Books, London, p.13.
3. Whitley, M. J. (1989), *German Capital Ships of World War Two*, Arms and Armour Press, London, p.31.
4. On *Graf Spee's* first and only war cruise see Powell, M. (1973), *The Last Voyage of the Graf Spee*, New English Library, London.
5. It was initially suspected that the pocket battleship brought to action was in fact the *Admiral Scheer* 'Naval Battle in the South Atlantic', *The Times*, 30 December 1939, p.8.
6. 'Full Story of Naval Battle', *The Chicago Herald*, 14 December 1939, p.1. 'Three British Cruisers Shell Nazi Pocket Battleship in Greatest Battle of War', *The Montana Standard*, 14 December 1939, p.1. '2 Cruisers Trap *Graf Spee*: British Rush More Warships', *The New York Post*, 14 December 1939, p.1. 'German vessel to remain at Montivideo', *The Montana Standard*, 15 December 1939, p.1. '*Graf Spee* hints at Dash for Sea', *St Paul Dispatch*, 15 December 1939, p.1. 'Trapped Raider Gets Reprieve', *The Fargo Forum*, 15 December 1939, p.1. 'Uruguay Orders German Vessel to Leave Port, *The Montana Standard*, 16 December 1939, p.1. 'Germans Scuttle *Graf Spee*', *The Montana Standard*, 18 December 1939, p.1. 'Sink *Spee* on Hitler Order', *Chicago Daily Tribune*, 18 December 1939, p.1.
7. See report on Salvage operations, The National Archives, British National Archives (hereinafter TNA:PRO) ADM1/10467 and Sir Henry Tizard's Report on Radio Direction Finding in the German Navy, TNA: ADM1/10794. See assessment of the wreck by Admiralty Intelligence TNA: ADM228/84–86. See also Whitley, M. J. (1989), *German Capital Ships of World War Two*, Arms and Armour Press, London, p.102.
8. See comments by Admiral Krancke, Bennett, G. H. & R. (2004), *Hitler's Admirals*, United States Naval Institute Press, Annapolis, p.64.
9. See Busch, F. O. (2001), *The Drama of the Scharnhorst*, Wordsworth Editions, London, pp.26–29 and 'The Tragedy of HMS Glorious', *The War Illustrated*, vol. 10, No.240, 30 August 1946, pp.291–292.
10. On *Pinguin* see Brennecke, H. J. (1954), *Cruise of the Raider HK-33*, Thomas

Crowell, Binghamton. On *Kormoran* see Detmers, T. (1959), *The Raider Kormoran*, Kimber, London; Ward, H. T. (1970), *Flight of the Cormoran*, Vantage Press, New York City. On *Atlantis* see Hoyt, E. P. (1988), *Raider 16*, Avon Books, New York City; Sellwood, U. M. & A. V. (2005), *Phantom Raider*, Cerberus Publishing, Bristol; Rogge, B. & Frank, W. (1956), *German Raider Atlantis*, Ballantine Books, New York; Slavick, J. P. (2003), *The Cruise of the German Raider Atlantis*, Naval Institute Press, Annapolis. On *Orion* see Weyher, K. (1955), *The Black Raider*, Elek, New York City. Overall see Woodward, D. (1955), *The Secret Raiders*, W. W. Norton, New York; Schmalenbach, P. (1979), *German Raiders: A History of Auxiliary Cruisers of the German Navy, 1895–1945*, Naval Institute Press, Annapolis; Edwards, B. (2001), *Beware Raiders: German Surface Raiders in the Second World War*, Naval Institute Press, Annapolis; Muggenthaler, A. K. (1977), *German Raiders of World War II*, Prentice-Hall, Englewood Cliffs; Duffy, J. P. (2001), *Hitler's Secret Pirate Fleet: The Deadliest Ships of World War II*, Praeger,Wesport. On the blockade runners and network of ships which supported the raiders while at sea, see Brice, M. H. (1981), *Axis Blockade Runners of World War II*, Naval Institute Press, Annapolis.

11. Conference of the Commander-in-Chief Navy with the Führer, 14 November 1940, Führer *Conferences on Naval Affairs*, Greenhill Books, London, 1990, p.151.

12. Mohr, U. & Sellwood, A.V. (1955), *Atlantis: The Story of a German Raider*, Werner Laurie, London, pp.186–187.

13. For the Royal Navy's own files on the affair see ADM1/18899.

14. Duffy, J. P. (2005), *Hitler's Secret Pirate Fleet: The Deadliest Ships of World War II*, University of Nebraska Press, Lincoln, p.207. See also: Scott, G. (1962), *HMAS Sydney*, Horwitz Publications, Melbourne; Montgomery, M. (1981), *Who Sank the Sydney?*, Cassell, Auckland; Frame, T. (1993), *HMAS Sydney: Loss and Controversy*, Hodder and Stoughton, New South Wales. For an overview of the controversy see 'An insight into the Genesis and Evolution of the HMAS *Sydney* Controversy', http://www.defence.gov.au/sydneyii/WAM/ WAM.070.0010.pdf accessed 6/6/2011.

15. Actions against Raiders, despatch submitted to the Admiralty, 8 December 1941, by Vice-Admiral Willis published in *Supplement to the London Gazette*, 12 July 1948, pp.4009–4015.

16. See analysis of the difficulties of tracking German surface raiders 1939– 1944 and lessons learned by Government Code and Cypher School TNA: HW8/48.

17. Comment on the loss of *Atlantis*, *Kormoran* and the supply ship *Python* in Admiral Dönitz, (1958) *Memoirs: Ten Years and Twenty Days*, Weidenfeld and Nicolson, London, p.179.

18. See Prime Minister's File on *Scharnhorst* and *Gneisenau*, 1941–42, TNA: PREM 3/191/2A.

19. Diary entry 11 February 1942, Lochner, L. P. (1948) *The Goebbels Diaries 1942–1943*, Doubleday & Co, Garden City, p.78.

20. 'Channel Attack on German Ships', *The Daily Telegraph*, 13 February 1943, p.1.

21. Smith, P. C. (1984), *Hold the Narrow Sea: Naval Warfare in the English Channel 1939–1945*, Naval Institute Press, Annapolis, p.154.

22. See, for example, papers relating to the setting up of a joint board of Inquiry TNA: ADM1/11782 and notes on the publication of the Bucknill Committee's report, 1946, TNA: ADM/19325.

23. A.V. Alexander in debate on the 1942 Naval Estimates, *House of Commons Debates*, 26 February 1942, vol. 378, col. 375.

24. The *Komet* was completely blown to pieces in a massive explosion. British sources suggest that this was as result of a torpedo attack by *MTB236*. German sources suggest that gunfire from British destroyers led to a fire in No.2 hold which contained aviation spirit. This in turn may have led to the explosion of the forward magazine. See Smith, P. C. (1984), *Hold the Narrow Sea: Naval Warfare in the English Channel 1939–1945*, Naval Institute Press, Annapolis, pp.170–171.

25. Conference of the Commander-in-Chief Navy with the Führer, 6 January 1943, Führer *Conferences on Naval Affairs*, Greenhill Books, London, 1990, pp.306–308.

26. Admiral Dönitz, (1958), *Memoirs: Ten Years and Twenty Days*, Weidenfeld and Nicolson, London, p.373.

27. For a German perspective on the loss of *Scharnhorst* see Bekker, C. (1974), *Verdammte See*, Verlag Ullstein, Berlin, pp.328–350.

28. Whitley, M. J. (1989), *German Capital Ships of World War Two*, Arms and Armour Press, London, p.203.

29. '*Scharnhorst*: We did not lose a single ship', *The Daily Express*, 28 December 1943, p.1. '*Scharnhorst* fell into Trap', *The Daily Mail*, 28 December 1943, p.1. 'British Naval Force Sinks Nazi Battleship *Scharnhorst*', *San Francisco Chronicle*, 28 December 1943, p.1. '*Scharnhorst* Sinking', *Toronto Daily Star*, 27 December 1943, p.1. 'Battleship *Scharnhorst* is Sunk', *New York Times*, 28 December 1943, p.1. 'Nazi Battleship *Scharnhorst* Sunk', *Dallas Morning News*, 27 December 1943, p.1. 'Battleship *Scharnhorst* sunk by British', *Houston Post*, 27 December 1943, p.1. 'British Bare *Scharnhorst* Battle Story', *Los Angles Evening Herald Express*, 28 December 1943, p.1.

30. 'The War at Sea', *The War Illustrated*, vol. 7, No.172, 21 February 1944, p.518.

31. Conference of the Commander-in-Chief Navy with the Führer, 1–3 January 1944, Führer *Conferences on Naval Affairs*, Greenhill Books, London, 1990, p.379.

32. Koop, G. & Schmolke, K. P. (2000), *Pocket Battleships of the Deutschland Class*, Greenhill Books, London, p.220.

PART I

B.R. 1736

C.B. 3081 (19)

BATTLE SUMMARY No. 26

THE CHASE AND DESTRUCTION OF THE GRAF SPEE
1939
Including
The Battle of the River Plate
13 December, 1939

NOTE:- This book is based on information available
up to and including September, 1944

T.S.D. 682 April 4
Tactical, Torpedo And Staff Duties Division
(Historical Section)
Naval Staff, Admiralty, S.W.1.

CONTENTS

Chapter V
The *Admiral Graf Spee*

Chapter VI
The Battle of the River Plate

The South Atlantic, Early September

Introduction

Early in the war of 1914–1918 it was painfully evident that in favourable circumstances a small hostile cruiser could wreak great havoc amongst unescorted merchant ships on an ocean trade route. By 9 November, 1914, the German light cruiser *Emden*[1] had accounted for no less than 16 merchant ships in the Indian Ocean and Bay of Bengal totalling 66,146 tons, valued at more than two million pounds sterling.[2] She was finally brought to action off Cocos Island on 9 November by the Australian light cruiser *Sydney*,[3] which "had little difficulty in putting an end to the raider's career."[4]

The merit of the *Emden*'s cruise was fully appreciated in Germany for at the outbreak of the Second World War in September, 1939, the Third Reich possessed three small capital ships, or "Pocket battleships," designed specially for commerce raiding on an ambitious scale. Armed with six 11-in. guns in triple turrets they were far more powerful than the *Emden*. With a maximum speed of 27.7 knots they could out-distance all but five of the British and French capital ships, which were the only Allied ships able to oppose them in single combat with any certainty of success. Their destruction was therefore no easy problem. One of them was the *Admiral Graf Spee*.[5]

British Navy Policy, 1939

The broad lines of British Navy Policy for the protection of trade in the event of war with Germany and Italy were laid down in an Admiralty memorandum dated January, 1939, which also included the dispositions of the British and French forces for 1 August, 1939.[6]

This memorandum, anticipating attacks by raiders, including the three pocket battleships, in the Atlantic, Red Sea and Indian Ocean, specified the "traditional and well-proved methods" of protecting British trade. These, it stated, consisted in the dispersal of shipping, the stationing of naval patrols in focal areas where cruisers could concentrate in pairs against a superior enemy, and the formation of adequately escorted convoys. It added that detachments from the main fleet could also be used if required.

"By such means," says the memorandum, "we have in the past succeeded in protecting shipping on essential routes, and it is intended to rely on these methods again, adapting them to the problem under review."

The intended strategy therefore was to rely, on the outbreak of war – when sufficient forces for escorting ocean convoys would not be available – on evasive routeing and the patrol of focal areas. The memorandum, however, added that shipping could be escorted, if necessary, for the first portion of the homeward passage. Armed merchant cruisers, when available, could escort the convoys the whole way home. If it were absolutely necessary, warships could accompany convoys throughout their passage, though this would inevitably result in a serious slowing down of trade. Though the introduction of general convoy would rest with the Admiralty, Commanders-in-Chief on foreign stations could institute local convoys.

On the outbreak of hostilities on 3 September, 1939, the policy outlined in the memorandum was put into effect. No ocean escorts, however, were provided though a cruiser sometimes accompanied convoys from Freetown to the latitude of the Canaries. In South American waters a cruiser, or a destroyer, occasionally escorted convoys clear of land during daylight.

The South America Division, September, 1939

Immediately before the outbreak of war the designation of Vice-Admiral George D'Oyly Lyon, C.B., who had been Commander-in-Chief, Africa Station, since March, 1938, was changed to Commander-in-Chief, South Atlantic. On the creation of the new command the Admiral transferred his flag from the Cape to Freetown, Sierra Leone, and assumed general Naval control over British movements in the whole of the South Atlantic Ocean. At the same time the South America Division of the America and West Indies Squadron, which consisted of the cruisers *Exeter* and *Ajax* under the immediate command of Commodore Henry Harwood, O.B.E., was transferred to the new South Atlantic Station.[7]

On 23 August, 1939, the *Exeter* was at Devonport with her crew on foreign service leave when she was recalled to South American waters. Although Captain F. S. Bell assumed command of the ship two days later, she continued to fly Commodore Harwood's broad pendant as Commodore, South America Division. That evening she sailed for St. Vincent, Cape Verde Islands.

Next day, 26 August, as it seemed possible that two German pocket battleships might be in the Atlantic, the Admiralty ordered her to reinforce the escort of the transport *Dunera* from Ushant to Cape St. Vincent. She sighted the transport, escorted by the cruisers *Dauntless* and *Colombo*, broad pendant of Commodore, 11th Cruiser Squadron, at 1700.

Twelve and a half hours later, at 0530, 27 August, the British *Maidan* joined the convoy, but being unable to keep up was left behind to follow without escort. The *Exeter* left the convoy off Cape St. Vincent at 1200/28 and proceeded at 21 knots for the Cape Verde Islands.

Commodore Harwood was anxious to meet the Commander-in-Chief, and, as a result of a signal suggesting that he should meet him at Dakar or Freetown and fuel there, was ordered to meet the *Neptune* off Freetown. Bad visibility, however, prevented the meeting, and on 1 September the *Exeter* arrived at Freetown. That morning the Commodore met the Commander-in-Chief onboard the *Neptune*, and at 2100 sailed for the Cape Verde Islands and Rio de Janeiro.

Meanwhile four destroyers of the 4th Destroyer Division, Mediterranean Fleet, the *Hotspur*, *Havock*, *Hyperion* and *Hunter*, had left Gibraltar on 31 August for Freetown[8] to act against submarines in the event of war.

The *Ajax* was already off the coast of South America. At 1330 on 3 September, less than three hours after the British declaration of war, she intercepted the German SS *Olinda*, 4,576 tons, outward bound from Montevideo with a general cargo of wool, cotton, hides, scrap iron and wood. The position, 34° 58' S., 53° 32' W., off the River Plate, was over a thousand miles from the nearest British territory, the Falklands. The nearest British warship, the *Exeter*, was 2,500 miles away. The *Ajax*, having no prize crew available, sank the *Olinda* by gunfire at 1627 in 34° 58' S., 53° 27' W.[9] Twenty-four hours later, on the afternoon of 4 September, she intercepted the German SS *Carl Fritzen*, 6,954 tons, and sank her with gunfire in 33° 22' S., 48° 50' W., 200 miles E.S.E. of Rio Grande do Sul.[10]

Next day, 5 September, the *Hotspur* and *Havock* left Freetown to join the South America Division with orders to examine the island of Trinidade[11] on the way. They were followed three days later by the cruiser *Cumberland* from the 2nd Cruiser Squadron of the Home Fleet. She had reached Freetown from Plymouth on 7 September with orders to reinforce Commodore Harwood in the Rio de Janeiro area.[12]

On 7 September the *Exeter* had entered Rio de Janeiro, where Commodore Harwood had interviewed[13] the Brazilian Secretary-General for Foreign Affairs, who was handling all War and Neutrality questions, Sir Hugh Gurney, H.M. Ambassador to Brazil, and Sir Esmond Overy, H.M. Ambassador to the Argentine, who was passing through Rio on his way to Buenos Aires. Having informed himself of the situation the Commodore left Rio at 0100/8. A few hours later, having learned from the Admiralty at 0738 that the German merchant vessels *General Artigas*, *Monte Pascoal* and *Gloria* were assembling off the Patagonian coast, the extreme tip of South America, he decided to move both the *Exeter* and the *Ajax* south, and ordered the *Ajax* to meet him at 0800 on 9 September.

During the forenoon of 8 September the *Exeter* sighted the Panamanian SS *Culebra* and the British SS *Brittany*, and next morning, at 0700, met the *Ajax*. The Commodore thought that the German merchant vessels might embark reservists from Porto Alegré (Brazil) or from Puerto Madryn (Argentine) and raid the Falkland Islands. To guard against this he ordered the *Ajax* to proceed to Port Stanley at 20 knots. At the same time, to cover the very important Plate area, the *Exeter* proceeded there and patrolled from 10–18 September. On 10 September she sighted the British SS *Dunster Grange*, and later that day the British SS *Queensberry*, which she chased until identified. That evening the British Consul at Porto Alegré informed Commodore Harwood that any attempt to embark German reservists was most unlikely. As it appeared probable that the German merchant vessels might be converting themselves into armed raiders the Commodore decided to start short distance convoys from the Santos–Rio and Plate areas. He therefore ordered the *Cumberland* to refuel at Rio on her arrival there on 15 September and to organise and run "out" convoys in that area with the *Havock* as an anti-submarine escort. The convoys were to leave at dawn and be protected against submarines and surface raiders till dusk. The ships were then to be dispersed so that they would be far apart by dawn the next day. At the same time the Commodore ordered the *Hotspur* to join him in the Plate area after refuelling at Rio de Janeiro, so that similar convoys could be started from Montevideo. If a German pocket battleship arrived off the east coast of South America the *Cumberland* was to abandon the convoy scheme and join the *Exeter*.

On 10 September Commodore Harwood was informed by the Admiralty that the German SS *Montevideo* was leaving Rio Grande do Sul for Florianopolis (Brazil), but decided not to try and intercept her as this would divert the *Exeter* 500 miles from the focal area off the Plate.

On the night of 12 September the Commodore was informed by the British Naval Attaché, Buenos Aires, that a concentration of German reservists was taking place in Southern Argentina with the Falklands as a possible objective. The therefore ordered the *Ajax* to remain at the Falklands till situation cleared, and proceeded south of the Plate area to be in closer touch with her and yet remain within easy reach of the Plate. During the next few days he intercepted several British and neutral vessels.

In view of a report that the German ships *Porto Alegré* and *Monte Olivia* were leaving Santos on 15 and 16 September Commodore Harwood decided to start the short distance convoys from Montevideo as soon as possible. The *Cumberland* had arranged a twelve-hour convoy system from Santos. Ships from Rio de Janeiro for Freetown would sail at dawn on odd numbered days, and ships for the south on even numbered days with the *Havock* as an anti-submarine escort and the *Cumberland* in distant support. The *Cumberland* left Rio de Janeiro on 16 September and during the next eight days sighted 15 British and neutral ships while on patrol.[14]

Meanwhile the *Exeter* had met the British SS *English Trader* on 17 September and next day the British SS *Sussex* bound for Montevideo. That day the *Hotspur* joined her to patrol the Plate area. The *Exeter*, after a short visit to Montevideo, resumed this patrol on 20 September, refuelling as necessary from the oiler *Olwen* in the mouth of the River Plate.

Soon after leaving Montevideo on 20 September Commodore Harwood learned from the British Naval Attaché, Buenos Aires, that the local German authorities were endeavouring to inform German ships at sea that the British SS *Lafonia* was on her way to the Falklands with reservists for the Falkland Island defence force. About the same time the reporting officer at Punta Arenas signalled that an unknown warship had passed to the eastward on 17 September.

In view of these reports and of others pointing to the likelihood of armed raiders being fitted out in southern waters the Commodore ordered the *Hotspur* to escort the *Lafonia* to Port Stanley on the dispersal of the local convoy of 22 September. As the volume of British trade was greater from the Plate than in the Rio de Janeiro–Santos area, he ordered the *Havock* to come south for anti-submarine duties with the local Plate convoys.

The first local convoy outward from Montevideo sailed on 22 September. It consisted of the British ships *Sussex*, *Roxby* and *El Ciervo*, in addition to the *Lafonia*, and was escorted by the *Hotspur*. The *Exeter* met it during the forenoon and covered it throughout the day. At dusk the merchant ships were dispersed on prearranged courses, while the *Exeter* remained within supporting distance and the *Hotspur* escorted the *Lafonia* to Port Stanley.[15]

On 24 September Admiral Lyon and Commodore Harwood learned from the Naval Attaché, Buenos Aires, that "according to a reliable source," arrangements had been made for a number of German ships, which might include the Luft Hansa carrier *Westfalen*, the *General Artigas*, the *Monte Pascoal*, the *Poseidon*, and a cruising submarine, to meet a position 120° S.W. of Ascension[16] on 28 September.

As it was possible to send a cruiser there without uncovering the focal points for more than three days, Commodore Harwood ordered the *Cumberland* to proceed to the rendezvous forthwith and the *Ajax*, recalled from the Falklands on 21 September, to take her place in the Rio de Janeiro area.

He was only anticipating the wishes of the Commander-in-Chief, who, when the report reached him, at once recalled the *Neptune* to refuel and ordered the *Cumberland* to proceed at top speed (21 knots) to the German rendezvous. On 25 September the destroyers *Hyperion* and *Hunter* sailed from Freetown for the same position.

The *Neptune* and the two destroyers were spread off the rendezvous on 28 September. It was fruitless and the entire force proceeded to Freetown arriving there on 2 October with the *Cumberland* short of fuel.

While the *Cumberland* was sweeping for the German ships, the *Exeter* and the *Ajax* were watching off the Plate and in the Rio de Janeiro–Santos area respectively. Commodore Harwood had ordered the *Ajax* to return to the Rio de Janeiro area after fuelling from the *Olwen* eastward of English Bank. She had shown herself off Rio Grande do Sul to deter the German merchant vessels there from breaking out, and had examined a few neutral ships and small fishing craft on the way. In the meantime the *Havock* had remained with the *Olwen* in the lee of English Bank previous to escorting a convoy consisting of the British ships *Sarthe*, *Miguel de Larrinaga* and *Pilar de Larrinaga* out of the River Plate on 27 September. Next day a local convoy consisting of the British ships *Waynegate*, *Cressdene*, *Lord Byron*, *Ramillies*, *Adellan* and *Holmbury* was escorted out of the Plate by the *Exeter* and *Havock*.

At daylight on 29 September the *Ajax* was off Rio de Janeiro ready to escort ships sailing northward. She sighted none till the early afternoon when she met the SS *Almeda Star* and, a few hours later, the SS *San Ubaldo*. That night several neutral steamers were sighted off Rio and on 30 September the British SS *La Pampa* was met and escorted during daylight on her way to Santos. This ended the work of the South America Division for September. Commodore Harwood's three cruisers, busy with the task of patrolling the focal areas, had not yet been concentrated as a single force.

South America Division, Fuelling Policy, September, 1939

One of Commodore Harwood's most pressing anxieties was the problem of refuelling his ships. Operating as he was off a neutral coast, with the nearest British base, the Falklands, 1,000 miles to the southward, the selection of suitable anchorages was no easy matter.

Under the stipulations of the Thirteenth Hague Convention, 1907, belligerent warships are only allowed to take in sufficient fuel to enable them to reach the nearest port in their own country. In some neutral countries who interpret the rule to that effect, they may also fill up all bunkers built to carry fuel, but when they have once fuelled in a neutral port they may not within the succeeding three months replenish their supply in a port belonging to the same power.[17]

This meant that the Commodore could only refuel his ships in any port of each of the three neutral republics, Brazil, Uruguay and the Argentine, once every three months. When he visited Rio de Janeiro on 7 September, he discussed with Vice-Admiral José Guisasola, the Argentine Commander-in-Chief who was also visiting Rio, the question of refuelling his ships, especially his destroyers, off the entrance to the Plate. The Admiral raised no objections and strongly advised him to use the lee of Rouen Bank[18] in the Plate Estuary, as it afforded much calmer conditions than English Bank and was well clear of all normal shipping routes. (Plan 1).

During this visit His Majesty's Ambassador, Sir Hugh Gurney, and the Commodore saw the Brazilian Secretary-General for Foreign Affairs on the same subject. After laying stress on the recent sinking of the *Athenia*, they suggested that, as the British destroyers were coming out to protect ships against sinking at sight, they were entitled to look for preferential treatment in the case of fuelling and repairs. They received a most friendly reply and permission to refuel at frequent intervals, provided that such visits were made discreetly and at different ports.

When the Commodore visited Montevideo in the *Exeter* on 19 September he cited to the Uruguayan Minister for Foreign Affairs

Germany's infringement of international agreements in sinking ships at sight, as an argument towards obtaining extra facilities for his destroyers to visit Uruguayan ports more than once a quarter. The British Minister, Mr. E. Millington-Drake, felt sure that under the repair clause of the Thirteenth Hague Convention he could arrange for occasional visits by the destroyers, if they did not fuel more than once every three months.

The small number of the ships available and the severe limitations on fuelling in neutral countries were grave handicaps. They made it impossible to keep a close watch on German ships in all ports on the east coast of South America. The best the Commodore could hope for was to pay sporadic visits which would deter them for a time, but could hardly be expected to lead to their permanent detention and internment.[19]

The stirrup method of oiling ships in exposed anchorages would have been very useful in the River Plate Estuary, but as neither the oiler *Olwen* nor the *Olynthus*, which subsequently relieved her,[20] was fitted for the purpose, nothing could be expected in this direction.

Although an enemy submarine was reported off Natal (Brazil) on 24 September, the Admiralty recalled the 4th Destroyer Division on 28 September to meet the serious destroyer shortage in the Home Fleet. Next day the submarine was reported south of Natal and the Commander-in-Chief was informed that the *Hotspur* and *Havock* might patrol the area while on passage to Freetown.[21] The first day of October, however, saw a dramatic change in the situation. A powerful German surface raider had appeared off Pernambuco and the recall of the 4th Destroyer Division was immediately cancelled.

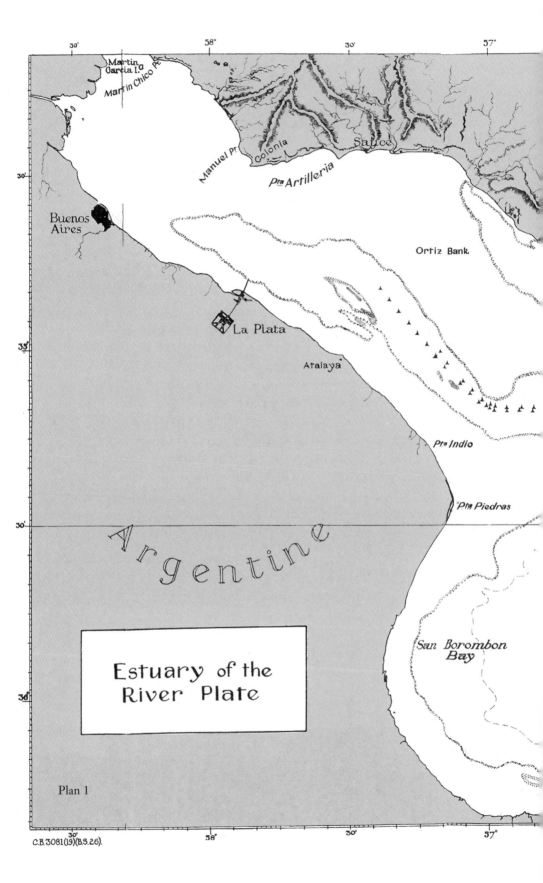

Estuary of the
River Plate

Plan 1

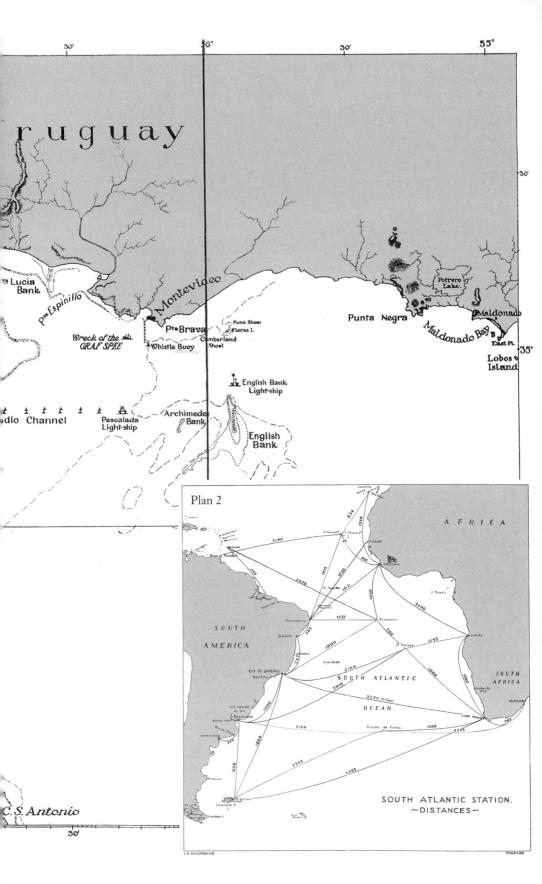

r u g u a y

ta Lucia
Bank

Pta Espinillo

Montevideo

Pta Brava

Wreck of the
GRAF SPEE

Whistle Buoy

Puno Shoal
Flores I.
Cumberland
Shoal

Punta Negra

Potrero
Lake.

Maldonado

Maldonado Bay

East Pt.

Lobos
Island

English Bank
Light-ship

dio Channel

Pescalada
Light-ship

Archimedes
Bank

English
Bank

Plan 2

AFRICA

Canaries

S¹ Vincent   S¹ Vince P¹

DAKAR

Freetown

S. Thomé

Ascension

S¹ Helena

Lobito

SOUTH

AMERICA

Pernambuco

BAHIA

RIO DE JANEIRO
Santos

Trinidada

SOUTH ATLANTIC

Luderitz Bay

SOUTH

AFRICA

DURBAN

RIO GRANDE
do Sul

MONTEVIDEO
BUENOS AIRES
BAHIA BLANCA

OCEAN

CAPE TOWN

Tristan da Cunha

Pt Stanley
Falkland Is.

C.S. Antonio

SOUTH ATLANTIC STATION.
~DISTANCES~

The South Atlantic, October

A Surface Raider Reported

When a report that the British SS *Clement* had been sunk by a "surface raider" 75 miles S.E. of Pernambuco[22] at 1400/30 September reached the Admiralty at 1600 on 1 October, the Commander-in-Chief was immediately informed that he should retain the 4th Destroyer Division[23] and that his command would be reinforced by the cruisers *Effingham*, *Emerald*, *Enterprise*, *Norfolk* and *Cape Town*. The battleships *Resolution* and *Revenge* and the aircraft carrier *Hermes* would proceed to Freetown or Jamaica. These dispositions never materialised being superseded on 5 October by a more general policy which cancelled them. The new policy may have been under consideration on 2 October for that evening the 9th Cruiser Squadron was recalled from the South Atlantic Station. By the end of the month it was widely dispersed.[24]

On 3 October the Commander-in-Chief was informed that[25] Commodore Harwood must not for the sake of temporary benefit accept departures from strict neutrality laws which might prove prejudicial if the enemy obtained reciprocal concessions. The Commodore replied that only benevolency so far accepted was the embarkation of stores at Montevideo by the *Olwen*. As Uruguay had only one port and no unfrequented anchorages he considered it easy to control the approaches and neutralise the value of concessions to the enemy. He emphasised the value of concessions for extra fuelling facilities in Brazil, whose Government had shown great willingness to stretch a point in his favour. He pointed out the desirability of keeping ships out of the Pernambuco area where British trade was comparatively small and it was impossible to maintain a patrol owing to fuelling restrictions. Fuelling at sea was seldom possible on account of the heavy swell, and anchorages such as Abrolhos[26] were open to submarine attack. (Plan 2).

In view of these difficulties the Commodore decided to make more use of Port Stanley in the Falklands where ships could also carry out minor repairs and have the occasional stay in harbour which the Commander-in-Chief considered essential for their welfare.[27]

The Institution of Hunting Groups

Details of the new measures for dealing with enemy raiders reached the Commander-in-Chief in an Admiralty telegram on 5 October. Eight hunting groups of sufficient strength to destroy any pocket battleship or *Hipper* class cruiser were being formed in the Atlantic and Indian Ocean:–

Force.	Hunting Group.	Area.	From.
"F"	*Berwick* *York*	North America and West Indies.	Halifax Escort Force.
"G"	*Cumberland* *Exeter*	S.E. Coast America	South Atlantic.
"H"	*Sussex* *Shropshire*	Cape of Good Hope	Suez.
"I"	*Cornwall* *Dorsetshire* *Eagle*	Ceylon	China Station.
"K"	*Ark Royal* *Renown*	Pernambuco	Home Fleet.
"L"	*Dunkerque*, three 6-in. gun cruisers and aircraft carrier *Bearn*	Brest	–
"M"	Two 8-in. cruisers	Dakar	–
"N"	*Strasbourg* *Hermes*	West Indies	Plymouth Command.

Hunting groups were to keep wireless silence when searching for raiders unless their presence had been disclosed. As Commanders-in-Chief might not always know their position they were to be given discretion to disregard their orders if necessary. All available information was to be passed to them by "I" method, and they were to be careful not to be enticed from "areas where trade was thick."

This was an entirely new policy very different from the patrol of focal areas visualised in the January 1939 memorandum, and carried out by the South America Division since the outbreak of war.[28]

It was not the only measure instituted against raiders on 5 October. That day the *Resolution*, *Revenge*, *Enterprise* and *Emerald* were ordered[29] to sail in company to Halifax, Nova Scotia, to escort homeward bound convoys. The *Effingham* was to join them later. The *Ramillies* left Gibraltar on 5 October for the same duty but was recalled next day when the *Malaya* and *Glorious* were ordered from the Mediterranean to the Indian Ocean as an additional hunting group, Force "J." This force was to work against raiders thought likely by the Admiralty to attack shipping in the Socotra area, at the entrance to the Gulf of Aden, though according to the Commander-in-Chief, South Atlantic, no enemy intelligence had been received which pointed to this objective. The appearance of an enemy raider off Pernambuco had led to the formation of nine Allied hunting groups and to the despatch of two battleships and three cruisers to Halifax for escort duties. This entailed the withdrawal of two battleships, one battlecruiser, two aircraft carriers, and three cruisers from home waters; and one battleship, one aircraft carrier, and two cruisers from the Mediterranean.

The selection of the cruisers *Berwick* and *York* as Force "F" on the America and West Indies Station, entailed their withdrawal from the Halifax Escort Force. They were still working independently, however, when the *Berwick* docked at Bermuda on 19 October. Two days later a report reached the Commander-in-Chief, North America and West Indies Station, Vice-Admiral Sir Sydney Meyrick, K.C.B., that the Norwegian ship *Lorentz W. Hansen*, 1,918 tons, had been stopped on 14 October by a pocket battleship 300 miles east of Newfoundland. She had, in fact, been sunk that day by the *Deutschland*[30] in 49° 5' N., 43° 44' W., 420 miles east of Newfoundland.[31] Orders were at once given to the *Enterprise* and *York* to concentrate in the focal area south of Halifax where the *Berwick* would join them as soon as possible.

These orders were never carried out. Shortly after they were issued the Admiralty ordered the *Berwick* and *Perth* to leave Bermuda[32] and steer 060° at high speed. The *York* was to proceed from Halifax along the route of Convoy H.X.5 which had sailed on 17 October and was still in the threatened area.[33] On 28 October the *Berwick* arrived back at Bermuda to complete her repairs and left there on 7 November to join the Home Fleet.

Two days later, the *York* developed defects too serious for local repair. She left Bermuda on 17 November and escorted Convoy H.X.10 home from Halifax on 26 November. After refitting in the United Kingdom, she too joined the Home Fleet. Busy with other tasks and urgent repairs the two cruisers had never worked together as Force "F."[34]

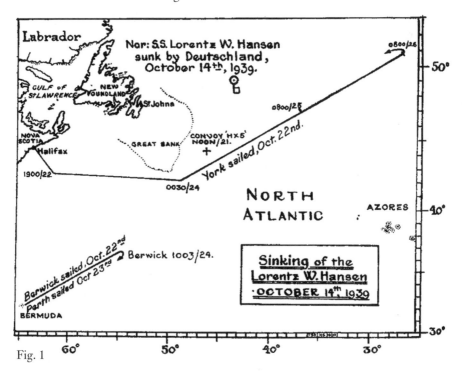

Fig. 1

Meanwhile the *Malaya* and *Glorious* had left Aden on 14 October for their initial patrol of the Socotra area as Force "J." The patrol continued with short breaks for refuelling and without result till 6 December, when the *Glorious* was detached to Colombo and the *Malaya* to Halifax. In the meantime the search for the missing raider had ranged far and wide over the waters of the South Atlantic Ocean.

A sequel to the appearance of the raider off Pernambuco was closer co-operation between British and French forces in the South Atlantic. Though Rear-Admiral J. H. C. F. Moreau, Commander of the French 5th Squadron, had arranged to co-operate with the Commander-in-Chief, South Atlantic, Admiral Lyon had so far received little information concerning the French dispositions and movements at Dakar. He therefore invited Vice-Admiral

Duplat, who had arrived at Dakar in the French cruiser *Algerie* on 14 October, to meet him at Freetown. The Admiral welcomed the suggestion and visited Freetown on 19 October. The meeting led to a greater understanding between the British and French commands. To maintain it Commander Kenneth Cary Helyar was appointed British Naval Liaison Officer at Dakar with Lieutenant-Commander Frank C. R. Younghusband as his assistant.

The French were maintaining more or less regular patrols. During the month Dakar forces accounted for two German ships. On 16 October the German SS *Halle*, outward bound from Bissau in the Bissagos Islands, was intercepted off Dakar by the cruiser *Duguay-Trouin* and scuttled herself. On 25 October Force "X", consisting of the French cruisers *Algerie* and *Dupleix* and the battlecruiser *Strasbourg* with two French destroyers in company captured[35] the German SS *Santa Fé* which had escaped from Rio de Janeiro on 14 October, and brought her into Dakar.[36]

Meanwhile on 9 October[37] the Commander-in-Chief South Atlantic had informed the Admiralty and Commodore Harwood of his intention to co-ordinate the movements of Force "G" (*Cumberland* and *Exeter*), Force "H" (*Sussex* and *Shropshire*) and Force "K" (*Ark Royal* and *Renown*). As this would entail long periods of wireless silence in Force "G" he proposed that Commodore Harwood should transfer to the *Ajax*, leaving Captain Fallowfield of the *Cumberland* as its senior officer. The Admiralty approved of this, and Captain Fallowfield was ordered to co-ordinate his movements with those of Forces "H" and "K." The Commodore, after stating his intention of transferring his broad pendant in the River Plate on 27 October, suggested that the *Exeter*, which had only half the endurance of the *Cumberland*, should be relieved by a 10,000-ton cruiser. He also expressed his view that the relative importance of areas off the east coast of South America appeared to be:–

(1) River Plate focal area.
(2) Rio de Janeiro–Santos focal area.
(3) Diverted routes in a semicircle of 600 miles radius from a point roughly midway between the Plate and Rio de Janeiro.
(4) Diverted routes within a circle 500 miles from position 20 S., 28° W.

and suggested that unless an enemy warship were known to be in the vicinity, Area 4 might normally be covered by an armed merchant cruiser.

The inclusion of the *Exeter* in Force "G" created a new problem.[38] Owing to her small fuel capacity she could not work far from her fuelling base in the Plate but no suitable cruiser was available to relieve her.[39]

On 12 October the first of the new forces arrived on the station. The *Ark Royal*, flying the flag of the Vice-Admiral, Aircraft Carriers, Vice-Admiral L. V. Wells, C.B., D.S.O., reached Freetown that morning from the United Kingdom with the *Renown*. They were followed by the destroyers *Hardy*, *Hostile* and *Hasty* from the Mediterranean Fleet. Next day the cruisers *Sussex* and *Shropshire* reached Simonstown from the Mediterranean,[40] and on 14 October the *Hermes* reached Dakar from Plymouth.

On the passage south aircraft from the *Ark Royal* had sighted a vessel to westward of the Cape Verde Islands[41] which claimed to be the United States SS *Delmar*. She was lying stopped with her crew fishing hundreds of miles from land, but "owing to the absence of destroyers in company" no attempt was made to intercept her. Later on the Admiralty ascertained that the real *Delmar* was in New Orleans, and the Commander-in-Chief, South Atlantic, remarked that the ship sighted by the *Ark Royal*'s aircraft "might well have been an enemy supply ship."

South America Division, Early October[42]

When news that an enemy warship was in the South Atlantic reached the Commander-in-Chief at Freetown on 1 October[43] he immediately suspended sailings from Pernambuco and Natal (Brazil) and sent the *Havock*[44] and *Hotspur* to escort British ships clear of the area. But next morning he cancelled these dispositions and ordered Commodore Harwood to concentrate the *Exeter*, *Ajax* and the destroyers 1,000 miles further south off Rio de Janeiro. By this time, however, the raider was far away from the South American coast.

From a steam of contradictory reports emanating from Bahia, Pernambuco and Rio de Janeiro during the next 10 days it appeared that the raider might be a *Hipper*, *Leipzig* or *Schwabenland* class cruiser, though descriptions by more reliable witnesses indicated that she was a pocket battleship, probably the *Admiral Scheer*.

The Commodore being far from certain that the raider was in fact a pocket battleship, however, hesitated to abandon the valuable British shipping in the Plate area. He thought that the intention behind the appearance of a raider to the northward might be to divert his ships from the Plate, opening the way for others to attack British shipping where it was thickest. Before the Commander-in-Chief's order to concentrate in the Rio de Janeiro area reached him, he had informed Admiral Lyon[45] that he intended to concentrate the *Exeter* and *Ajax* off Rio and to send the *Hotspur* to cover the Rio de Janeiro–Santos area while keeping the *Havock* off the Plate.

He ordered the *Ajax* to join him in the Rio area[46] at 1700 on 3 October, and directed the Consular Shipping Adviser at Montevideo to suspend the local Plate convoys and to revert to diverted routeing as far from the coast as possible.

At the same time he instructed the Consular Shipping Advisers at Rio de Janeiro and Santos to suspend sailings for four days so as to give the *Hotspur* time to reach the area vacated by the *Ajax*.

The *Exeter*, after fuelling from the *Olwen* off English Bank in the Plate estuary[47] on 2 October joined the *Ajax* at 18 knots. When he received the Commander-in-Chief's order to concentrate[48] the Commodore instructed the destroyers to meet him after fuelling, but not later than 0800 on 4 October.

The Admiralty now informed him that the New Zealand cruiser *Achilles*, Captain W. E. Parry, would reinforce his division from the west coast of South America. On 3 October the Commander-in-Chief directed that, failing any further raider developments in the immediate future, the *Ajax*, *Achilles* and the two destroyers should protect trade in the Rio de Janeiro and Plate areas. The *Exeter* and *Cumberland* were to carry out their initial sweep as a hunting unit as far north as their fuel supplies allowed.

Reports that the raider was not a pocket battleship continued coming in. The Commodore was still anxious not to leave the Plate trade exposed to attack by a hostile armed merchant vessel while all the British warships were drawn off to the north. He therefore amended his previous order and instructed the *Havock* to return to the Plate. She was to maintain 75 per cent of fuel, ready to rejoin him with *Despatch* if, after all, the raider proved to be a pocked battleship and showed signs of coming south.

When a report from Bahia confirmed that the *Clement* had been sunk by the *Admiral Scheer*[49] he no longer felt justified, however, in departing from the Commander-in-Chief's order to keep his ships concentrated and again directed the *Havock* to meet him in the Rio area. She joined him at 1300 on 4 October. In the meantime the *Ajax* had joined him at 1700/3 and the *Hotspur* at 0500/4 . The *Cumberland*, which had returned to Freetown on 2 October to fuel after sweeping for German ships off Ascension on 28 September, had left Freetown at 1900 on 3 October to meet him in the same area.

Commodore Harwood's Policy against Raiders[50] and a Raider Report

Commodore Harwood had decided to keep his forces concentrated and, failing any further raider reports, to patrol the Rio de Janeiro area, in accordance with the Commander-in-Chief's order.

If he met a pocket battleship in daylight he intended to shadow it till dusk. He would then close and attack in the dark hours. If, on the other hand, he made contact at night, his destroyers would at once close the enemy's beam and attack her with torpedoes.

On 5 October, the British ship *Martand* informed the *Cumberland* in 1° 10' S., 19° 20' W., that a German armed raider had attacked an unknown ship – which was in fact the British SS *Newton Beech* – 900 miles away on the Cape–Freetown route in 9° 20' S., 6° 19' W. According to the Commander-in-Chief the value of this information, which if acted upon might, in his opinion, have led to the early destruction of the *Graf Spee* and her supply ship, the *Altmark*, was apparently not appreciated by the *Cumberland*. At the time she was 700 miles from Freetown, and Captain Fallowfield assumed that the message would be intercepted and passed on to the Commander-in-Chief by ships on the Cape–Freetown route, even if it were not intercepted by a shore station. He also considered wireless silence particularly important and decided against breaking it. The Admiralty, however, were strongly of opinion that the report should have been passed to the Commander-in-Chief. As it was, Admiral Lyon knew nothing of it till 21 January, 1940.[51]

By 5 October, 1939, the *Exeter*, *Ajax*, *Havock* and *Hotspur* were concentrated in the Rio de Janeiro area ready to engage the raider if she came south from the neighbourhood of Pernambuco. The *Achilles* was on her way round Cape Horn to reinforce the South America Division.

When the *Ajax* visited Rio on 7 October Commodore Harwood directed her to suggest to the Consular Shipping Advisers there, and at Santos, that, owing to the small volume of shipping leaving these ports, the local convoy systems, which had been instituted on 22 September against armed merchant raiders, should be suspended, and Allied ships routed independently.

The Commodore intended to meet the *Cumberland* at 1700 on 8 October at the rendezvous given to her by the Commander-in-Chief. At 1600 on 7 October, however, a message reached him from the Consular Shipping Adviser at Rio who desired to sail a 13-knot convoy at 0430 the next day and asked him if an escort could be arranged as this convoy had received much local publicity.

The Commodore thought that this "publicity" might draw the reported pocket battleship into the area. He therefore took his entire force back towards Rio to meet the convoy at dawn on 8 October, sending the *Hotspur* on ahead to make contact and keeping the *Exeter*, *Ajax* and *Havock* in support. The convoy consisted of the British ships *Highland Chieftain* and *Nariva* and the French *Alsina*, which having great difficulty in keeping station greatly hampered it by her erratic behaviour.

Meanwhile the Commodore had directed the *Cumberland* to meet him at dawn on 9 October. When the convoy was dispersed at 1800 August the *Exeter* and *Ajax* steered to meet her and the *Havock* parted company to fuel at Montevideo. At 2200 the Commodore detached the *Ajax* with orders to keep clear of the *Cumberland* during the night.

When the *Cumberland* joined the Commodore at 0500, the *Exeter*, being short of fuel, was unable to carry out the sweep northwards ordered by the Commander-in-Chief on 3 October.[52] He therefore decided to work down to the Plate keeping the *Hotspur* with him as long as possible.

On 12 October Rio Grande do Sul reported the German ship *Rio Grande* about to sail. The Commodore at once closed with the *Cumberland* to intercept her. He arrived off Rio Grande do Sul at 1600 next day, but finding all quiet in the harbour shaped course for the Plate at nightfall. Meanwhile he had ordered the *Hotspur* to refuel at Montevideo when the *Havock* left there next morning.

About this time the *Olwen* informed[53] him that the German SS *Bahia Laura* was leaving Montevideo at 1000 next morning and might protest if the *Havock* was sailed the same day. Instead, therefore, of entering Montevideo the *Hotspur* at once refuelled from the *Olwen* and then remained out on patrol. The *Bahia Laura*, however, showed no signs of leaving and at 0800 the *Havock* put to sea. Four hours later the *Hotspur* entered Montevideo. That day the *Exeter* and *Cumberland* fuelled from the *Olwen* in San Borombon Bay at the southern entrance of the Plate estuary. When the *Havock* joined them at 1430 Commodore Harwood ordered her to watch Montevideo for the *Bahia Laura*, and when the *Exeter* finished fuelling he put out to sea. The *Cumberland* rejoined him at 0700 next day, 15 October. He then ordered the *Havock* to join him on patrol.

On 16 October he learned that the *Bahia Laura* had sailed at 1015 the previous day. When the signal reached him she was far out in the open sea, well past his patrol line, but as the whole area was enveloped in dense fog he considered that her interception would have been most unlikely.

South America Division, Late October[54]

Meanwhile Commodore Harwood had informed the Commander-in-Chief on 13 October that as the *Exeter* required certain minor repairs he proposed to proceed to the Falklands on 17 October and to return to the Plate on 27 of the month. The Commander-in-Chief replied that he would prefer the *Exeter* to stay in the Plate area till the Commodore transferred his Broad Pendant to the *Ajax* on 27 October. As the *Achilles* was due in the Plate by this date, she and the *Cumberland* could then operate as Force "G" in the *Exeter*'s absence.

This meant that there would be no cruiser in the Rio de Janeiro area till the *Exeter*, on her return, relieved the *Achilles* in Force "G." The Commodore therefore ordered the *Havock* to sail on 21 October for a four days' patrol in the Rio–Santos area, where the *Hotspur*, which could remain at sea till 2 November, would relieve her. From that date till the relief of the *Achilles* there would be no ship in the area. The Commodore therefore asked the Commander-in-Chief to allow Force "G" to work there from 2 to 10 November.

When the *Hotspur* joined the *Exeter* and *Cumberland* from Montevideo on 17 October the Commodore ordered her to patrol off Rio Grande do Sul to intercept the German ships *Rio Grande* and *Montevideo* if they came out, and sent the *Havock* to patrol inshore with orders to anchor at night clear of the shipping route.

This proved to be the last duty of these two destroyers with the South America Division. On 20 October the Admiralty ordered their transfer to the West Indies. Three days later the Commodore sent them into Buenos Aires to fuel, and as the distance to Trinidad, 4,000 miles, was almost the limit of their endurance, also obtained permission to refuel them at Pernambuco. They left Buenos Aires on 25 October and, after bidding the Commodore farewell, proceeded northwards. They sailed from Pernambuco on 1 November, but on 3 November the *Havock* was diverted to Freetown with engine trouble. The two remaining destroyers of the 4th Division, the *Hyperion* and *Hunter*, had left Freetown with Convoy S.L.6 on 23 October. Off Dakar their duties were taken over by the French cruiser *Duguay-Trouin*. They fuelled at Dakar on 27 October and sailed for Trinidad next morning.

Meanwhile the *Cumberland* had entered Montevideo at 0800/26. An hour later the *Achilles* joined the *Exeter* off the Plate and, after fuelling from the *Olwen* sailed to meet the *Cumberland* off Lobos next day with orders to cover the Rio–Santos area with her as Force "G." The *Olwen* was proceeding to the West Indies and the *Ajax*, which had arrived from the Rio area on 26 October, took all her remaining fuel except 500 tons for her passage to Trinidad. That morning, 27 October, Commodore Harwood transferred his Broad Pendant to the *Ajax* and the *Exeter* sailed for Port Stanley.

Meanwhile the newly constituted Forces "H" and "K" were busy on the other side of the South Atlantic. Force "H," the *Sussex* and *Shropshire*, had reached the Cape on 13 October.[55]

As the *Cumberland* had not passed on the *Martand*'s report, no news of the raider had reached the Admiralty or Commander-in-Chief since 1 October and on 14 October Force "H" sailed to search for her along the Cape–Freetown route as far as the latitude of St. Helena. That day Force "K" (the *Ark Royal* and *Renown*) left Freetown with the *Neptune*, *Hardy*, *Hero* and *Hereward* to search westward towards St. Paul Rocks, the direction of their sweep being determined by the complete lack of any further raider information.

A Raider Report and Sweeps by Forces "H" and "K"

The three weeks' old mystery of the raider's whereabouts was partially solved on 22 October when the British SS *Llanstephan Castle* intercepted a signal from an unknown ship: "Gunned in 16° S., 4° 3' E., at 1400 G.M.T."[56] There was, however, no immediate confirmation of her report, and the Commander-in-Chief ordered Force "K," the *Neptune* and the destroyers on their return to Freetown on 23 October to remain there at four hours' notice and clean boilers. Force "H" had returned to the Cape ports on 22 October, and the *Shropshire*, which had sailed from Capetown at 0600 on 23 October to rejoin the *Sussex* off Port Elizabeth, was recalled and Force "H" kept at short notice.[57]

Although the southern half of the Freetown–Cape route had been swept by Force "H" between 14 and 22 October, the Commander-in-Chief decided, in view of the *Llanstephan Castle's* report, on a new and complete sweep of the whole route. He ordered Force "H" to sail after dark on 27 October for the latitude of St. Helena. At noon on 31 October it was in 15° S., 2° 51' E., the north-eastern limit of its patrol, when a Walrus aircraft failed to return to the *Sussex* from a reconnaissance flight. It was never found, though the two cruisers spent three and a half days searching for it. Being short of fuel they then returned to the Cape by the route on which they had swept outwards.

Sweep by Force "K"

To cover the northern end of the route as far as St. Helena, Force "K" left Freetown on 28 October with the *Neptune* and the destroyers *Hardy*, *Hasty*, *Hero* and *Hereward*. The *Neptune* was to sweep independently from 3° 20' S., 1° 10' W., through 14° 30' S., 16° 50' W., back to Freetown.

On 30 October a report from Dakar stated that the German SS *Togo* had left the Congo on 26 October, that the German SS *Pioneer* had sailed from Fernando Po on 28 October and that five German ships had left Lobito the same day. When the Vice-Admiral, Aircraft Carriers, received this information he detached the *Hardy* and *Hasty* to sweep north-westward for the *Pioneer*, while Force "K" and the remaining destroyers searched for her to the south-westward. Both searches were unsuccessful. Meanwhile, a message from Lobito had stated that the five vessels reported to have sailed from there were still in harbour. On 5 November the German SS *Uhenfels*, which had escaped from Lourenço Marques on 16 October, was sighted by an aircraft from the *Ark Royal*. Only energetic action on the part of the *Hereward* saved her from being scuttled.[58] She was brought into Freetown by the *Hereward* on 7 November, a few hours behind Force "K."[59]

The South Atlantic, November

Forces "H" and "G", Early November, 1939

The first half of November was comparatively quiet on both sides of the South Atlantic. At the opening of the month Forces "H" and "K" were still on the diverted shipping route between Sierra Leone and the Cape.

On 3 November the Admiralty informed the Commander-in-Chief[60] that all German capital ships and cruisers were apparently in Home Waters. It appeared, therefore, that the pocket battleship, which was still thought to be the *Admiral Scheer*, had returned home and that the raider reported by the *Llanstephan Castle* on 22 October was nothing but an armed merchantman. Here was a good opportunity for resting the hunting groups, and on 4 November the Admiralty issued orders[61] that Forces "G" and "H" should exchange areas. This exchange would not only give Force "G" an opportunity of resting and refitting at the Cape, but would also provide Commodore Harwood with the hunting group of long endurance that he so greatly desired.

The Commander-in-Chief had planned that Force "H," which had returned to the Cape ports on 7 November, should sweep towards Durban, arriving there on 16 November. This would have taken it within 160 miles of the *Graf Spee* when she sank the *Africa Shell* of Lourenço Marques on 15 November. On 5 November, however, he ordered it to sail on 11 of the month and effect, westward of St. Helena, on the evening of 17 November, the exchange of areas with Force "G."

Although on 8 November the Admiralty, cancelling the suppositions of the former signal (3 November), informed the Commander-in-Chief that the *Admiral Scheer* was believed to be in the Indian Ocean, Force "H" duly left the Cape on 11 November. Bad weather had, however, delayed Force "G" in the Plate, where the *Exeter* had been considerably damaged by her oiler casting off in a heavy sea. Before the exchange of areas could take place it was cancelled.[62]

South America Division, First Half of November, 1939

After hoisting Commodore Harwood's Broad Pendant on 27 October, the *Ajax* had swept the Plate focal area. When the Commodore received the Commander-in-Chief's order of 5 November for the change over of Forces "H" and "G" on 17 November, he ordered the *Cumberland* to proceed to the Plate at 20 knots and refuel. About this time a message reached him from Buenos Aires that the Argentine Foreign Minister had drawn attention to cases of fuelling in the Plate by the *Exeter* and *Ajax*. Although the Argentine Government had no apparent intention of raising the issue, he decided to cut down fuellings in the inshore waters of the Plate as much as possible. He therefore cancelled the fuelling of the *Exeter*, due to take place there on 7 November from the oiler *Olynthus*, which had relieved the *Olwen*, and ordered the *Cumberland* to fuel at Buenos Aires on 9 November. The *Exeter*, which had arrived at the Falklands on 31 October, sailed on 4 November to meet the *Cumberland* off the Plate on 10 November, but the Commodore ordered her to enter Mar del Plata[63] on 9 November for a 24-hour visit. As this gave her some time in hand, he ordered her to cover the Plate while he visited Buenos Aires in the *Ajax* from 6 to 8 November to discuss with the Argentine naval authorities the question of fuelling his ships in the River Plate Estuary.

As the Northern, or Lobos Island, exit from the Plate was covered by the approach of the *Cumberland* from the Rio area, the *Exeter* took up a patrol between Rouen Bank and Cape San Antonio. She sighted only one vessel, the British SS *Harcalo*, outward-bound from Buenos Aires to Freetown, which she met on 8 November, 95 miles east of Cape San Antonio.

During his visit to Buenos Aires, the Commodore discussed the question of the English Bank fuelling with the Argentine Minister of Marine and his Chief of Naval Staff. They both suggested that he should use San Borombon Bay. This was most acceptable. He had in fact been using it for some time.

When the *Ajax* left Buenos Aires on 8 November she patrolled the Plate area. The *Exeter* made fast alongside the Escollera Norte at Mar del Plata next day. A strong south-westerly gale was blowing, which would have made it impossible for her to leave the wall even if circumstances had demanded it. As fuel could not be obtained at Mar del Plata, the Commodore ordered her to fuel from the *Olynthus* in San Borombon Bay on 10 November and instructed the *Cumberland* to meet her 35 miles south of Lobos Island[64] at 0600 November.

By the morning of 10 November the gale had blown itself out and the *Exeter* left Mar del Plata. The *Ajax* was fuelling from the *Olynthus* in San Borombon Bay. At 1600 the *Exeter* started fuelling with the *Ajax* at anchor close by. The gale sprang up again. The *Olynthus* was forced to cast off, severely damaging the *Exeter*, which was still 600 tons short of fuel. As she could not reach the Cape without a full supply the sailing of Force "G" to exchange areas with Force "H" was delayed. The *Exeter* finally finished fuelling on 13 November and sailed with the *Cumberland* for Simonstown. Before the exchange of areas could be effected, however, a raider was reported off Lourenço Marques and the order was cancelled.[65]

Another Raider Report[66]

On 16 November the Naval Officer-in-Charge, Simonstown, reported that the British SS *Africa Shell* had been sunk off Lourenço Marques the previous day by a raider identified as a pocket battleship. After the usual conflicting reports from eye-witnesses during the next few days, however, it was doubtful how many raiders there were or whether they were pocket battleships or heavy cruisers.

The presence of an enemy heavy ship or ships off Lourenço Marques called for new dispositions. When the raider report reached Whitehall on 17 November, the Admiralty, cancelling the exchange of areas between Force "H" (*Sussex* and *Shropshire*) and Force "G" (*Cumberland* and *Exeter*) ordered the return of Force "H" to the Cape and the retention of Force "G" on the East Coast of South America. They also ordered the *Despatch* of Force "K" towards the Cape with instructions to go on to Diego Suarez in Madagascar. That morning a report reached the Commander-in-Chief that the German ships *Windhuk* and *Adolf Woermann* had left Lobito. He at once ordered Force "H," which was west of St. Helena in the approximate latitude of Lobito[67]" to spend three days searching for them.

Next day Force "K" left Freetown with the *Neptune*, *Hero*, *Hardy* and *Hostile*, to sweep west of St. Helena through 16° 30' S., 10° W., and thence to Diego Suarez. The destroyers parted company at 2300 that night to search for the German ships. On 20 November the Commander-in-Chief ordered Force "H" to return to the Cape if nothing had been sighted. Both cruisers reached Cape ports on 23 November.

The *Adolf Woermann* had not escaped. Early on 21 November the British SS *Waimarama* reported her in 12° 24' S., 3° 31' W. At 1127 Force "K"

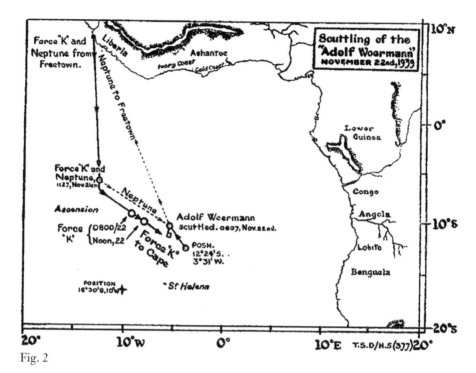

Fig. 2

(*Ark Royal* and *Renown*), which was in 5° 55' S., 12° 26' W., altered course to close, and the *Neptune* went ahead at high speed. Shortly after 0800/22 she made contact with the *Adolf Woermann* in 10° 37' S., 5° 11' W., and went alongside. Despite strenuous efforts to save her the German vessel was scuttled, and when the *Neptune* reached Freetown early on 25 November she had 162 German survivors onboard.[68]

Forces "H" and "K", Late November[69]

As the search for the *Adolf Woermann* had taken Force "K" nearly 200 miles to the eastward, the Vice-Admiral, Aircraft Carriers, decided to proceed towards the Cape by the route east of St. Helena to save fuel. This may have resulted according to the Commander-in-Chief in the escape of the German supply ship *Altmark*, which was awaiting the return of the *Graf Spee* to the Atlantic in the unfrequented areas west of the Cape Shipping Routes, through which Force "K" would have swept. On 23 November, while Force "K" was still north-west of Cape Town, the Commander-in-Chief ordered Force "H" to sail from the Cape next day and patrol the "Diversive Routes" as far as 33° E. till 28 November.

At the northern end of the South Atlantic Station the *Neptune*, *Hardy*, *Hero*, *Hostile*, *Hasty* and the submarine *Clyde*, after parting company with Force "K" on 21 November, had established a patrol to intercept escaping German merchant ships or raiders between 22 and 25 November[70] on a line joining Freetown and Cape San Roque, Brazil. It was maintained without result till all units were recalled to Freetown on 30 November.

In the meantime the Admiralty had ordered[71] Force "H" (*Sussex* and *Shropshire*) and Force "K" (*Ark Royal* and *Renown*) on 27 November to form a patrol to the southward of the Cape. At noon Force "K" was in 34° 10' S., 13° 23' E., 250 miles 273° from Cape Point.[72] Force "H" was approaching the Cape ports and the Commander-in-Chief ordered its ships to refuel before joining Force "K" for the combined patrol on the meridian of 20° E.[73] The two forces met early on 1 December. (Plan 3)

The plan, according to the Commander-in-Chief, appeared to be a "good one in theory," but was found unsuitable in practice on account of local weather conditions. These permitted flying from a carrier only once in five or six days, so that the patrol could not be extended far enough to the south to intercept a raider bent on evasion. In fact, only once, on 2 December, during the time Force "K" was on patrol, from 28 November – 2 December, was the weather suitable for flying.[74]

South America Division, Late November

After the *Cumberland* and *Exeter*, Force "G", had sailed from San Borombon Bay for Simonstown on 13 November, the *Ajax* patrolled the Plate area and escorted the French SS *Massilia*, bound for Europe from Buenos Aires with French reservists. After parting from the *Massilia* she closed Rio Grande do Sul and ascertained that the German ships *Rio Grande* and *Montevideo* were still there. For the next two days she patrolled the normal peace-time shipping routes.

When the Admiralty cancelled the exchange of areas between the *Exeter* and *Cumberland*, Force "G," and the *Shropshire* and *Sussex*, Force "H," on 17 November, Commodore Harwood sent Force "G" to cover Rio de Janeiro. He ordered the *Achilles* to refuel from the *Olynthus* in the Plate on 22 November and then relieve Force "G" in the Rio de Janeiro–Santos focal area. As the *Exeter* would require fuel on 26 November he instructed her and the *Cumberland* to meet the *Olynthus* in the Plate area that day. They would then patrol the Plate while the *Ajax* visited the Falklands.

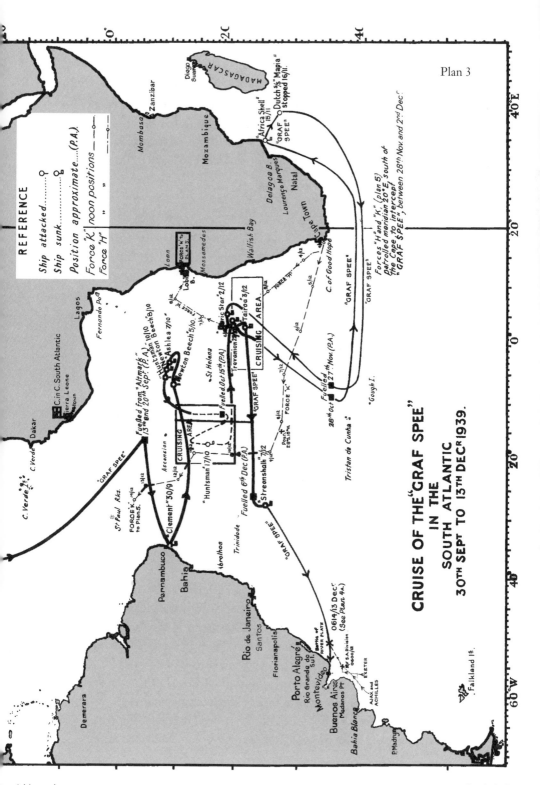

CRUISE OF THE "GRAF SPEE"
IN THE
SOUTH ATLANTIC
30TH SEPT TO 13TH DEC.R 1939.

Plan 3

REFERENCE

Ship attacked.........Q
Ship sunk.............Q
Position approximate.....(P.A.)
Force "K" noon positions ——
Force "H"   "   "

On 18 November the Commodore was informed that the German SS *Ussukumu* might sail from Bahia Blanca for Montevideo at any time. He at once ordered the *Olynthus* to watch for her between Medanos and Cape San Antonio and took the *Ajax* south to the same vicinity.[75]

At 0700/22, the *Achilles* heard the German SS *Lahn* calling Cerrito by wireless, and when the *Ajax* arrived half an hour later a search was carried out. It was unsuccessful for both the *Lahn* and the German SS *Tacoma* reached Montevideo safely during the forenoon.

The two cruisers fuelled from the *Olynthus* in San Borombon Bay next afternoon. The *Achilles* then sailed for the Rio area. She had orders to move up to Pernambuco and show herself off Cabadello and Bahia as a number of German ships in Pernambuco were reported ready to sail to Cabadello to load cotton for Germany. She was to return at once to the Rio area if any raiders were reported in the South Atlantic.

The *Ajax* left the Plate on 25 November and sent up a seaplane to reconnoitre Bahia Blanca. The *Ussukumu* showed no signs of sailing, and she proceeded to the Falklands, arriving there on 27 November.

By this time the *Cumberland* and *Exeter* were in urgent need of refits after long periods at sea, and Commodore Harwood ordered the *Exeter* to proceed to the Falklands forthwith. She arrived at Port Stanley on 29 November and her defects were taken in hand.

8 December was the twenty-fifth anniversary of the Battle of the Falklands, and thinking that the enemy might attempt to avenge the defeat the Commodore ordered the *Cumberland* to join the *Exeter* there on 7 December. She was to patrol off the Islands for two days before entering Port Stanley for repairs and rest.[76]

French Forces, Dakar, November, 1939[77]

During November the most important event at Dakar, where the French were maintaining a number of more or less regular patrols, was the reorganisation of Force "X." On 1 November the French destroyer[78] *Audacieux* sailed from Dakar westward to 26° W. and thence south-west in search of the German SS *Togo*. She returned on 4 November without sighting anything. That day the *Duguay-Trouin* sailed to sweep round the Cape Verde Islands and on to St. Paul Rocks. She returned on 10 November. The old Force "X," the *Algerie*, Flag of Vice-Admiral Duplat, *Dupleix* and *Strasbourg*, had sailed on 7 November to sweep west of the Cape Verde Islands. It returned on

13 November. Meanwhile French submarines based on Casablanca were maintaining a continuous patrol round the Canary Islands between 25° and 30° N.

On 18 November the French 5ᵗʰ Squadron was disbanded. Admiral Duplat shifted his flag to the *Dupleix* and assumed command of the new Force "X." This now consisted of the French cruisers *Dupleix* and *Foch* and the British aircraft carrier *Hermes*. On 21 November the *Algerie*, flag of Admiral Moreau, *Strasbourg*, *Le Terrible* and *Le Fantasque*, left Dakar for European waters, and next day Force "X" sailed with the *Milan* and *Cassard* to cruise towards 8° N., 30° W. That day, 22 November, the *Audacieux* sailed with a convoy for Casablanca.

On 25 November the *Duguay-Trouin* sailed to patrol the parallel of 19° N. between 25° and 30° W., and two days later the British submarine *Severn* docked at Dakar. On 30 November the *Dupleix* and *Foch* arrived from patrol, being followed next day by the *Hermes*, *Milan* and *Cassard*.

British Movements Leading to the Battle of the Plate

Dispositions of South Atlantic Forces

At the beginning of December the *Ark Royal*, flag of the Vice-Admiral, Aircraft Carriers, and *Renown*, Force "K," were patrolling the meridian of 20° E. south of the Cape with the *Sussex* and *Shropshire*, Force "H," to intercept the raider reported off Lourenço Marques on 15 November.

In the north the cruiser *Neptune*, the destroyers *Hardy*, *Hero*, *Hostile*, *Hasty*, and the submarine *Clyde*, were returning to Freetown after patrolling between there and Cape San Roque for escaping German merchant ships or raiders. The French cruisers *Dupleix* and *Foch* and the British aircraft carrier *Hermes*, Force "X," accompanied by the French destroyers *Milan* and *Cassard*, were approaching Dakar from a patrol parallel to and 130 miles N.N.W. of the British line. The French cruiser *Duguay-Trouin* was patrolling the parallel of 19° N. between 25° and 30° W. and the British submarine *Severn* was refitting at Dakar.

Across the South Atlantic, Commodore Harwood, in the *Ajax*, was at Port Stanley with the *Exeter*. The *Cumberland*, which was due at Port Stanley on 9 December, was still in the River Plate area, and the *Achilles* was off Rio de Janeiro.

Forces "H" and "K"[79]

No further reports had been received of the raider which had sunk the *Africa Shell* off Lourenço Marques on 15 November, and it seemed clear that she had either gone further into the Indian Ocean or had doubled back into the Atlantic well south of the Cape, after achieving her apparent object of drawing a large proportion of the British South Atlantic forces into the area east of Cape Point. On 2 December the Admiralty ordered Forces "K" and "H" to return to their patrol line south of the Cape after refuelling, and the Commander-in-Chief at once ordered them to proceed to the Cape ports for fuel. That day a reconnaissance aircraft of the South African Air

Force reported a suspicious ship south of Cape Point at noon. The *Sussex* intercepted her, but her crew set her on fire. She proved to be the German SS *Watussi* (9,600 tons), and was sunk by the guns of the *Renown*. Her survivors were taken into Simonstown by the *Sussex*.

No news of the missing raider had come in since 16 November. Then the mystery shrouding her whereabouts was again partially solved. At 1530 that afternoon, 2 December, a raider signal "R.R.R. 19° 15' S., 5° 5' E. gunned battleship" reached the Commander-in-Chief from the British SS *Doric Star*. As this signal placed the raider in the South Atlantic the Commander-in-Chief at once decided to abandon the patrol south of the Cape, and ordered Force "H" to cover the trade routes between the Cape and the latitude of St. Helena at 20 knots on completion of fuelling. As it was too late for Force "K" to reach the Freetown–Pernambuco area in time to intercept the raider if she made for the North Atlantic, he proposed to the Admiralty that Force "K" after fuelling should sweep direct from the Cape to a position in 20° S., 15° W., and thence to Freetown. He added that he believed from previous experience that if the raider reported on 2 December was proceeding south and east she would probably keep well clear of the trade routes. Early next morning the Admiralty placed Force "K" at his disposal and indicated that he should assume that the raider would not proceed south and east round the Cape of Good Hope.[80]

That morning, 3 December, Force "H" reached Simonstown three-quarters of an hour before Force "K" arrived at Cape Town. The Commander-in-Chief ordered the Vice-Admiral, Aircraft Carriers, to make for the position in 20° S., 15° W. This was changed at the request of the Vice-Admiral to 28° S., 15° W., to place his Force in a more central position for proceeding to Freetown, to the Falklands, or to Rio de Janeiro.[81] At 1030 a report reached the Commander-in-Chief that the pocket battleship *Admiral Scheer* had been in 21° 20' S., 3° 10' E.[82] at 0501, clearly indicating that the raider was moving westward, clear of the Cape–Sierra Leone trade route. Force "H" left Simonstown at 1700 that afternoon, 3 December, and Force "K" sailed from Cape Town at 0915 next morning after a short delay during which its aircraft were being made serviceable. The search of the broad waters of the South Atlantic for the elusive raider was once more in full swing. Again it could be likened to the hunt of the proverbial needle in a haystack and once again the hunt proved fruitless. When Force "H" reached the area where the *Graf Spee* had been working off Walfish Bay the raider was already a thousand miles away to the westward. No better fortune attended Force "K," which crossed the raider's track in 23° S., 19° W.[83] on 9 December, about four days too late to intercept her.

Although the Commander-in-Chief had been instructed to assume that the raider would not proceed round the Cape, and though there were clear indications that she was moving westward in the South Atlantic, the Admiralty, taking no chances, ordered the *Cornwall*, *Eagle* and *Gloucester*[84] on 4 December to establish a new patrol south of the Cape. They were to work under the Commander-in-Chief, South Atlantic, in conjunction with the South African Air Force. On 8 December, however, the Admiralty replaced them under the Commander-in-Chief, East Indies, who recalled them to Durban, where they arrived on 12 December.

The Commander-in-Chief, South Atlantic, estimated that if the raider proceeded northward she would, at 15 knots, cross the Freetown–Pernambuco line between 9 and 10 December. He therefore arranged that Vice-Admiral Duplat, the Senior Officer of Force "X," should take the *Neptune* and her destroyers under his orders and patrol the parallel of 3° N. between 31° W. and 38° W. from 10 – 13 December. Force "K" would meet the *Neptune* and destroyers on 14 December and return to Freetown and refuel. The destroyers, the 3rd Division of the 2nd Destroyer Flotilla (*Hardy*, *Hostile* and *Hero*[85]), left Freetown on 6 December with the RFA *Cherryleaf*. They had orders to meet the *Dupleix* (Flag of Vice-Admiral Duplat), *Foch*, *Hermes*, Force "X," the French destroyers[86] *Milan* and *Cassard*, and the *Neptune*, in 3° N., 31° W., on 10 December. On 7 December Force "X" left Dakar for the rendezvous. That day the submarine *Clyde* left Freetown to patrol between 3° N., 23° W., and 3° N., 28° W., and thence to 5° 15' N., 23 W., between 9–13 December.[87]

On the evening of 8 December the German ship *Adolf Leonhardt* (3,000 tons) sailed from Lobito for South America. Force "H," which by then was between St. Helena and the west coast of Africa, was at once ordered to intercept her. The *Shropshire*'s aircraft made contact at 0952 next morning and alighted alongside in 13° S., 11° 44' E. At 1250 the *Shropshire* came up, but despite her strenuous action the *Adolf Leonhardt* was scuttled. Force "H" then returned to Cape Town, arriving on 14 December.[88]

At 0800/11 the submarine *Severn* left Freetown for Port Stanley at 15 knots. She was to protect the whaling industry in South Georgia and intercept hostile raiders or supply ships. The cruiser *Dorsetshire*, which had arrived at Simonstown from Colombo on 9 November to relieve the *Exeter*, left Simonstown on 13 November for Port Stanley with orders to call at Tristan da Cunha on the way. On that day, 13 December, was fought the action between the British South America Division and the German pocket battleship *Admiral Graf Spee*, known as the Battle of the River Plate.

South America Division[89]

At the beginning of December the *Ajax* and *Exeter* were at Port Stanley, the *Cumberland* was in the River Plate. The *Achilles* was patrolling the Rio de Janeiro area.

On 2 December the *Ajax* sailed for the River Plate. That evening Commodore Harwood learned that the *Doric Star* had been sunk by a raider south-east of St. Helena. Two days later the Commander-in-Chief informed him that the *Dorsetshire* would arrive at Port Stanley in the Falklands on 23 December to relieve the *Exeter*, which was then to refit at Simonstown.

Early on 5 December the British Naval Attaché at Buenos Aires reported that the German SS *Ussukuma*, 7,800 tons, had left Bahia Blanca at 1900 the previous evening. The Commodore immediately ordered the *Cumberland*, which was on the way south to the Falkland Islands, to search the southern arcs of the *Ussukuma*'s possible course. Meanwhile the *Ajax* turned south at 22 knots after closing the Argentine coast in the case the *Ussukuma*, which was known to be short of fuel, should attempt to reach Montevideo inside territorial waters. At 1910/5 the *Ajax* sighted her smoke to the north-north-east, but the Germans scuttled their ship which, in spite of the efforts of the *Ajax* to save her, sank during the night.[90] At 0615 the *Cumberland* came up and embarked the German survivors. The *Ajax* then refuelled in San Borombon Bay from the *Olynthus*.

About this time the Brazilian authorities asked that the *Achilles* should not refuel in any Brazilian port at an interval of less than three months. The Commodore, therefore, ordered her to return south and fuel at Montevideo on 8 December. During 8/9 December the *Ajax* intercepted three British ships, the *Baronesa*, *Cordillera* and *South Wales*, off the Plate. The *Achilles* joined her from Montevideo at 1000 October in 35° 11' S., 51° 13' W., 230 miles east of English Bank, and at 0650 next day they stopped the British SS *Norman Star* in 32° 58' S., 51° 4' W. They then met the *Exeter* in 36° 54' S., 53° 39' W., 150 miles east of Medanos Light, at 0600 on 12 December.

Ever since the beginning of the war Commodore Harwood's cruisers had worked off the east coast of South America either as single units or in pairs. The concentration of the *Ajax*, *Achilles* and *Exeter* in the River Plate area on 12 December was, however, no mere matter of chance.

Concentration of British Force in the River Plate Area[91]

When a pocket battleship was located in 19° 15' S., 5° 5' E., on 2 December by the sinking of the *Doric Star*, her position was over 3,000 miles from any of the South America focal areas. The Commodore, however, recognised that her next objective might be the valuable British shipping on the South American coast. He estimated that, at a cruising speed of 15 knots, she could reach the Rio de Janeiro area by 12 December, the Plate by 13 December, or the Falklands by 14 December. More than 1,500 miles separated these areas, but the most important of the three was the focal area of the large and very valuable grain and meat trade off the River Plate. He therefore decided to concentrate all his available forces off the Plate estuary by 12 December. On 3 December he cancelled his previous dispositions[92] and ordered the *Exeter* to leave the Falklands on 9 December, and the *Achilles* to meet the *Ajax* in the Plate area at 1000 on 10 December. On her way north the *Exeter* acted as cover for the British SS *Lafonia*, which was bringing back to Buenos Aires the British contingent which had volunteered for service in the Falkland Islands Defence Force, and at 0600 on 12 December met the *Ajax* and *Achilles* 150 miles east of Medanos Point.

The three cruisers then proceeded towards 32° S., 47° W., which was "in the centre of the thickest of the British diverted shipping routes off the Plate at the time." That evening the Commodore signalled:– "My policy with three cruisers in company versus one pocket battleship – attack at once by day or night. By day act as two units, First Division and *Exeter* diverged to permit flank marking. First Division will concentrate gunfire. By night ships will normally remain in company in open order."

At 0614 next morning, 13 December, the *Ajax* sighted smoke bearing 324° in 34° 28' S., 49° 5' W., and Commodore Harwood ordered the *Exeter* to investigate it.[93]

Opposite, Plan 4

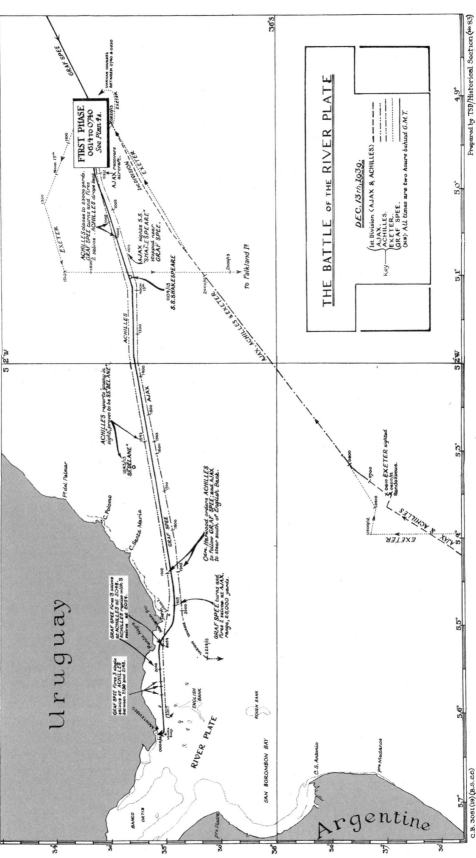

THE BATTLE of the RIVER PLATE

DEC. 13th, 1930.

Key:
- 1st Division (AJAX & ACHILLES).
- AJAX.
- ACHILLES.
- EXETER.
- GRAF SPEE.
- (Note): All times are two hours behind G.M.T.

FIRST PHASE
0614 TO 0740
See Plan #4.

ACHILLES closes to 23000 yards.
GRAF SPEE turns and fires
2 salvos. ACHILLES drops back.

AJAX recovers aircraft.

AJAX sights S.S.
'SHAKESPEARE'
stopped near
GRAF SPEE.

1104/13 S.S. SHAKESPEARE

ACHILLES reports enemy in
sight, proves to be the S.S. DELANE.

1541/13 S.S. DELANE

C.in C./Harwood orders ACHILLES
to follow GRAF SPEE; and AJAX
to steer south of English Bank.

GRAF SPEE burns at AJAX.
Fires 2 salvos at 25,000 yards.

GRAF SPEE fires 3 salvos
at ACHILLES at 2048.
ACHILLES replies at 2054.

GRAF SPEE fires 3 single
salvos at ACHILLES
between 2130 and 2145.

Uruguay

RIVER PLATE

Argentine

Various courses between 0700 & 0930

To Falkland Is.

Prepared by T.S.D./Historical Section (No. 83)

C.B. 3081 (19) (S.S. 26)

The *Admiral Graf Spee*

The Cruise of the *Graf Spee*[94]

Commodore Harwood's foresight in concentrating his three available cruisers off the Plate Estuary on 12 December was fully justified by events, for the smoke sighted by the *Ajax* at 0614 on 13 December proved to be that of the *Graf Spee*.

Officially the *Admiral Graf Spee* was a ship of 10,000 tons displacement, though her actual displacement was probably nearer the 12,000-ton mark. She carried a main armament of six 11-in. guns in triple turrets and a secondary armament of eight 5.9-in. guns. Her captain was Kapitän zur See Hans Langsdof, an officer of the old Imperial Navy who had fought at Jutland.

She had left Germany late in August, and by 13 September was some 240 miles north of Ascension, where she fuelled from her supply ship, the *Altmark*, which had filled up with oil in Texas towards the end of August. She fuelled from the *Altmark* again, in the same position, on 20 September and on 27 of the month steered westward towards Pernambuco. At 1400/30 she met her first victim, the Booth liner *Clement*, 5,051 tons, bound from Pernambuco to Bahia, and sank her in 9° 5' S., 34° 5' W., 75 miles south-east of Pernambuco.[95] She then made a cast eastwards and between 5 and 10 October claimed three more victims. About 0630/5 in 9° 35' S., 6° 30' W., flying the French flag, she captured the British SS *Newton Beech*, 4,651 tons, bound from Cape Town to Sierra Leone and the United Kingdom with a cargo of maize. Two days later, in the forenoon of 7 October, she boarded in 9° S., 3° W., the British SS *Ashlea*, 4,222 tons, bound from Cape Town to Freetown with a cargo of sugar, and after transferring her crew to the *Newton Beech*, sank her with bombs. She embarked the crews of the *Newton Beech* and *Ashlea* next day, and at 1900 exploded a bomb alongside the *Newton Beech*, which sank about midnight. Two days later, on 10 October at 1740, in approximately 8° 30' S., 5° 15' W.,[96] she placed a prize crew onboard the British SS *Huntsman*, 8,196 tons, homeward bound from Durban with a general cargo.

Five uneventful days passed; then on 15 October she met the *Altmark* and refuelled. Two days later she transferred the crew of the *Huntsman* to the tanker and sank their vessel with bombs in 16° S., 17° W. Next day she transferred the crews of the *Newton Beech* and *Ashlea* to the *Altmark*. Then she parted company with her for another 10 days. For the first day or two she cruised westward of St. Helena before steering towards the African coast to claim her fifth victim. This was the British SS *Trevanion*, 5,299 tons, homeward bound from Port Pirie with a cargo of a concentrates, which she sank in 19° 40' S., 4° 2' E., on the afternoon of 22 October, after embarking her crew. When the *Trevanion* sighted her at 1430 the raider was flying a big French ensign, her usual practice when approaching her victims.

She refuelled from the *Altmark* near Tristan du Cunha on 28 October, and transferred the crew of the *Trevanion* to her. She then parted from the oiler for another month and paid a short visit to the Indian ocean. There, on 15 November in 24° 45' S., 35° E., 160 miles north-east of Lourenço Marques, she sank the small British tanker *Africa Shell*, 706 tons, bound from Kuelimare to Lourenço Marques in ballast. Next day she stopped the Dutch SS *Mapia* but let her go.

It was 11 days later, 27 November, that the Admiralty ordered Forces "H" and "K" to patrol south of the Cape on the meridian of 20° E. to intercept her if she attempted to break back into the South Atlantic.[97] It was too late. She had rejoined the *Altmark* in the South Atlantic on 26 November. Next day she fuelled from her 300 miles from Tristan da Cunha. Two days later she re-embarked from her all the merchant service officers she had captured, with the apparent intention of taking them back to Germany. She then returned to the area where she had sunk the *Trevanion* on 22 October. There at 1300 on 2 December in 19° 15' S., 5° 5' E., she sank with gunfire and torpedo her seventh and largest victim, the British SS *Doric Star*, 10,086 tons bound from Auckland to London with a cargo of meat and dairy produce, and armed with a 4-in. gun. This attack Captain Langsdorf no doubt regarded as his greatest success, but in the end it was to prove fatal to him.

The *Graf Spee* steamed away at high speed after disposing of the *Doric Star*. Perhaps Captain Langsdorf was anxious to get clear of the area knowing that the *Doric Star* had reported him. This knowledge, however, did not prevent his sinking the British SS *Tairoa*, 7,983 tons, bound from Melbourne to Sierra Leone with a cargo of meat, wool and lead, in 21° 30' S., 3° E. shortly after 0400 next morning, 3 December. This was the day on which Commodore Harwood ordered his three cruisers to concentrate off the Plate on 12 December. Three days later the *Graf Spee* refuelled from the *Altmark* for the last time. She was then far away to the westward in 23° S., 26° W.,[98] nearly half-way between St. Helena and the River Plate area, roughly 1,700 miles from Montevideo.

After leaving the *Graf Spee* the *Altmark* steamed past Ascension and then steered to the southward where she remained till 24 January, 1940. Meanwhile the *Graf Spee* continued towards the Plate, hoping to intercept the British SS *Highland Monarch* outward bound from Buenos Aires. At 1630 next day, 7 December, 1939, she sank in 25° 1' S., 27° 50' W., her last victim, the British SS *Streonshalh*, 3,895 tons, bound from Montevideo to Freetown and Europe, with a cargo of wheat. She had destroyed nine British ships totalling 50,089 tons[99] without the loss of a single life. At 0614 on 13 December, her smoke was sighted by the South America Division.

Plan 5

C.B. 3081(19) (B.S. 26).

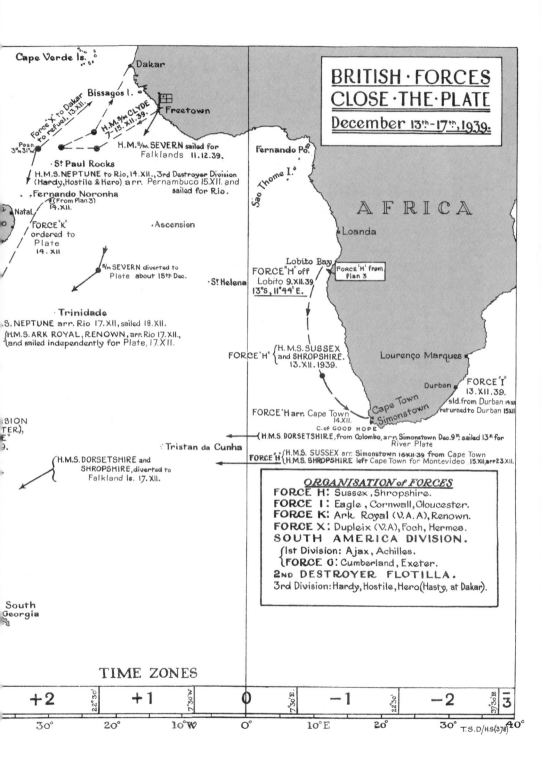

Cape Verde Is.

Dakar

Bissagos I.

Force "X" to Dakar to refuel, 13.XII.

Freetown

H.M.S/m CLYDE 7-15.XII.39.

Posn. 3°N31'W

H.M.S/m.SEVERN sailed for Falklands 11.12.39.

Fernando Po.

·St Paul Rocks

H.M.S.NEPTUNE to Rio, 14.XII., 3rd Destroyer Division (Hardy, Hostile & Hero) arr. Pernambuco 15.XII. and sailed for Rio.

Sao Thome I.

.·Fernando Noronha {(From Plan 3) 14.XII.

Natal.

"FORCE "K" ordered to Plate 14.XII

·Ascension

A F R I C A

·Loanda

Lobito Bay

S/m SEVERN diverted to Plate about 15th Dec.

·St Helena

FORCE"H" off Lobito 9.XII.39 13°S, 11°44' E.

FORCE "H" from Plan 3

· Trinidade

S. NEPTUNE arr. Rio 17.XII, sailed 18.XII.
(H.M.S. ARK ROYAL, RENOWN, arr.Rio 17.XII., and sailed independently for Plate, 17.XII.

FORCE"H" {H.M.S.SUSSEX and SHROPSHIRE. 13.XII.1939.

Lourenço Marques

Durban   FORCE "I" 13.XII.39.

FORCE"H"arr. Cape Town 14.XII.

Cape Town
Simonstown

sld.from Durban 14.XII returned to Durban 15XII

C. of GOOD HOPE
(H.M.S. DORSETSHIRE, from Colombo, arr. Simonstown Dec.9th, sailed 13th for River Plate

·SION TER), E" 9.

· Tristan da Cunha

FORCE "H" {H.M.S. SUSSEX arr. Simonstown 18.XII.39 from Cape Town {H.M.S. SHROPSHIRE left Cape Town for Montevideo .15.XII, arr 23.XII.

(H.M.S. DORSETSHIRE and SHROPSHIRE, diverted to Falkland Is. 17.XII.

BRITISH · FORCES CLOSE · THE · PLATE
December 13th-17th, 1939.

ORGANISATION of FORCES

FORCE H: Sussex, Shropshire.
FORCE I: Eagle, Cornwall, Gloucester.
FORCE K: Ark Royal (V.A.A), Renown.
FORCE X: Dupleix (V.A), Foch, Hermes.
SOUTH AMERICA DIVISION.
{1st Division: Ajax, Achilles.
{FORCE G: Cumberland, Exeter.
2ND DESTROYER FLOTILLA.
3rd Division: Hardy, Hostile, Hero (Hasty, at Dakar).

South Georgia

TIME ZONES

+2	22°30'	+1	7°30'W	0	7°30'E.	−1	22°30'	−2	37°30'E	3

| 30° | 20° | 10° W | 0° | 10° E | 20° | 30° T.S.D/H.S(378) | 40° |

The Battle of the River Plate[100]

The Battle, First Phase

When Commodore Harwood detached the *Exeter* at 0614[101] on 13 December to investigate smoke bearing 324°,[102] his squadron was in 34° 28' S., 49° 5' W. It was steering 060° at 14 knots in single line ahead in the order *Ajax*, broad pendant, Commodore H. H. Harwood, Captain C. H. L. Woodhouse, 6,985 tons, eight 6-in., four 4-in. A.A. guns; *Achilles*, Captain W. E. Parry, 7,030 tons, eight 6-in., eight 4-in. A.A. guns; and *Exeter*, Captain F. S. Bell, 8,390 tons, six 8-in., eight 4-in. A.A. guns. Events followed quickly. At 0616 the *Exeter* signalled "I think it is a pocket battleship."[103] Two minutes later the *Graf Spee* opened fire.

The movements of the British cruisers and the *Graf Spee* during the battle can best be followed by referring to the included plans.[104] When the *Graf Spee* opened fire, the 1st Division, the *Ajax* and *Achilles*, increased speed and turned to 340° to close the range and engage the enemy from the eastward. At the same time the *Exeter* turned westward at full speed to engage her from the southward and to carry out the Commodore's plan of attacking simultaneously from widely different bearings.[105]

When the Commodore signalled that his policy with three cruisers in company versus one pocket battleship was to act as two units, on divergent courses to permit of flank marking,[106] he apparently intended the *Exeter* to take station on a line of bearing from the enemy at approximately right angles to the line of fire of the First Division.

To put this into effect the *Exeter's* first intention was to engage the enemy on her port bow. Seeing that this might hamper the 1st Division, however, she turned to 280° and at 0620 opened fire to starboard at 18,700 yards with her two foremost 8-in. gun turrets. These tactics were most effective. With two or more targets to engage, an enemy will always have the difficulty of choosing between engaging one ship or dividing his armament amongst them, no matter what formation the target ships are in. The difficulty was enhanced in this case by the wide dispersion of the targets. The enemy having to choose between leaving one of the British units disengaged by her 11-in. guns or dividing her main armament between them, chose the second alternative and opened fire with one turret against the *Ajax* and the other against the *Exeter*. The *Exeter*'s 8-in. salvoes appeared to worry her, however, for after shifting targets rapidly once or twice she concentrated all six 11-in. guns on her and quickly straddled. At this point the *Exeter*'s after turret opened fire.

At 0623 an 11-in. shell of the *Graf Spee*'s third salvo, bursting short amidships, killed the *Exeter*'s starboard tubes' crews and damaged her searchlights, communications, funnels and aircraft. One minute later, when the *Exeter* had fired eight salvoes, another 11-in. shell knocked out her "B" turret. Its splinters swept the bridge, killing or wounding all the bridge personnel except Captain Bell and two others, and wrecked the wheelhouse communications. She was no longer under control from forward and Captain Bell made his way aft. He had hardly left the bridge before her head began to swing rapidly to starboard. Although the lower conning position at once took over the steering, she was in danger of masking her after turret. The torpedo officer, Lieutenant-Commander C. J. Smith, had been momentarily stunned, but recovered in time to get an order through to bring her back to a westerly course. By this time she had received two more direct hits forward and damage from shells bursting short. Her aircraft were extensively riddled. Petrol from the port machine was spraying over the after conning position. There was a serious danger of fire and both aircraft were jettisoned.

Captain Bell arrived aft only to find communications broken down between the after conning position and the steering flat. He was obliged to pass his orders through a chain of messengers. In a ship still heavily engaged this was a task of extreme difficulty, but it was successfully accomplished till the cumulative results of extensive damage eventually forced Captain Bell to break off the action.

While the *Graf Spee* was fiercely engaging the *Exeter* with 11-in. salvoes she was firing alternately at the *Ajax* and *Achilles* with her secondary armament. Some of her 5.9-in. salvoes fell very close, but none actually hit. Meanwhile the *Ajax* and *Achilles* were hitting back hard with 'concentrated fire' at a rapidly closing range. Their shooting was effective, for at 0639 the *Graf Spee* shifted one of her main turrets to the *Ajax*, halving the volume of fire against the *Exeter*. At 0631 three 11-in. salvoes straddled the *Ajax* and the 1st Division turned away a point or two to confuse the enemy's fire. Three minutes later, however, the *Ajax* turned back to port to close the range, and at 0637 catapulted her aircraft with Lieutenant E. D. G. Lewin as pilot.

Meanwhile the *Exeter* had fired her starboard torpedoes in local control, and at 0637 the *Graf Spee*, apparently finding the British attack too hot, turned 150° to port and retired north-westward under cover of a smoke screen. The 1st Division immediately hauled round at full speed, first to north, then to west, to close the range and regain bearing. Three minutes later the *Exeter* turned several points to starboard to bring her port tubes to bear, and at 0643 fired her port torpedoes. She then steered north-east to close the 1st Division, but at 0645 turned back once more to a westerly course to keep within range. By this time she had received two more direct 11-in. hits, one of them on "A" turret, and was showing signs of acute distress. Her foremost turrets were out of action. She was burning fiercely amidships. Her one remaining turret was in local control. Her compasses were destroyed.

Meanwhile the *Graf Spee* was heavily engaging the 1st Division. At 0640 an 11-in. shell burst on the water in line with the bridge of the *Achilles*. It killed or seriously wounded four ratings in her director control tower, stunned the gunnery officer, Lieutenant R. E. Washbourn, and slightly wounded Captain Parry. Her director tower, however, was undamaged, and her rate of fire unaffected as she was in concentration firing.

At 0646 her fire control wireless set broke down, and thereafter she carried on in individual control. She had great difficulty at first in finding the range and her salvoes fell short. Reports of these salvoes were transmitted by the *Ajax*'s aircraft. The *Ajax*, however, not knowing that the *Achilles* was no longer in concentration firing, accepted them as referring to her own salvoes, and corrected accordingly. At this time the enemy was making a smoke screen and spotting conditions were extremely bad. As a result the *Ajax*'s salvoes fell far beyond the target. The range was not found again till 0708.

At 0650 the *Exeter* was steering west with her remaining turret still in action. She had a 7° list to starboard and several forward compartments flooded. At 0656 the 1st Division hauled round north-westward, and for a time the *Graf Spee* kept altering course frequently to confuse its fire. At 0710 the range was still 16,000 yards. To shorten it the Division turned westward at full speed. Six minutes later the *Graf Spee* made a large turn to port and under cover of smoke steered straight for the *Exeter* in an apparent attempt to finish her off. The 1st Division at once turned to the rescue, firing so accurately that the enemy was set on fire amidships and forced to turn back north-west to re-engage the *Ajax*. The British cruiser was immediately straddled at 11,000 yards by three 11-in. salvoes, though the enemy's secondary armament was shooting wildly.

At 0725 an 11-in. shell knocked out the *Ajax*'s after turrets. She at once retaliated by turning to starboard and firing four torpedoes at 9,000 yards. The enemy avoided them with a wide turn[107] to port, but almost at once turned back north-westward in an apparent attempt to close the 1st Division. At 0728 the Division turned to 280° to close the range still further. At 0731, however, the *Ajax*'s aircraft reported "Torpedoes approaching; they will pass ahead of you."[108] Commodore Harwood decided to take no chances, and, turning south, engaged the enemy on his starboard side, with the range still closing rapidly. One minute later the *Graf Spee* turned westward under cover of smoke to confuse the accurate gunfire of the 1st Division. At 0736 she turned south-west, again bringing all her guns to bear. Two minutes later one of her salvoes brought down the topmast and wireless aerial of the *Ajax* at 8,000 yards.

Meanwhile the *Exeter* was dropping slowly astern with her after turret still firing. At 0730 pressure in this turret failed. She could keep up no longer, and at 0740 turned slowly south-east to repair damage.

About this time a report reached the Commodore that only 20 per cent. of the *Ajax*'s ammunition remained.[109] With the *Exeter* out of action, and with two of the *Ajax*'s turrets knocked out, the available British gun power was little superior to that of the enemy's secondary armament. The *Graf Spee*'s shooting was still very accurate and she appeared little damaged. The prospects of continuing a successful daylight action were anything but rosy. The Commodore therefore decided to break off the fight till dark, when there would be a better chance of closing to a range at which his lighter armament and torpedoes would be most effective. At 0740 the *Ajax* and *Achilles* turned away east under cover of smoke. Thus ended the first phase of the battle. It had lasted one hour and twenty-two minutes.

According to Captain Parry, of the *Achilles*, the *Graf Spee*'s rate of fire averaged one salvo a minute throughout this phase of the action. His estimate includes some 20 to 25 salvoes fired at the 1st Division and presumably about

60 salvoes fired at the *Exeter*. He states that the *Graf Spee*'s fore turret was out of action for some time early in the engagement. It is not possible to estimate the number of rounds she expended between 0618 and 0740 as there is no evidence to show how many guns she included in each salvo.

The Battle, Second Phase

When the *Ajax* and *Achilles* turned away at 0740 the *Graf Spee* did not follow them. After opening the range for six minutes under cover of smoke Commodore Harwood turned back westward. The action now developed into a procession, the *Graf Spee* in the van steering at 22 knots straight for the River Plate with the 1st Division disposed quarterly 15 miles distant, the *Achilles* on the raider's starboard quarter and the *Ajax* on her port quarter. Even at this extreme range the battleship's conspicuous control tower made her an easy quarry to follow.

At 0800 the *Ajax* was in 34° 25' S., 49° 29' W. Seven minutes later and every hour thereafter the British cruisers broadcast the enemy's position, course, and speed to warn merchant vessels to keep out of danger. By 0814 the *Exeter* was out of sight and Commodore Harwood ordered his aircraft to tell her to close. At 0910 the aircraft signalled that the *Exeter*, though badly damaged, was joining him as best she could.[110] Two minutes later the *Ajax* recovered the aircraft. Although the *Exeter* was doing her best to rejoin the 1st Division, Captain Bell, with only an inaccurate boat-compass to steer by, could not make contact. He therefore reduced speed to enable the *Exeter* to be brought to an even keel and her bulkheads to be shored up. At 0930 he turned westward for the nearest land, and at 0946 the Commodore ordered the *Cumberland*, which was still at the Falklands, to close the Plate at full speed. His signal was some time getting through for when the *Cumberland* sailed at noon it was on the initiative of her commanding officer, Captain W. H. Fallowfield, who up till then had received only very jumbled messages. She increased to full speed when the Commodore's signal eventually reached her.

Shortly after 1000 the *Achilles*, over-estimating the speed of the *Graf Spee*, closed the range to 23,000 yards, and at 1005 the enemy, turning suddenly, opened fire on her. Her first salvo was short, but the second fell almost alongside. Nothing could be gained by risking unnecessary damage. The *Achilles* therefore turned away at full speed behind a smoke screen to resume shadowing at a safe distance, and the enemy ceased fire.

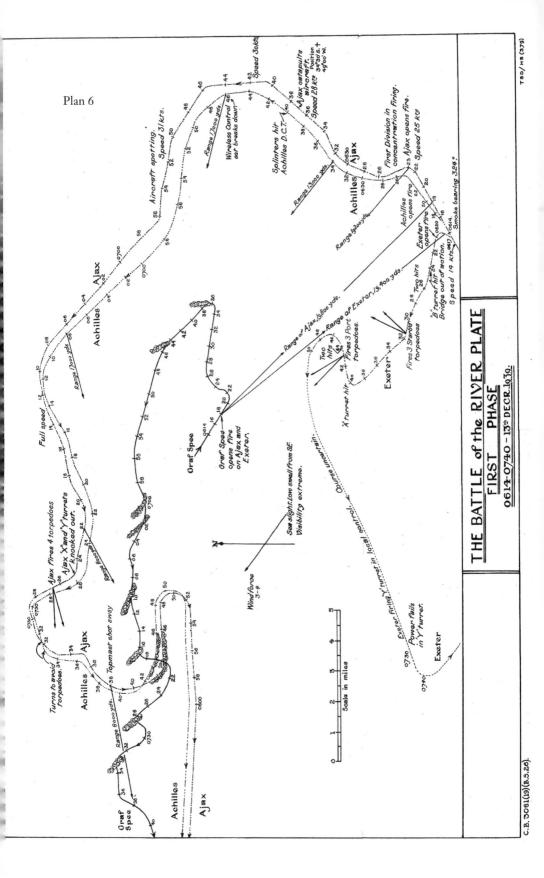

Plan 6

THE BATTLE of the RIVER PLATE
FIRST PHASE
0614-0740 - 13th DECR. 1939.

Scale in miles

C.B. 3081(19)(B.5.26).

TSD/MS(379)

The next hour was uneventful. Then, at 1104, the *Ajax* sighted the British SS *Shakespeare*, stopped near the *Graf Spee*. A few minutes later the raider asked her[111] and the *Achilles* to pick up the lifeboats of the English steamer. When he reached her, however, the Commodore found all the *Shakespeare*'s boats hoisted and that she was in no need of assistance. The *Graf Spee*'s signal must be regarded as an unsuccessful ruse to shake off her unrelenting pursuers.

At 1105 the *Exeter* signalled that though she was flooded forward and had all her turrets out of action she could still steam at 18 knots. Some time later she was able to report that one of her after turret guns could be fired in local control. It was clear, however, that she had no further fighting value, and at 1340 the Commodore ordered her to make for the Falklands. At 1510 she turned south.[112]

Meanwhile the early afternoon had passed quietly in the 1st Division. Then at 1543 the dramatic signal "Enemy in sight 297°" flashed from the *Achilles*. Shortly afterwards she identified the new enemy as an 8-in. gun cruiser.[113] This was grim news. The Division was in no state to take on an additional enemy in a fight which in any case could have only one result. Fortunately the alarm proved to be false. At 1559 the approaching vessel was identified as the SS *Delane*. Her streamlined funnel had given her the appearance of a *Blücher* class cruiser at long range.

The 1st Division shadowed the *Graf Spee* without further incident till 1900. By that time the raider's intention to enter the River Plate was becoming clear, and at 1902 the Commodore ordered the *Achilles* to follow her if she went west of Lobos Island.[114]

At 1915 the *Graf Spee* turned and fired two salvoes at the *Ajax*. The range was 26,000 yards. The first salvo was short, but the second fell in the cruiser's wake as she turned away behind a smoke screen. The *Achilles*, too, turned away on seeing the gun flashes, but soon resumed her westerly course. About 2000 the *Ajax* turned south to frustrate any attempt on the part of the *Graf Spee* at doubling back to elude the British cruisers. Commodore Harwood was then off Lobos Island in 35° 8' S., 54° 49' W., 50 miles east of English Bank.

For more than twelve hours the *Graf Spee* had closed the Plate at a steady 22 knots with the two small British cruisers hanging grimly on to her heels. As soon as she passed Lobos Island the whole duty of shadowing her devolved upon the *Achilles*. At 2014 Captain Parry increased speed to close before dusk. In half an hour he had reduced the distance to 23,000 yards. At sunset, 2048, the enemy, apparently as a counter to the shortening of the range, turned and fired three salvoes. The first two fell short as the *Achilles* turned away at full speed, but the third fell only just astern. Two minutes later the *Achilles* turned northward to keep the full advantage of the after glow, and at 2054 fired five salvoes which appeared to straddle. She then turned west once more and increased to 30 knots to keep in touch. Between 2130 and 2145 the enemy fired three final salvoes from her after turret. These Parthian shots were more in the nature of a gesture than an effective action. All three fell short, and the *Achilles*, not wishing to give away her own position, did not return the fire.

By 2200 she had closed to 5 miles, but finding it increasingly difficult to see her quarry, altered course 2213 to silhouette her against the lights of Montevideo. She continued her westerly course for another hour. Then, at 2317, the *Ajax* ordered her to withdraw. Shortly after midnight the *Graf Spee* entered Montevideo. Thus ended the second phase of the Battle of the River Plate. During it the raider had fired another ten salvoes, five of them from one turret only.

The Watch on the River Plate

When Commodore Harwood recalled the *Achilles* at 2317 the *Graf Spee's* intention to enter Montevideo was quite clear. The main question was how long would she stay there. It was also of the utmost importance that the British cruisers should keep to seaward of her if she came out. It was equally important that they should not be caught against the light of dawn. At 2350, therefore, the 1st Division withdrew temporarily from the Plate, the *Achilles* to patrol the northern area between the Uruguayan coast and a line 120° from English Bank, and the *Ajax* to patrol the southern area. The night passed without incident. Both ships moved back towards Montevideo as soon as the danger of the dawn light had passed.

For the moment these two small British cruisers stood alone between the enemy and the open sea. Both had been heavily engaged the previous day and both were short of fuel. They had no hope at all of destroying the *Graf Spee* unless they were concentrated, nor were the geographical factors in their favour. From the River Plate Estuary, which is 120 miles wide between Cape S. Antonio and Lobos Island, run three widely separated deep-water channels, the northernmost between the English Bank Lightship and

Cumberland Shoal, the second between English Bank and Rouen Bank, and the southernmost, nearly 30 miles wide, between Rouen Bank and the Argentine coast.[115] The difficulties of the situation were great and the Commodore could look for little immediate assistance.

On the morning of 13 December, the day of the battle, the *Sussex* and *Shropshire*, Force "H" were sweeping off Lobito, on the west coast of Africa, 4,000 miles away from the River Plate estuary; the *Eagle*, *Cornwall* and *Gloucester*, Force "I", of the East Indies Station, were at Durban; the *Cumberland* was at the Falklands, nearly 1,000 miles away to the south; the *Ark Royal* and *Renown*, Force "K", the most powerful force on the South Atlantic Station, were off Pernambuco, 2,000 miles to the northwards; while the French cruisers *Dupleix* and *Foch*, and the British aircraft carrier *Hermes*, Force "X", with the *Neptune*, *Hardy*, *Hostile* and *Hero* were further north still off St. Paul Rocks.[116] The submarine *Severn* was about half way between St. Helena and Bahia, on her way from Freetown to the Falklands, and the submarine *Clyde* was approaching Dakar from a patrol in the St. Paul Rocks area.

Throughout 14 December the *Ajax* and *Achilles* kept a constant watch over as much of the River Plate estuary as possible. That night they received a much needed reinforcement when the *Cumberland* arrived from the Falklands at 2200 having made the long passage northwards in 34 hours. This enabled Commodore Harwood to watch all three deep-water channels during the night, with the *Cumberland* in the centre, the *Achilles* to the north and the *Ajax* to the south. If the *Graf Spee* came out she was to be shadowed till the three cruisers had concentrated far enough to seaward to make a concerted attack on her. The Commodore's avowed object was the destruction of the enemy.[117]

Next day, 15 December, the problem of refuelling had to be faced. Fortunately the *Olynthus* was at hand and the Commodore ordered her to meet the *Ajax* in San Borombon Bay, while the *Cumberland* closed to cover them in case the *Graf Spee* came out without warning. Although the weather was so bad that the securing wires, including two spans of "hurricane hawsers," parted, the *Ajax* took in 200 tons of fuel. She then proceeded to join the *Cumberland*.

Shortly after this the Commodore learned that the *Graf Spee*, which had been hit between 60 and 70 times and was more extensively damaged than had hitherto appeared likely, had been given permission to remain at

Montevideo another 72 hours to make herself seaworthy. There could be no guarantee, however, that she would stay there, and the British cruisers were in no way able to relax their instant readiness for action.

Thus, when just before dawn next morning, 16 December, the *Ajax*, *Achilles* and *Cumberland* were concentrated off San Antonio in the southern part of the estuary the *Ajax* flew off her aircraft to reconnoitre. It returned at 0830 with a report that though visibility was extremely bad it had been fired on near the Whistle Buoy. This indicated that the enemy might be leaving and the three cruisers went to action stations. It was a false alarm, however, for a report from Montevideo started shortly afterwards that the battleship was still in the harbour. The day passed without further incident. The squadron spent the night patrolling north and south five miles east of English Bank.

Next morning, 17 December, the *Ajax* and *Cumberland* covered the *Achilles* while she refuelled from the *Olynthus* off Rouen Bank. The whole squadron then cruised in company throughout the afternoon ready to take up its night patrols at dusk.

British Forces Close the Plate, 13–17 December

While the cruisers of the South America Division were watching the Plate between 13 and 17 December, strong British forces were steadily closing in on Montevideo. Their movements can best be followed by reference to Plan 5.[118]

On the afternoon of 13 December, the day of the battle, the Admiralty placed the cruisers *Cornwall* and *Gloucester* and the aircraft carrier *Eagle*, Force "I", which had returned to Durban from the South Atlantic Station on 12 December,[119] once again at the disposal of the Commander-in-Chief, South Atlantic, as a searching force. He immediately ordered them to proceed to the Cape ports with all despatch. They sailed next morning, but a few hours later the Admiralty replaced them under the command of the Commander-in-Chief, East Indies, for work in connection with Australian and New Zealand troop convoys. The Commander-in-Chief, East Indies, at once recalled them to Durban, where they arrived on the afternoon of 15 December.

On the afternoon of 13 December, the *Sussex* and *Shropshire*, Force "H," were on their way south from the neighbourhood of Lobito Bay to Cape Town. They had still some 400 miles to go at 1752 when the Commander-in-Chief, South Atlantic, ordered them to proceed to the Cape with all possible speed and refuel. Next morning[120] he instructed them to sail for Freetown when fuelled. When the Admiralty recalled Force "I" to the East Indies Station that afternoon, however, he ordered them to remain at the Cape. At 1745/15 the Admiralty ordered the *Dorsetshire*, which had arrived at Simonstown from Colombo on 9 December, to proceed with the *Shropshire* to the River Plate. Their order had been partly anticipated by the Commander-in-Chief for the *Dorsetshire* had sailed for the Plate on 13 December. The *Shropshire* therefore sailed alone; steaming 20 knots in order to arrive off Montevideo on 23 December. The *Sussex* left Cape Town for Simonstown that day, 15 December, and arrived there early next morning. She was kept at short notice ready to sail for position 20° S., 15° W., if the *Graf Spee* cleared the River Plate.

The *Dorsetshire* had orders to call at Tristan du Cunha on 16 December, but the Admiralty cancelled them on 15 December and two days later ordered her and the *Shropshire* to close the Falklands at 25 knots to counter any attempt of the *Graf Spee* to escape to the southward. At 0043 on 18 December[121] they were diverted to the Falklands at economical speed. An hour later, at 0148, the Admiralty placed them under the orders of the Rear-Admiral,[122] South Atlantic Division to intercept the German SS *Tacoma* if she escaped from Montevideo.

The *Ark Royal* (V.A.(A)) and *Renown*, Force "K," had left Cape Town on 4 December to sweep through a position in 28° S., 15° W. By 13 December they were in the neighbourhood of Pernambuco en route to meet the *Neptune* and the destroyers of the Third Division off St. Paul Rocks.[123] As the *Renown* had barely enough fuel to reach the Plate and none for a protracted chase in the South Atlantic, the Commander-in-Chief ordered the Vice-Admiral, Aircraft Carriers, to meet the *Neptune* at the rendezvous as quickly as possible and then to proceed to Freetown and refuel. His signal reached the Vice-Admiral at 1900.

Early next morning, however, the Admiralty ordered Force "K" to the River Plate. When this order reached the Vice-Admiral at 0215 he immediately steered for the Plate at 20 knots. Some four and a half hours later, however, the Commander-in-Chief ordered him to refuel at Rio de Janeiro and he increased to 25 knots. He reached Rio at 0600/17. Twelve hours later, when the *Ark Royal* had finished fuelling, he sailed at 25 knots for the Plate, leaving instructions for the *Renown* and *Neptune* to meet him off the Plate in due course. Just before midnight,[124] however, he ordered them and the destroyers to meet him off Rio in 22° 50' S., 40° W., at 1800/18.

Further north the French cruisers *Dupleix* and *Foch*, and the British aircraft carrier *Hermes*, Force "X", with the French destroyers *Milan* and *Cassard* and HMS *Neptune* in company had met the *Hardy*, *Hostile* and *Hero*,[125] and the RFA *Cherryleaf* in 3° N., 31° W., off St. Paul Rocks, at noon on 10 December according to plan.[126] The French destroyers then withdrew to refuel at Dakar before returning to accompany Force "X" back to base. The remaining vessels patrolled the parallel of 3° N. between longitude 31° W. and 38° W. until 13 December. The Franco-British force are stated to have worked well together during the patrol. Force "X" parted from the *Neptune* and the British destroyers at noon on 13 December at the original rendezvous in 3° N., 31° W., and withdrew to refuel at Dakar. The *Neptune* had ordered to meet Force "K" off St. Paul Rocks with her destroyers next day before returning to Freetown. When she received the Admiralty's signal ordering Force "K" to the River Plate, however, she ordered the destroyers to make for Rio de Janeiro. But the Commander-in-Chief when he ordered Force "K" to refuel at Rio had also ordered the destroyers to refuel at Pernambuco before meeting the Vice-Admiral off Rio or off the River Plate. They reached Pernambuco at 2300 on 15 December and sailed for a position off Rio an hour later. The *Neptune* reached Rio at 1600/17, 10 hours behind Force "K." She sailed again at 1230 next afternoon to meet the Vice-Admiral at the rendezvous off Rio in 22° 50' S., 40° W., at 1800. Meanwhile the *Graf Spee* had met with an ignominious end.

The End of the Graf Spee

At 1540 on 17 December Admiral Harwood learned that the *Graf Spee* was transferring 300 or 400 men to the German SS *Tacoma*. At 1720 a further report reached him that over 700 men, with baggage and provisions, were being transferred. Shortly afterwards he learned that the *Graf Spee* was weighing anchor. He immediately increased to 25 knots and turning to close the Whistle Buoy, flew off the *Ajax*'s aircraft to report the *Graf Spee*'s position.

The *Graf Spee* left the harbour at 1815 and followed by the *Tacoma* steamed slowly westward. The British cruisers were in a state of instant readiness. At 2054 the *Ajax*'s aircraft, after reporting the enemy in shallow water six miles south-west of Montevideo, made the dramatic signal "*Graf*

Spee has blown herself up."

The British squadron steamed on towards Montevideo, passing the wreck of the German battleship[127] in the darkness. It was ablaze from stem to stern with flames reaching to the top of the control tower, a magnificent and awe-inspiring sight. This was the ignominious fate of the ship which Hitler had triumphantly designated "the pride of the German Navy." Her inglorious end may have been prompted by the wide publicity given after the battle to highly coloured reports of a great concentration of Allied forces off the Plate. Actually, though strong British forces were steadily closing in, no further reinforcement for Admiral Harwood was immediately at hand. To him therefore and to his three gallant cruisers, the *Ajax*, *Exeter* and *Achilles*, belongs the paramount credit for the *Graf Spee*'s destruction, which, in the words of Mr. Winston Churchill, then First Lord of the Admiralty,[128] "came like a flash of light and colour on the scene, carrying with it an encouragement to all who are fighting, to ourselves, and to our Allies."[129]

Appendix A

Board Of Admiralty
December, 1939

First Lord: The Rt. Hon. Winston L. Spencer Churchill, C. H., M. P.

First Sea Lord and Chief of Naval Staff: Admiral of the Fleet Sir A. Dudley P. R. Pound, G.C.B., G.C.V.O. (12.6.1939.)

Second Sea Lord and Chief of Naval Personnel: Admiral Sir Charles Little, K.C.B. (30.9.1938.)

Third Sea Lord and Controller: Rear-Admiral B. A. Fraser, C.B., O.B.E. (1.3.1939.)

Fourth Sea Lord and Chief of Supplies and Transport: Rear-Admiral G. S. Arbuthnot, C.B., D.S.O. (1.10.1937.)

Fifth Sea Lord and Chief of Naval Air Services: Vice-Admiral G. C. C. Royle, C.B., C.M.G. (21.11.1939.)

Deputy Chief of Naval Staff: Rear-Admiral T. S. V. Phillips, C.B. (1.6.1939.)

Assistant Chief of Naval Staff: Rear-Admiral H. M. Burrough, C.B. (10.1.1939.)

Parliamentary and Financial Secretary: Geoffrey Shakespeare, Esq., M.P.

Civil Lord: Captain A. U. M. Hudson, M.P.

Permanent Secretary: Sir R. H. Archibald Carter, K.C.B., K.C.I.E.

Dates are dates of appointment.

Appendix B

Forces, South Atlantic Command
At Outbreak of War, September, 1939

Commander-In-Chief

Vice-Admiral George Hamilton D'Oyly Lyon, C.B.

(Flag flown on shore at Freetown, Sierra Leone.)

		Commanding Officer.[130]
	Sixth Cruiser Squadron	
Neptune	(8 6-in.)	Captain J. A. V. Morse, D.S.O.
	Ninth Cruiser Squadron	
Despatch (Brd. Pdt.)	(6 6-in.)	Captain A. Poland, D.S.O. (Commodore 2nd Class).
Dauntless	(6 6-in.)	Captain G. D. Moore, R.A.N.
Danae	(6 6-in.)	Captain A. C. Collinson.
Durban	(6 6-in.)	Captain Maxwell Hyslop, A.M.
	South America Division	
Exeter (Brd. Pdt.)	(6 8-in.)	Captain H. H. Harwood, O.B.E. (Commodore 2nd Class) Captain F. S. Bell, C.B.
Ajax	(8 6-in.)	Captain C. H. L. Woodhouse.
Cumberland	(8 8-in.)	Captain W. H. G. Fallowfield.
	Seaplane Carrier	
Albatross	(4 4.7-in.)	Captain W. G. Andrewes.

Second Destroyer Flotilla (4th Division)

Hyperion	(4 4.7-in.)	Commander H. St. L. Nicolson.
Hunter	(4 4.7-in.)	Lieut.-Commander L. de Villiers.
Hotspur	(4 4.7-in.)	Commander H. F. H. Layman.
Havock	(4 4.7-in.)	Lieut. J. F. A. Ashcroft.

Submarines

Clyde	Commander W. E. Banks.
Severn	Lieut.-Commander B. W. Taylor.

Forces, South Atlantic Command
13 December, 1939

Battlecruiser

Renown (Force "K")   Captain C. E. B. Simeon.

Aircraft Carriers

Ark Royal (Flag of V. A.(A)) (Force "K")   Vice-Admiral L. V. Wells, C.B., D.S.O.
Flag-Captain A. J. Power, C.V.O.

Hermes (Force "X")   Captain F. E. P. Hutton.

Seaplane Carrier

Albatross   Captain W. G. Andrewes.

Cruisers

Ajax (Brd. Pdt., South America Division)   Captain H. H. Harwood, O.B.E. (Commodore, 2nd Class).
Captain C. H. L. Woodhouse.

Cumberland (South America Division).   Force "G"   Captain W. H. G. Fallowfield (S.O. Force "G").

Exeter (South America Division)   Captain F. S. Bell, C.B.

Dorsetshire (Force "G" vice *Exeter*[131])	Force "G"	Captain B. C. S. Martin.
Achilles (N.Z.) (South America Division)		Captain W. E. Parry.
Shropshire (Cape of Good Hope)		Captain A. W. La. T. Bisset.
Sussex (Cape of Good Hope)	Force "H"	Captain A. R. Hammick.
Neptune (6th C.S.), Dakar		Captain J. A. V. Morse, D.S.O.

Second Destroyer Flotilla
(3rd Division)

Hardy (Captain D.2)	Captain B. A. W. Warburton-Lee.
Hostile	Commander J. P. Wright.
Hero	Commander C. F. Tower.
Hasty	Lieut.-Commander L. R. K. Tyrwhitt.
Havock	Lieutenant J. F. A. Ashcroft.

Seventh Submarine Flotilla

Maidstone (Depot, Captain S.7)	Captain E. H. Longdon.
Clyde	Commander W. E. Banks.
Severn	Lieut.-Commander B. W. Taylor.

French Forces Based on Dakar[132]
13 December, 1939

Cruisers

Dupleix (Flag of V.A.) (Force "X")

Foch (Force "X")

Duguay-Trouin

Contre-Torpilleurs

Cassard

Milan

Sloop

D'Entrecasteaux

South Atlantic Command

Organisation of "Forces" as Hunting Groups Against Raiders, October, 1939

Admiralty Telegram 1409/5 October, 1939

From: Admiralty.

To: C.-in-C., South Atlantic, etc.

Part I

(1) Admiralty policy for dealing with German Raiders on Trade Routes is as follows.

(2) Present information indicates that raider off Brazil may be either pocket battleship or *Hipper* class. Further warship raiders must be expected, also armed merchant ship raiders. Enemy activities may be extended soon to North Atlantic and to Indian Ocean.

(3) It is necessary to maintain the flow of trade and accept such losses as are inevitable. Full convoy system in South Atlantic and Indian Ocean would result in unacceptable delay even if escorts could be provided. Halifax and Freetown inward convoys will continue. Kingstown convoys will cease and trade from Caribbean and Panama will be routed up American coast to join Halifax convoys. Arrangements for escort of convoys follow in Part II.

(4) Hunting groups will be as follows:–

Force.	Composition.	Area.
"F"	*Berwick, York*	North America and West Indies.

"G"	*Cumberland* and *Exeter*	East coast of South America.
"H"	*Sussex* and *Shropshire*	Cape of Good Hope area.
"I"	*Cornwall, Dorsetshire* and *Eagle*	Ceylon area.
"K"	*Renown, Ark Royal* and one 6-in. gun cruiser to be detailed by C.-in-C., South Atlantic.	Pernambuco–Freetown area.
"L"	*Dunkerque,* three 6-in. gun cruisers and *Bearn.*	Brest.
"M"	Two 8-in. cruisers	Dakar.
"N"	*Strasbourg, Hermes*	West Indies.

(5) When hunting raiders it is essential that W/T silence should be maintained except when it is known that the presence of the hunting group has been disclosed. Hence the Commander-in-Chief of the station may not always be aware of the position of the hunting groups, which must therefore have more than ordinary latitude to disregard any orders they may receive. All available information will be passed for hunting groups by Commanders-in-Chief by the "I" method.

(6) Hunting groups should be cautious of being lured away from areas where trade is thick, because the raiders must come to these areas to do serious damage.

(7) The strength of each hunting group is sufficient to destroy any German armoured ship of the *Deutschland* class or armoured cruiser of the *Hipper* class.

(8) It is also to be remembered that raiders are vitally dependent on their mobility being so far from repairs facilities. Hence a weaker force, if not able to effect immediate destruction may, by resolute attack, be able to cripple an opponent sufficiently to ensure a certain

subsequent location and destruction by other forces.

(9) U-boats may work in conjunction with surface ships for their destruction.

(10) The location and destruction of enemy supply ships is an important factor in rounding up raiders. It seems more probable that raiders will meet their supply ships on the high seas than attempt to use out of the way anchorages. Care must be taken in examining likely supply ships as they may have submarine in company.

Appendix C

Selection of Signals

C1. Assistant Naval Attaché,
Rio de Janeiro

To: Commodore Commanding,
South America
Division, etc.
29.9.39.

Strongly suspect German submarine operating from inlets of the south of Natal, possibly Bahia da Traiçao, latitude 6 degrees 44 minutes south, longitude 34 degrees 53 minutes west.

Brazilian Naval authorities have promised to send warship to this area week commencing 30 September.

Regard submarine reported at 1600 on 24 September off Natal as reliable. (1800/28.)

C2. Admiralty.

To: C.-in-C., South Atlantic
29.9.39.

IMPORTANT.

Following received from A.N.A., Rio de Janeiro, begins: "Strongly suspect German submarine operating from inlets neighbourhood of (corrupt) possibly Bahia da Traiçao, latitude 6 degrees 44 minutes south, longitude 34 degrees 53 minutes west. Brazil Naval authorities promise to station man-of-war in this area from week commencing 30 September. German merchant ships at Pernambuco Bahia are sailing with fair regularity and boldness." Ends. In view of the foregoing and with reference to my 1329/28 and your 1703/28, if fuelling situation will admit and if you consider it desirable, *Hotspur* and *Havock* may patrol the above area while on passage to Freetown. The consequent delay in their return to UK can be accepted. (1311/29.)

C3. N.C.S. Officer, Pernambuco.

To: Admiralty.
Repeated S.O. (1), Freetown,
Sierra Leone.
1.10.39.

IMPORTANT.

British ship MBBL (*Clement*) sunk by surface raider 75 miles south-east of Pernambuco, 1400 local time yesterday. (1100/1.)

C4. Commodore Commanding,
South America Division.

To: C.-in-C., South Atlantic.

Repeated Admiralty.
3.10.39.

Admiralty message 1859, 1 October. Sooner or later it appears probable that German submarines will operate in South America. Against future withdrawals of destroyers, *vide* Admiralty message No. 1329, 28 September, and if anti-submarine escort vessels are not available to replace them, suggest that five modern oil-burning whalers be taken up and fitted with trawler type anti-submarine gear for use in South America.

"Gun 6" type not repetition not suitable; see my 1940, 28 November, 1938, not to C.-in-C., Africa. Suitable whalers might now be in Norway or South Africa. Failing that, those in South Georgia could be docked and fitted there. (1814/1.)

C5. Admiralty.

To: C.-in-C., South Atlantic.
Repeated commodore, S.A. Divisino, etc.
1.10.39.

IMMEDIATE.

My 1329/28. 4th Destroyer Division are to be retained in the South Atlantic for the present. (1859/1.)

C6. C.-in-C., South Atlantic.   To: Admiralty.
Repeated S.O., Force "K," etc.
2.12.39.

IMMEDIATE.

My 1625, 2 December. I propose that Force "K," on completion of fuelling, should carry out a sweep direct from the Cape to position 020 south, 015 west, repeated 020 south, 015 west, sweeping north to Freetown from this position. Believe appearing from previous experience that raiders after tip and run attack on trade routes disappear to unfrequented areas, and if the raider reported in S.N.O., Simonstown's 1615, 2 December, is proceeding south and east, she will probably proceed well clear of trade routes. (1721/2.)

C7. Admiralty   To: C.-in-C., South Atlantic.
Repeated: S.O., Force "K," etc.

IMPORTANT.

Your 1721/2 to Admiralty, S.O., Force "K," and S.N.O., Simonstown only. Force "K" is at your disposal. It should be assumed that raider will not repetition not proceed round the Cape. In due course it is desired that *Dorsetshire* should relieve *Exeter*, as in my 2113/30, but until present situation is cleared up she may be used as an independent unit as you desire. Let me know if anything is required from Paris to assist you in obtaining full co-operation from French. (0144/3.)

Appendix D

The Battle of the River Plate
13 December, 1939

Selection of Signals[133]

D1. From C.C.S.A.D. *Ajax* to *Exeter*.
Investigate smoke bearing 324°. If this is a British merchant ship bound for the Plate due to get into harbour soon, transfer your signal (*sic*) to her. (0608.)

D2. From *Exeter* to C.C.S.A.D.
I think it is a pocket battleship. (0616.)

D3. From *Ajax* to *Achilles*.
Cross my stern. (0730.)

D4. From Aircraft to *Ajax*.
Torpedoes approaching; they will pass ahead of you. (0731.)

D5. C.C.S.A.D. *Ajax* to *Achilles*.
I am nearly out of ammunition. Continue the action if you are well off. (0745.)

D6. From C.C.S.A.D. *Ajax* to *Achilles*.
Broadcast in plain language to all British merchant ships. One pocket battleship, latitude 34° S., 47° W.[134] Course 275°. Report to Admiralty. (0805.)

From *Achilles* to A.B.M.S.
Am engaging pocket battleship in 34° S., 49° W.[135] (0817)

D7. From *Ajax* to Aircraft.
  What is course of enemy?
  Reply: 275°. (0809.)

  From *Ajax* to Aircraft.
   Tell *Exeter* to close. (0814.)

  From Aircraft to C.C.S.A.D., *Ajax*.
   Exeter is badly damaged, but is joining you as best she can.
   (0910.)

D8. From *Ajax* to Aircraft.
  Be ready to land shortly. (0848.)

  From *Ajax* to *Achilles*.
   I am turning to recover my aircraft. (0855.)

D9. *Exeter* to C.C.S.A.D., *Ajax*.
  18 knots. One gun in "Y" turret available in local control. All
  other main armament permanently out of action. One 4-in. gun
  available only in ship. (1107.)

D10. *Exeter* to C.C.S.A.D., *Ajax*.
  Immediate.
  All guns out of action. (1127.)

D11. *Graf Spee* to *Ajax* (pre-war call sign) and *Achilles*.
  Please pick up lifeboats of English steamer. *Ajax* did not reply.

  From *Achilles* to *Ajax*.
   Have you received message from *Graf Spee*? Reply: Yes. (1123.)

  From *Ajax* to unknown Steamship.
   Are you all right? If so, hoist International "C." (1123.)
   Steamer hoister International "C." (1125.)

D12. C.C.S.A.D. *Ajax* to *Achilles*.

Did you fire any torpedoes. (1437.)

Reply: No. (1547.)

D13. *Achilles* to C.C.S.A.D., *Ajax*.

Enemy in sight bearing 297°. (1544.)

C.C.S.A.D. to *Achilles*.

What is it? (1543.)

Achilles to C.C.S.A.D.

Suspect 8-in. cruiser; am confirming.

Achilles to C.C.S.A.D.

False alarm. (1559.)

D14. *Exeter* to C.C.S.A.D., *Ajax*.

My position, course and speed at 1600, 34° 19' S., 50° 57' W., 180°, 20 knots. Am endeavouring to make Falklands Islands. (1603.)

D15. C.C.S.A.D. *Ajax* to *Achilles*.

I am leaving him to you this side. Make frequent enemy reports. (1829.)

From C.C.S.A.D. to *Ajax* and *Achilles*.

If enemy passes west of Lobos *Achilles* is to follow him in. *Ajax* will proceed south of English Bank in case he doubles out. Be careful you are not caught at dawn up sun, as even if he anchors he may come out to sea again any time. He is not to be relied on to respect territorial waters. (1851.)

C.C.S.A.D. *Ajax* to *Achilles*.

As you get near territorial waters take advantage of them to close up to enemy. (1925.)

Appendix E

Commodore Harwood's Signals
3 and 15 December, 1939

E1. Text of Commodore Harwood's Signal to the South American Division, Timed 1315, of 3 December, 1939

"In view of reported pocket battleship, amend previous dispositions. *Cumberland* self-refit at Falkland Islands as previously arranged, but keep at short notice on two shifts. *Achilles* leave Rio de Janeiro area so as to arrive and fuel Montevideo 0600 (Zone + 2), 8 December. *Exeter* leave Falkland Islands for Plate, a.m., 9 December, covering SS *Lafonia* with returning volunteers. *Ajax*, *Achilles* concentrate in position 35 degrees south, 50 degrees west, at 1600 (Zone + 2) 10 December. *Exeter* to pass through position 090 degrees Medanos light 150 miles at 0700, 12 December. If concentration with *Ajax* and *Achilles* is not effected by that time, further instructions will be issued to *Exeter*. Oiler *Olynthus* is to remain at sea rendezvous until situation clears instead of proceeding to Falkland Islands."

E2. Text of Commodore Harwood's Signal to the South America Division, Timed 1135, of 15 December, 1939.

"My object destruction. Necessities concentrating our forces. Increased risk of enemy escape accepted. *Achilles* is now to watch north of English Bank and *Cumberland* to west of English Bank, latter showing herself off Montevideo in daylight. If enemy leaves before 2100, ships in touch shadow at maximum range – all units concentrate on shadower. If enemy has not left by 2100, leave patrol positions and concentrate in position 090 degrees, San Antonio 15 miles, by 0030; *Ajax* will probably join *Cumberland* on her way south.

If enemy leaves Montevideo after sunset, *Cumberland* is at once to fly off one aircraft to locate and shadow enemy, if necessary landing in a lee risking internment and trying to find a British ship in the morning. If plan miscarries, adopt Plan B, all units concentrate in position 36 degrees south, 52 degrees west, at 0600."

Appendix F

Events at Montevideo Preceding Scuttling Graf Spee[136]

A British observer who inspected the *Admiral Graf Spee* in Montevideo harbour on 14 December as closely as was possible in the circumstances reports that the visible signs of damage were: the port midship 6-in. gun disabled; starboard pair of anti-aircraft guns probably out of action; rangefinders on fore superstructure probably also out of action; aeroplane wrecked; one searchlight damaged; large hole and other smaller holes on the port side of the hull; four holes in the control tower, the efficiency of which was probably seriously impaired; two holes below the waterline. In all there were signs of between 50 and 60 hits and there was reason to suspect that one if not two of the 11-in. guns in the foremost turret had been put out of action.

After the arrival of the *Admiral Graf Spee* every precaution which could be taken without violating Uruguayan neutrality was adopted by the British in order to keep a watch on the German ship and communicate any movement she might make as soon as possible to those concerned.

On the night of 14 December, Mr. Millington-Drake, the British Minister, handed a note to the Uruguayan Government asking for the *Admiral Graf Spee* to be interned should her stay in harbour exceed 24 hours, on the grounds that, having steamed into harbour at a high speed, she was in a seaworthy condition. The Minister for Foreign Affairs informed the British Minister that technical experts were onboard examining the damage, and would report to him in due course as to her seaworthiness.

On Friday, 15 December, the British ship *Ashworth* was sailed at 1700, and a note was handed in and accepted to the effect that the *Admiral Graf Spee* should not be allowed to sail for 24 hours after her departure.

That night the British Minister presented a second note to the Uruguayans complaining that the *Graf Spee* was receiving assistance in skilled labour and material from the shore to make good her damage. It was represented to the Minister for Foreign Affairs that the measures adopted by the Uruguayan Government to hold her were in no way adequate should she decide to break out in spite of our merchant ship having sailed, and it was suggested to him that, as there was no Uruguayan warship nor shore defence that could ensure that she did not sail, he should place an armed guard onboard. He thereupon telephoned to the Minister for Defence, who informed him that he could not put an armed guard onboard, but that he would put a tug with an armed party alongside and that this would be done forthwith. The tug was provided, but actually remained at anchor close to her quarters.

On Saturday, 16 December, the British Naval Attaché tried to get an interview with the Minister for Defence in order to suggest that further precautions should be taken by the removal of certain parts of the main armament of the *Admiral Graf Spee*, but diplomatic etiquette made this impossible.

Meanwhile an extension up to 72 hours in all for making good sea-going defects had been granted, from the time of the completion of the inspection by the Uruguayan Authorities. The *Admiral Graf Spee* would, therefore, have to sail not later than 2000 on Sunday, 17 December, or be interned. This was highly satisfactory as an assertion of Uruguayan neutrality, the more so as the British had complained of the amount of assistance which the Germans had received from the shore, for large oxygen cylinders, steel plates and other material for repair, as well as workmen from the shore – all of which and whom probably came from Buenos Aires – were openly seen to be taken onboard.

At 1700 on Friday, 15 December, another British merchant ship was sailed, and a note again handed in and accepted to the effect that the *Admiral Graf Spee* should not proceed until 24 hours after the departure of that ship.

On Saturday, 16 December, every effort was apparently being made by the Germans to complete the repairs as soon as possible. The *Admiral Graf Spee* had provisioned but not oiled; but it was improbable that she required much oil as she had completed from the *Altmark* only a week previously,[137] and it looked as if she might try to get away that night.

On Sunday, 17 December, during the forenoon, all repair materials were taken ashore. The Uruguayan authorities had issued a note prohibiting the sailing of any British ship after 2000 the previous day as the *Admiral Graf Spee* was due to sail at 2000 that evening. Late in the forenoon some extra boat traffic was observed and then the wounded men were brought ashore. Soon after 1400 boat-loads of men and personal effects were seen to be transferring to the *Tacoma* lying a short distance away across the harbour. At first attempts were made to preserve secrecy. Canvas screens were rigged up over the gangway so that observers from outboard could not see what was being put into the boats, and the men going onboard the *Tacoma* were once sent below. Later in the afternoon, however, all efforts to preserve secrecy were abandoned and boats full of men were openly ferried across the harbour. By 1700 over 700 men had been counted as having left.

Accordingly a note was handed in pressing the Uruguayans to intern the *Tacoma* on the grounds that she had become a naval transport.

At 1817 the *Admiral Graf Spee* hoisted a large ensign on the foremast as well as at the main and left the harbour, followed soon afterwards by the *Tacoma*. Having left the harbour, the *Admiral Graf Spee* steamed to the south-westward and stopped about five miles from the entrance. The *Tacoma* anchored about two miles to the north-east of her. Several boats then left the *Admiral Graf Spee* for the *Tacoma*, and two tugs and a lighter arrived from Buenos Aires. Her destruction was made as dramatic as possible. The first explosion took place exactly as the sun set, while all her crew were lined up on the deck of the *Tacoma* making the Nazi salute. The whole procedure was watched by vast crowds from the shore.

Reported Events in *Graf Spee* Preceding Scuttling[138]

The *Admiral Graf Spee* had been repairing at top speed from the morning of Thursday, 14 December, onwards. On Saturday, 16 December, it was anticipated that repairs would be completed sometime during Saturday night, or early on Sunday morning. The Uruguayan officials were so confident that she would make a break out sometime during that night that they prohibited all Allied ships from leaving the port.

Captain Langsdorf came ashore at 8 p.m. on Saturday to consult the German Minister. He apparently cabled to Hitler about that hour, and a reply ordering the scuttling of the ship was probably received about midnight. Captain Langsdorf returned onboard the *Admiral Graf Spee* shortly after midnight, and all repair work was suspended. At the same hour arrangements were made with Buenos Aires for two large German-owned Argentine tugs to tow a large barge over to receive the crew of the *Admiral Graf Spee* after the ship had been scuttled, and take them to Buenos Aires.

During the previous afternoon (Saturday, 16 December) barge loads of provisions had been embarked by the *Admiral Graf Spee*, and also a lot of lifebelts and other gear from the German merchant ship *Tacoma*. On Sunday morning this process was reversed. The lifebelts and gear were all returned to the *Tacoma* and the provisions embarked were transferred to that ship. From noon to 5.30 p.m. on Sunday about 900 of the *Admiral Graf Spee*'s officers and men were also transferred to the *Tacoma*.

Appendix G

Battle of the River Plate

Expenditure of Ammunition[139]

Ajax (8–6-in.)

Turret.	Rounds fired.
"A"	307
"B"	194
"X"	142
"Y"	180
Total rounds fired	823

Achilles (8–6-in.)

Turret.	Rounds fired.
"A"	340
"B"	349
"X"	290
"Y"	263
Total rounds fired	1,242

Exeter (6–8-in.)

Turret.	Rounds fired.
"A"	Not stated
"B"	8 salvoes
"Y"	177

Graf Spee
See pages 68-75.

Expenditure of Torpedoes

Ajax (8–21-in. tubes, quadrupled)

Torpedo tubes.	Torpedoes fired.
Starboard tubes	Nil
Port tubes	4

Achilles (8–21-in. tubes, quadrupled)

Torpedo tubes.	Torpedoes fired.
Starboard tubes	Nil
Port tubes	Nil

Exeter (6–21-in. tubes, tripled)

Torpedo tubes.	Torpedoes fired.
Starboard tubes	3
Port tubes	3

Graf Spee (8–21-in. tubes)
See pages 68-72.

Appendix H

Extract from Commodore Harwood's Report on the Battle of the River Plate[140]

Paragraph 6. Concentration of all three ships was effected by 0700, Tuesday, 12 December, and I then proceeded towards position 32 degrees south, 47 degrees west. This position was chosen from my shipping plot as being at that time the most congested part of the diverted shipping routes, i.e., the point where I estimated that a Raider could do most damage to British shipping.

Paragraph 7. On concentrating I made the following signal timed 1200, 12 December to my force:–

"My policy with three cruisers in company versus one pocket battleship. Attack at once by day or night. By day act as two units. 1st Division (*Ajax* and *Achilles*) and *Exeter* diverged to permit flank marking. 1st Division will concentrate gunfire. By night ships will normally remain in company in open order. Be prepared for the signal ZMM, which is to have the same meaning as MM except that for Division read Single Ship."

Paragraph 8. I amplified this later in my signal 1813, 12 December, as follows:–

"My object in the signal ZMM is to avoid torpedoes and take the enemy by surprise and cross his stern. Without further orders ships are to clear the line of fire by hauling astern of the new leading ship. The new leading ship is to lead the line without further orders so as to maintain decisive gun range."

I exercised this manoeuvre during the evening of 12 December.

The Action
Wednesday, 13 December, 1939. 0530–0623.

Paragraph 10. Captain F. S. Bell, Royal Navy, of HMS *Exeter*, hauled out of the line and altered course to the westward in accordance with my plan, in order to attack the enemy from a widely different bearing and permit flank marking...

Endnotes

1. The *Emden*, Korvettan-Käpitan von Müller, 3,592 tons, 10–4.1-in. guns, 24 knots.
2. She also captured and released one Allied and 12 neutral merchant ships, totalling 53,544 tons.
3. The *Sydney*, Captain John L.T. Glossop, R.N., 5,600 tons, 8–6-in. guns, 26 knots.
4. Naval Staff Monograph, "The Eastern Squadron," 1914, O.U. 5413 (C), page 101.
5. The *Admiral Graf Spee*, German pocket battleship, Kapitän Zur See Hans Langsdorf, 10,000 tons, 6–11-in, 8–5.9-in. and 6–4.1-in. H.A. guns. The others were the *Deutschland* renamed *Lützow*, December, 1939 and *Admiral Scheer*.
6. M.00697/39, War Memorandum (European). South Atlantic dispositions were:– Cape Verde Force (Freetown), *Neptune*; Freetown Force, two escort vessels (from Africa) Pernambuco Force (in Rio de Janeiro area initially), *Exeter* and *Ajax*.
7. See page 28.
8. They reached Freetown on 4 September.
9. The *Olinda* papers in M.013821/39, M.012635/39, and M.013530/39.
10. M.012637/39. Details in M.013820/39.
11. Formerly Trinidada.
12. The *Cumberland*, R. of P.
13. Details are in M.013752/39.
14. The *Cumberland*, R. of P.
15. Signal 1230/24, C.-in-C.'s War Diary, para 15.
16. Approximately 9° 35' S., 15° 35' W.
17. Thirteenth Hague Convention, 1907. Articles 17–20.
18. 45 miles off Cape San Antonio, south entrance to the Plate. See Plan 1.
19. Commodore S.A.D.'s L. of P. No. 5/39.
20. In November, 1939. Commodore S.A.D.'s L. of P. 6/39.
21. Appendix C. It now seems certain that these submarine reports were incorrect.
22. i.e., in 9° 5' S., 34° 5' W.
23. Appendix C.
24. Despatch to Bermuda; *Dauntless*, *Durban* and *Danae* to China Station.
25. October 3/2332.
26. 17° 58' S., 38° 42' W. See Plan 2.
27. For "Fuelling and other Facilities for H.M. Ships on South Atlantic Station" see M.0201/40.
28. See Appendix B for full text of telegram.

29. A.T. 1822/5.
30. Renamed *Lützow* in December, 1939.
31. O.U. 6353A (41).
32. The *Perth* sailed 22 October and *Berwick* 23 October.
33. The *York* sailed 22 October.
34. North America and West Indies War Diaries.
35. In 9° 15' N., 28° 12' W.
36. From South Atlantic Station R. of P., paras 34, 41 and 42, and War Diary, B.N.L.O., Dakar, 7 September, 1939-30 January, 1940.
37. October 9 /1001.
38. R.A.S.A.D's L. of P. No. 7, para 55.
39. South Atlantic Station R. of P. and Commodore S.A.D.'s L of P. No. 6/39.
40. Via Suez.
41. In 14° 18' N., 31° 48' W. on 9 October.
42. From South Atlantic Station R. of P. Commodore S.A.D.'s L of P. No. 6/39, and *Ajax's* L. of P. No. 10/39.
43. From Pernambuco, Oct. 1/1810.
44. The *Havock* was escorting a convoy of four British ships, the *Zouave, Sheridan, St. Clears* and *St. Margaret* from the Plate with the *Exeter* in support.
45. October 2/0340.
46. In 32° 40' S., 48° W., 240 miles east of Rio Grande do Sul.
47. Plan 1.
48. C.-in.-C. to C.A.S.D., Oct. 2 October01.
49. She was, in fact, sunk by the *Graf Spee*.
50. From Commodore S.A.D.'s L. of P. No. 6/39.
51. M.04 031/40.
52. See pages 43-45.
53. This information was passed by *Hotspur* from *Olwen*.
54. Commodore S.A.D.'s L. of P. No. 6/39.
55. See pages 39-43.
56. The *Trevanion* was sunk by the *Graf Spee* that afternoon (22 October). At an interview with the Casualty Section of Trade Division her captain gave the position as 18° 20' S., 1° 30' E., but according to O.U. 6553 (41), the position was 19° 40' S., 4° 2' E.
57. South Atlantic Station R. of P., paras. 27, 32 and 43.
58. Position 6° 2' N., 17° 25' W. Details in N.L.5234/39.
59. South Atlantic Station R. of P. paras. 31, 45, 46 and 47.
60. November 3/1359.
61. Nov. 4/1334.
62. South Atlantic Station R. of P., paras. 53 and 54.
63. See Plan 2.
64. In 35° 36' S., 54° 53' W. See Plan 1.
65. R.A. S.A.D.'s Letter of Proceedings No. 7/39, 27 October to 13 December, 1939, and *Exeter* Letter of Proceedings No. 01/39, 27 October to 10 November, 1939.

66. South Atlantic Station Report of Proceedings, paras 56, 57, 58 and 59.

67. 12° 18' S.

68. M.016266/39.

69. South Atlantic Station Report of Proceedings, paras. 59, 60, 61 and 62.

70. The *Clyde* patrolled from 22 November, destroyers from 23 November. The *Neptune* reached Freetown on 25 November with *Adolf Woermann* survivors, and sailed again the same day.

71. Signal Nov. 27/2203.

72. Cape Point is one mile east of the Cape of Good Hope.

73. See Plan 3.

74. C.-in-C., War Diary, paras. 62 and 70.

75. Plan 2.

76. R.A.S.A.D.'s Letter of Proceedings No. 7, 27 October–13 December, 1939.

77. From War Diary B.N.L.O., Dakar, in T.S.D. 4132/40.

78. 2,569 tons classified in British Return of Fleets as light cruiser.

79. South Atlantic Station R. of P., paras. 63-65, 69, 70, 73-78.

80. Appendix C.

81. Plan 3.

82. The *Graf Spee* sank the *Tairoa* in 21° 30' S., 3° E., at 0400 on 3 December, 1939. See pages 64-68.

83. Approximate position. For tracks of raider and Forces "H" and "K" see Plan 3.

84. Force I, East Indies Station.

85. The *Hasty* was at Dakar.

86. 2,441 tons, five 5.4-in. guns, called by the French contre-torpilleurs (i.e., destroyers), but classified in British Return of Fleets as light cruisers.

87. Plan 5.

88. Details of sinking of *Adolf Leonhardt* are in N.L.799/40.

89. R.A.S.A.D.'s L. of P. No. 7/39.

90. Position of *Ajax* at 2000. 39° 39' S., 57° 32' W., and of *Ussukuma* at 2140, 39° 24' S., 57° 15' W. (100 miles south of Mar del Plata). Details of the destruction of the *Ussukuma* are in N.L.1717/40.

91. R.A.S.A.D.'s L. of P. No. 7/39, paras. 74, 77, 91-93 and 96.

92. See Appendix E.

93. Appendix D. Commodore Harwood's signal reads "Investigate smoke bearing 324°." Its code time is 0608, but the Commodore's Report in R.O. Case 5450, Vol. 1, says "At 0614 smoke was sighted bearing 320°, etc." The *Achilles* says "At 0614 smoke was sighted bearing 310°."

94. See Plan 3.

95. The *Clement*'s crew were landed at Maceio, 110 miles south of Pernambuco.

96. According to Mr. A. H. Tompson, Chief Officer of the *Huntsman*; but O.U. 6353 (40) gives position 8° S., 8° W.

97. See pages 53-58 and 58-61.

98. Position approximate.

99. These figures may be compared with 16 British ships totalling 66,146 tons sunk by the *Emden* in 1914.

100. Admiralty Record Office Case No. 5450, Vols. I and II. For Selection of Signals, see Appendix D.

101. All times are two hours behind G.M.T.

102. Appendix D.

103. Appendix D.

104. Plans 4 and 6.

105. See Appendix H.

106. "First Division and *Exeter* diverged to permit flank marking." Page 64.

107. 130°.

108. Appendix D.

109. Appendix D. This report was far from correct. The *Ajax* carried 1,600 rounds of ammunition, of which nearly 50 per cent. remained. (See Appendix G.)

110. Appendix D.

111. By wireless. The *Graf Spee* used the *Ajax*'s pre-war call sign. Appendix D.

112. The *Exeter*'s 1600 position was 34° 19' S., 50° 57' W., and her 2000 position 35° 35' S. 50° 57' W. Appendix D.

113. Appendix D.

114. Appendix D.

115. See Plan 1.

116. For subsequent movements of all these Forces see pages 77-79.

117. See Appendix E.

118. Plan 5.

119. See pages 58-61.

120. At 0950.

121. Following the destruction of the *Graf Spee*.

122. Commodore Harwood had been specially promoted Rear-Admiral with seniority 13 December, 1939, and awarded a K.C.B. for his part in the Battle of the River Plate.

123. See Plans 3 and 5.

124. After hearing of the scuttling of the *Graf Spee*.

125. 2nd Destroyer Flotilla, 3rd Division.

126. See pages 58-61.

127. See Plan 1.

128. Appendix A.

129. Speech at Guildhall on 15 February, 1940. For Report of Events at Montevideo immediately preceding scuttling of *Graf Spee*, see Appendix F.

130. The names of the Commanding Officers in Appendix B are from the contemporary Navy List.

131. The *Dorsetshire* was originally detailed for Force "I," East Indies Command (Appendix B), but her place in Force "I" was taken by *Gloucester*.

132. HMS *Hermes* was attached to Force "X" at Dakar.

133. N.B.–The Code Times of the *Ajax*'s signals, which in the originals are Zone + 4, have

been adjusted to Zone + 2 to confirm with Commodore Harwood's Report in Record Office Case 5450, Vol. I.

134. 47° W. in original.

135. 49° in original.

136. From N.I.D. Summary of Naval and Political News, No. 9, 5 January, 1940, pages 57, 60 and 61.

137. Actually 10 days previously, i.e., on 6 December. H.S./T.S.D.

138. From a report received by the Admiralty and issued to the Press, 26 March, 1940.

139. Ajax and *Achilles* carried 200 rounds per gun and *Exeter* 100 rounds per gun.

140. Case 5450. Vol. 1, page 29.

PART II

NAVAL STAFF HISTORY
SECOND WORLD WAR

BATTLE SUMMARY No. 24

SINKING OF THE SCHARNHORST
26 December 1943

This book is based on information available up to and
including October, 1948

T.S.D. 223/48
Tactical and Staff Duties Division (Historical Section),
Naval Staff, Admiralty, S.W.1.

Battle Summary No. 24, 'The Sinking of the *Scharnhorst*', was originally compiled in the early part of 1944, less than six months after the event. Naturally, at that time little was known of the German side of the incident.

The capture of German naval records on the conclusion of the war in Europe has thrown much light on most naval operations, and though in this particular instance the records are not so complete as could be desired, owing to the death of the German Admiral and all the officers onboard the *Scharnhorst*, the events which led up to the action, the German plan, and the fruitless peregrinations of the five destroyers which accompanied the battlecruiser on the venture, can now be stated with some accuracy. It is difficult to read the German staff records without reaching the conclusion that the German High Command really attached more importance throughout to preserving the *Scharnhorst* intact than to inflicting damage on the convoy, an attitude which reflected itself in what is known of Admiral Bey's handling of the operation at sea, and which may account in some degree for the disaster which overtook him.

CONTENTS

Overview

The sinking of the German battlecruiser *Scharnhorst*[1] by units of the Home Fleet operating in support of the Russian convoys on 26 December, 1943, deprived the enemy of the only effective capital ship – exclusive of "pocket battleships" – remaining to him at the time,[2] and thus greatly eased the strategical situation in Home, Atlantic and North Russian waters. The action, which took place in the winter darkness of an Arctic day, was directed by the Commander-in-Chief, Home Fleet,[3] wearing his flag in the *Duke of York*. The operations after first contact in the early forenoon lasted about 10 hours. Two attempts by the *Scharnhorst* to close the convoy were frustrated by a cruiser force under Vice-Admiral Burnett,[4] which then shadowed her throughout the afternoon until the arrival on the scene of the Commander-in-Chief. Battered by the *Duke of York*'s gunfire, she was finally sunk by cruiser and destroyer torpedo attack.

The sailing of convoys from the United Kingdom to the White Sea, which had been discontinued during the summer months, was resumed in November, 1943. The Germans opposed them with a strong force of aircraft, surface craft (including capital ships) and submarines based on Northern Norway (see Plan 1), and the passage of these convoys was always fraught with considerable risk.[5] The winter darkness afforded a large measure of protection against air attack, but ice conditions compelled the convoys to pass to the southward of Bear Island – within 250 miles of the enemy base at Altenfjord – and thus offered excellent opportunities for attack by surface craft and submarines. To meet these dangers, the convoys were strongly escorted by destroyers and small craft; a cruiser force operated in support, and battleship cover was provided during the critical period of the passage in the vicinity of Bear Island. Economy in covering forces was effected by arranging that east- and west-bound convoys should pass each other in this area.

The operations which culminated in the sinking of the *Scharnhorst* started with the sailing of a convoy of 19 ships – J.W.55A – from Loch Ewe on 12 December, 1943; a similar convoy – J.W.55B – was due to leave about a week later. Cover for these convoys was provided by two forces:–

Force 1[6], under Vice-Admiral Burnett, consisting of the cruisers *Belfast* (flag), *Norfolk*, *Sheffield*.

Force 2[7], under the Commander-in-Chief, consisting of the *Duke of York* (flag), *Jamaica* and four destroyers.

During the passage of convoy J.W.55A the Commander-in-Chief took the opportunity of visiting Kola Inlet between 16 and 18 December, in order to inform himself at first hand of affairs in Northern Russia, and also to establish personal contact with the Russian Commander-in-Chief, with a view to future co-operation. On the conclusion of this visit, Force 2 left Kola Inlet, and proceeded to Akureyri (Iceland) to fuel preparatory to covering convoy J.W.55B, and the west-bound convoy, R.A.55A, which was due to leave Kola Inlet on 22 December.

Vice-Admiral Burnett having remained in support of convoy J.W.55A till danger of attack was over, proceeded to Kola Inlet on 19 December, and remained there till 23 December, when he sailed to cover the first part of the passage of convoy R.A.55A.

Opposite, Plan 1

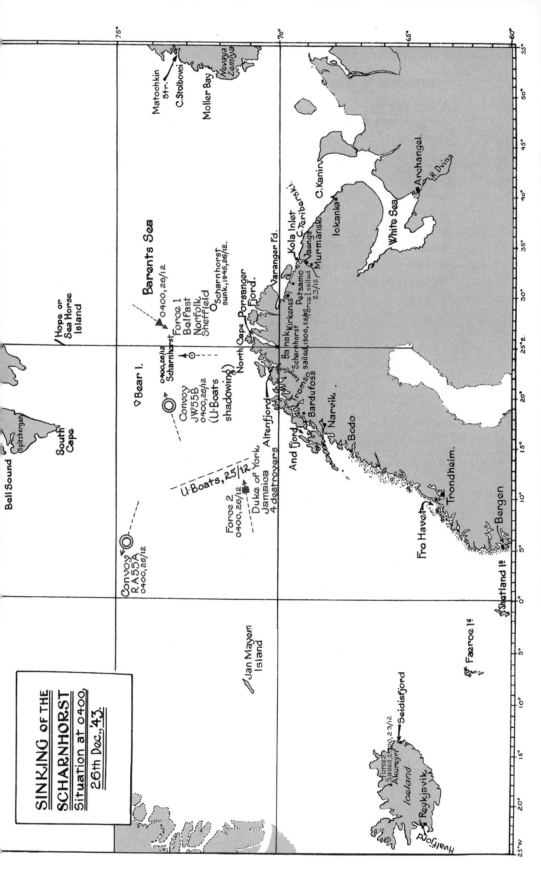

SINKING of the **SCHARNHORST**
Situation at 0400, 26th Dec., '43.

Barents Sea

0400, 26/12
Scharnhorst
Force 1
Belfast
Norfolk
Sheffield

○ Scharnhorst
sunk, 1945, 26/12.

Porsanger Fjord.
Varanger Fd.

North Cape

Kola Inlet
C.Teriborski
Vaanga Scharnhorst
Porsamo sailed 1900, 25/12 Force I sailed
Banak Kirkenes 23/12
From so
Bardufoss

Murmansk.
Iokankaa

C.Kanin

White Sea

Archangel.
R.Dvina

Hope or
Sea Horse
Island

◇ Bear I.

0400, 26/12
Scharnhorst ◉→

Convoy
JW55B
0400, 26/12
(U-Boats
shadowing)

Altenfjord

And Fjord

Narvik.

Bodo

Trondheim.

Fro Haven

Bergen

Shetland Is

Ball Sound

Spitsbergen

South
Cape

U-Boats, 25/12

Force 2
0400, 26/12
Duke of York
Jamaica
4 destroyers

Convoy
RA55A
0400, 26/12

Jan Mayen
Island

Faeroe Is

Iceland

Force 2
Sailed 1900, 23/12
Akureyri

Seidisfjord

Reykjavik

Hvalfjord

Matochkin
Str.
C.Stolbovoi

Moller Bay

Novaya
Zemlya

75°

70°

65°

60°

55°   50°   45°   40°   35°   30°   25°E.   20°   15°   10°   5°   0°   5°W.   10°   15°   20°   25°W.

The Commander-in-Chief's Intentions

Force 2 arrived at Akureyri on 21 December. With the safe arrival in Russian ports of convoy J.W.55A, the Commander-in-Chief "felt very strongly that the *Scharnhorst* would come out and endeavour to attack J.W.55B"; and before sailing from Akureyri on 23 December he held a meeting of the Commanding Officers of Force 2, at which he explained his intentions and stressed that for this operation "every officer and man must be doubly sure that he knew his night action duty."[8]

Since the endurance of his destroyers did not permit continuous cover to be given for the whole passage of the convoy, he intended to reach the covering position at a speed of advance of 15 knots, when the convoy was just east of Bear Island. This would allow him to spend some 30 hours in the area.

Should the *Scharnhorst* be encountered, he had decided:–

to close the enemy, opening fire with starshell at a range of about 12,000 yards;

to form the four destroyers of the screen into subdivisions, and release them in time to take up positions for torpedo attack;

to keep the *Jamaica* in close support of the *Duke of York*, but with freedom of action to take drastic avoiding action and open the distance if engaged.

Preliminary Movements
(Plan 1)

On 23 December, 1943, Vice-Admiral Burnett with Force 1 sailed from Kola Inlet, and at 2300[9] the same evening the Commander-in-Chief, with Force 2, left Akureyri.

Meanwhile convoy J.W.55B, which had left Loch Ewe on 20 December and was then some 450 miles to the north-eastward of Akureyri, had been located by enemy aircraft that day,[10] and during the morning of 24 December was continuously shadowed. This caused the Commander-in-Chief some anxiety; though the German surface forces had hitherto never made a sortie to the westward, such a contingency was possible. The convoy was entirely unsupported and had reached a position Lat. 70° 40' N., Long 3° 10' E. (about 400 miles from Altenfjord) by noon, 24 December. He therefore decided to break wireless silence at 1400, and reversed its course for three hours, at the same time increasing the speed of Force 2 to 19 knots.[11] No attack materialised, however, and the original intentions were resumed.

On Christmas Day it appeared that the west-bound convoy, R.A.55A, was passing Bear Island undetected by the enemy; this fact, combined with the shadowing of convoy J.W.55B, implied that U-boats, if present, might be concentrating on the latter. The Commander-in-Chief therefore requested the Rear-Admiral (D), Home Fleet,[12] to divert convoy R.A.55A, to the northward, clear of the area, and to detach four Fleet destroyers from its escort to reinforce convoy J.W.55B. This brought the destroyer strength of the latter up to fourteen, and Admiral Fraser then "felt confident that if the *Scharnhorst* attacked the convoy, Force 1 and the escort destroyers would either drive her off or inflict damage which would give me time to close."

During the night of 25/26 December, Force 2 steamed to the eastward at 17 knots. There was an unpleasant sea, and conditions in the *Duke of York* were most uncomfortable, few people obtaining any sleep. At 0339, 26 December, the Commander-in-Chief received from the Admiralty a message appreciating that the *Scharnhorst* was at sea.[13]

She had, in fact, left Langefjord (Altenfjord) with five destroyers,[14] at 1900 the previous evening (25 December), and was then steering to the northward, some 200 miles to the eastward of Force 2. Rear-Admiral Bey had hoisted his flag in her just before she sailed,[15] his staff of 30 bringing her company up to close on 2,000 men; of these, but 36 survived the ensuing twenty-four hours to tell the tale.

German Appreciation and Plan

The events which had led the Germans to undertake this operation were as follows. Reports indicating the renewed sailings of the convoys to Russia had been received in the middle of November, but earlier appreciations of both the Naval War Staff and Group Command, North, had ruled that the employment of the *Scharnhorst* against this traffic would be too risky, in view of the favourable conditions created by winter darkness and accentuated by the superiority of the British radar, for attack on her by escorting destroyers. For these reasons it seems to have been accepted by Group Command, North, that operations against the convoys would be confined to raids by destroyers, and that the *Scharnhorst* would not be employed before the days were lengthening in March, by which time also it was hoped that the *Tirpitz* would be repaired and able to take part.

But other forces were at work. For political reasons, Grand Admiral Dönitz, the Commander-in-Chief of the Navy, was anxious to demonstrate to Hitler the value of the capital ship, and at a conference held on 19 December he informed the Führer that he intended attacking the next convoy with the "Battle group," consisting of the *Scharnhorst* and 4th Destroyer Flotilla, and that meanwhile he was increasing the number of U-boats in Arctic waters. He believed the prospects of success were good, as since two convoys had already passed unmolested by German forces the enemy would probably be less prepared for trouble.[16]

Accordingly, after the convoy had been located on 22 December, the battle-group was brought to three hours notice for steam. As already mentioned, aircraft succeeded in maintaining contact throughout 23/24. In consequence of their reports the 8 U-boats, then assembled off Bear Island, were ordered to form a new patrol line to the westward, stretching approximately from Lat. 74° 24' N., Long. 13° E. to Lat. 72° N., Long. 16° E.

The Luftwaffe units in North Norway at this time were greatly under strength and inadequate for any offensive action, but they were relied on to provide continuous reconnaissance in the vicinity of the convoy, and in particular to search for any covering force of warships which might be within 300 miles of it. On these reconnaissance reports depended the decision whether the *Scharnhorst* would attempt the attack or not; it was laid down as essential that "the prospects of success were favourable," by which was meant that no risk was to be run of becoming involved with surface forces sufficiently powerful to do the German ships serious damage.

Contact with the convoy was temporarily lost after 1600/24, but during the night the U-boat patrol line was moved some 75 miles to the south-west, and at 0901/25, U.601 reported the convoy in Lat. 73° 32' N., Long. 12° 30' E. From then on the submarines continued to shadow,[17] replacing the aircraft which were unable to operate owing to bad weather. No increase of the British escort – which was believed to consist of 3 cruisers, 5 destroyers and 4 smaller craft – was reported, nor were there any indications of a heavier covering force being at sea. Accordingly, at 1410/25 the German Naval War Staff ordered the battle-group to commence operations, and some five hours later it put to sea.

The German plan was to intercept the convoy in approximately the longitude of North Cape; the *Scharnhorst* with two destroyers was to stand off, while the remainder shadowed till twilight broke and visibility improved sufficiently to enable the most effective use to be made of the battlecruiser's guns, when she would close in to the attack. If any enemy heavy ships should appear the operation was to be broken off immediately by the *Scharnhorst*, while the destroyers were to do as much damage as possible in a delaying action covering her withdrawal.

On clearing the land very heavy weather was encountered, and at 2116/25 Rear-Admiral Bey signalled to Group Command, North, that the destroyers were severely handicapped by it, both as regards their manoeuvrability and the use of their guns. The battle-group was then only a few hours steaming from the convoy and a speedy decision as to whether or not to break off the operation was vital. The matter was referred to Grand Admiral Dönitz himself, who decided that the operation was to proceed; if the destroyers could not remain at sea, the *Scharnhorst* might complete the task alone.[18] This decision he left to the Flag Officer afloat.

Orders to this effect were received by Admiral Bey at 0214/26, and the battle-group continued its course to the northward, the eight shadowing U-boats meanwhile keeping him supplied with valuable reports on the progress of the convoy.

Situation at 0400
(Plan 1)

At 0400, 26 December, the disposition of the Forces in the Bear Island area was as follows:–

The westbound convoy, R.A.55A, consisting of 22 merchant ships, was some 220 miles to the westward of Bear Island, in approximate position Lat. 74° 42' N., Long. 5° 27' E., steering 267°, 8 knots. Captain Campbell (D.3), in the *Milne*, was senior officer of the escort, which comprised six destroyers, three sloops and a minesweeper (see Appendix A). This convoy was apparently still undetected by the enemy.[19]

The eastbound convoy, J.W.55B, 19 merchant ships, was in position Lat. 73° 31' N., Long. 18° 54' E. (about 50 miles south of Bear Island), steering 070°, 8 knots. The escort, consisting of 14 destroyers, two sloops and a minesweeper (see Appendix A) was commanded by Captain McCoy (D.17), in the *Onslow*.

Vice-Admiral Burnett's cruisers were in Lat. 73° 52' N., Long. 27° 12' E. (150 miles to the eastward of J.W.55B), steering 235°, 18 knots, and the Commander-in-Chief with Force 2, some 350 miles to the south-west, in Lat. 71° 07' N., Long. 10° 48' E., had increased speed to 24 knots on course 080°. There was a strong south-westerly wind, and at this speed the destroyers had much difficulty to avoid broaching to in the heavy following sea, while the *Duke of York*'s bows were constantly under water.

"The stage was well set," wrote Admiral Fraser, "except that if the *Scharnhorst* attacked at daylight[20] and immediately retired, I was not yet sufficiently close to cut her off." Convoy J.W.55B had been consistently shadowed and reported by U-boats and aircraft throughout its passage, and he had no doubt that this was the *Scharnhorst*'s quarry; he therefore decided to divert the convoy to the northward, in order to increase the enemy's difficulties in finding it. This would entail breaking wireless silence and revealing the presence of covering forces, but he "decided that the safety of the convoy must be the primary object," and at 0401/26, directed Vice-Admiral Burnett and Captain McCoy to report their positions, at the same time informing them of his own. At 0628 the convoy was ordered to steer 045°, and Force 1 to close it for mutual support.

Vice-Admiral Burnett altered course to 270° at 0712, in order to approach the convoy from the southward, and thus, in the event of action, to avoid steaming into the strong south-westerly wind and heavy seas. He held this course for an hour, and after receiving the position, course and speed of the convoy, hauled up to 300° at 0815, increasing speed to 24 knots.

Meanwhile, the German battle-group had continued on its northerly course, and at 0730 was in estimated position Lat. 73° 52' N., Long. 23° 10' E. Soon after this the destroyers were detached, with orders to form a reconnaissance line 10 miles ahead of the *Scharnhorst*. This order was not received in its entirety by the destroyers; as a result, they moved ahead, but the area of their search was not the one intended. At 0800 the force altered course to 230°, probably on account of a submarine report giving a fresh position of the convoy.[21] At this time the destroyers were some 10 miles ahead of the battlecruiser, spread approximately in line abreast; but it seems that soon afterwards the *Scharnhorst* turned to the north-eastward, and all communications between her and the destroyers broke down. Communication was restored two hours later, but the destroyers never rejoined the flag.

First Contact with Enemy

At 0840, 26 December, the *Belfast*'s type 273 radar picked up the enemy at 35,000 yards, bearing 295°. The *Belfast*'s estimated position was then Lat. 73° 35' N., Long. 23° 21' E., and Vice-Admiral Burnett reckoned the convoy was bearing 287°, 48 miles, from him. At the same time Captain McCoy placed the enemy about 36 miles, 125°, from the convoy.

In the *Belfast* the range of the main echo decreased rapidly, and twenty minutes later – at 0900 – a second echo was obtained, bearing 299°, 24,500 yards. This second echo remained on a steady bearing till 0930, when, from its estimated speed of 8-10 knots, the Vice-Admiral considered that it was probably a merchant ship from the convoy, and disregarded it. It may well have been, however, one of the enemy destroyers, detached to shadow the convoy.[22]

At 0915 the main echo bore 250°, 13,000 yards, speed approximately 18 knots. At this time Force 1 was formed on a line of bearing 180°, in the order *Belfast*, *Sheffield*, *Norfolk*, the *Belfast* being the northern ship. The line of bearing had just been altered to 160°, when at 0921 the *Sheffield* reported the enemy in sight, bearing 222°, 13,000 yards.[23] Three minutes later (0924) the *Belfast* opened fire with starshell, and at 0929 Force 1 was ordered to engage with main armament, course being altered 40° towards the enemy, to 265°. The *Norfolk* opened fire at a range of 9,800 yards, but had to drop back to clear the *Belfast*'s range.[24] She continued firing till 0940 and obtained one hit, with her second or third salvo, either on the crow's nest or the bridge port director, which caused several casualties,[25] and possibly a hit on the forecastle. The 6-in. cruisers did not fire during this phase of the action, nor did the enemy, who altered course to about 150°, steaming at 30 knots. Force 1 altered to 105° at 0938, and to 170° at 0946 – by which time the range had opened to 24,000 yards – and chased to the southward, but the enemy drew away and the range continued to increase.

At 0955 the *Scharnhorst* altered course to the north-east, and Vice-Admiral Burnett at once appreciated that she was trying to work round to the northward of the convoy for a second attempt to attack it. Possibly this was the result of an exhortation from Admiral Dönitz which appears to have been received and read to her ship's company at about this time. In the prevailing weather conditions – wind force 7–8 from the south-west – Force 1's maximum speed was 24 knots, and as that of the enemy appeared to be 4 to 6 knots higher, the Vice-Admiral decided that he must get between the *Scharnhorst* and the convoy. He therefore altered course to 305° at 1000, and to 325° at 1014, with the result that six minutes later contact was lost with the enemy bearing 078°, 36,000 yards, and steering to the north-east at about 28 knots.

Meanwhile the Commander-in-Chief had ordered Captain McCoy to turn the convoy to the northward at 0930, and to send four destroyers to join Force 1 at 0937. The 36th Division[26] under Commander Fisher – *Musketeer*, *Opportune*, *Virago* and *Matchless* – was detached at 0951 and joined Vice-Admiral Burnett at 1024. By 1030, when it was clear to the Commander-in-Chief that Force 1 had lost touch with the enemy, and was again closing the convoy, he ordered J.W.55B to resume course 045°.

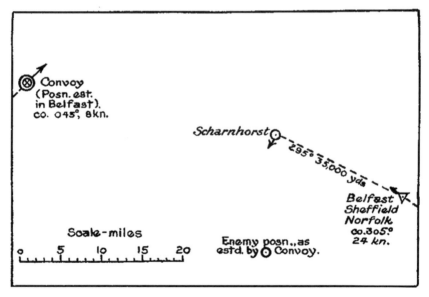

Fig. 1 Force 1: "First Radar Contact" 0840, 26 December, 1943
(positions are approximate)

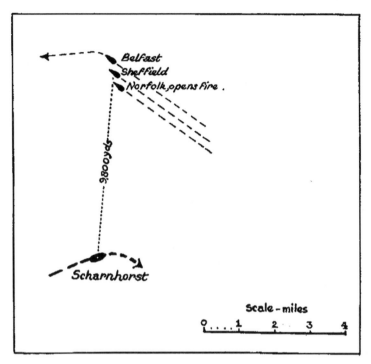

Fig. 2 Force 1: "Open Fire" 0929, 26 December, 1943
(positions are approximate)

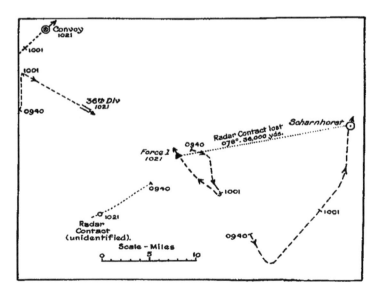

Fig. 3 Force 1: "Loses Radar Contact" 1021, 26 December, 1943
(positions are approximate)

Second Engagement of Force 1

(Plan 2)

Half an hour after losing touch with the enemy, Force 1 made radar contact with the convoy, bearing 324°, 28,000 yards, at 1050, and the cruisers commenced zigzagging 10 miles ahead of it, with the four destroyers of the 36th Division disposed ahead as a screen.

At 1058 the Commander-in-Chief informed Vice-Admiral Burnett that Force 2 would have little chance of finding the enemy unless some unit regained touch with him and shadowed; but, in view of the enemy's advantage in speed under the prevailing weather conditions, the Vice-Admiral "rightly considered it undesirable to split his force by detaching one or more ships to search, feeling confident that the enemy would return to the convoy from the north or north-east."[27]

An hour went by, and the Commander-in-Chief found himself faced with the difficult question of the destroyers' fuel situation. He had "either to turn back or go on to Kola Inlet, and if the *Scharnhorst* had already turned for home, there was obviously no chance of catching him."[27] This latter contingency was by no means improbable, for Force 2 had been shadowed from the starboard quarter by three enemy aircraft since about 1000, and their reports had presumably been passed to the *Scharnhorst*.[28] Then, at 1205, came a signal from the *Belfast* reporting radar contact again with the enemy, and he knew that there was every prospect of cutting him off.

The convoy had remained on a course 045° till just before noon, when Captain McCoy, who had been ordered by the Commander-in-Chief at 1122 to use his discretion as to its course, altered to 125° in order to keep Force 1 between the convoy and the probable direction of the enemy. The *Norfolk* had reported a radar contact at 27,000 yards at 1137, but had lost it a few minutes later, and by noon, when the convoy was turning to 125°, Force 1 was in Lat. 74° 11' N., Long. 22° 18' E., steering 045°, 18 knots, with the convoy about 9 miles on the port quarter. Five minutes later (1205) the *Belfast's* radar picked up the enemy bearing 075°, 30,500 yards. Vice-

Admiral Burnett concentrated his four destroyers on his starboard bow, and at 1219 altered course to 100°; the enemy course and speed was estimated at 240°, 20 knots. A minute later the *Scharnhorst* appeared to alter course slightly to the westward, and at 1221 the *Sheffield* reported "enemy in sight." Force 1 immediately opened fire, and the destroyers were ordered to attack with torpedoes, but were unable to reach a firing position owing to the weather conditions, and the enemy's hurried retirement.[29]

This second action, fought by the cruisers at ranges of from 9,000 to 16,000 yards, lasted about 20 minutes, and again the *Scharnhorst* was "most effectively driven off the convoy by Force 1's determined attack."[30] The enemy altered course from west round to south-east, increasing speed to 28 knots, and the range soon began to open. Several hits were claimed by the cruisers, but only one, which struck the port side aft and apparently failed to explode, was subsequently confirmed by prisoners. The *Musketeer*, however, which was herself engaging the enemy at a range of 4,500 yards, considered there were others, and the prisoners agreed that the cruisers' fire was unpleasantly accurate and filled the air with fragments.

At 1233 – 12 minutes after the action started – the *Norfolk* received two hits, one through the barbette of "X" turret, which was put out of action, and one amidships. All radar, except Type 284, became unserviceable and there were several casualties; one officer and six ratings were killed and five seriously wounded. At the same time an 11-in. salvo straddled the *Sheffield*, and several pieces of shell, described by Vice-Admiral Burnett as "up to football size" came inboard; fragments penetrated the ship at various points.

By 1241 the enemy was on a course 110° steaming 28 knots, and the range had opened to 12,400 yards. Vice-Admiral Burnett decided to check fire, and to shadow with his whole force until the *Scharnhorst* could be engaged by Force 2; he therefore increased speed to 28 knots, and at 1250 the enemy range and bearing were steady at 13,400 yards, 138°. The destroyers, to the westward of the cruisers, continued to pursue the enemy in line ahead, their range opening to 20,000 yards and then remaining steady.

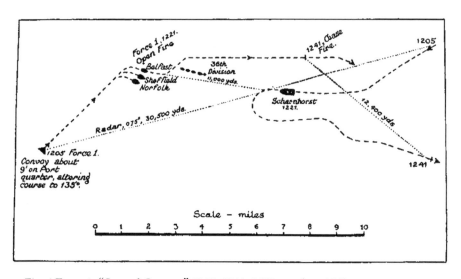

Fig. 4 Force 1: "Second Contact" 1205-1241, 26 December, 1943
(positions are approximate)

Opposite, Plan 2

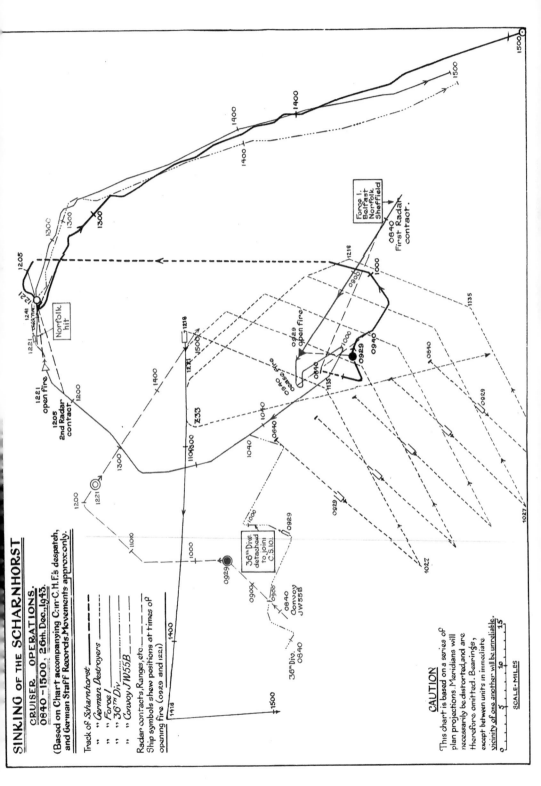

SINKING OF THE SCHARNHORST

CRUISER OPERATIONS.
0840-1500, 26th Dec., 1943.

(Based on Chart accompanying C-in-C.H.F.'s despatch,
and German Staff Records. Movements approx only.)

Track of Scharnhorst
  " " German Destroyers
  " " Force I
  " " 36th Div.
  " " Convoy JW55B

Radar contacts, Ranges, etc.
Ship symbols shew positions at times of
opening fire (0929 and 1221)

Force I.
Belfast
Norfolk
Sheffield

0840
First Radar
contact.

Norfolk
hit

1221
open fire
1205
2nd Radar
contact.

0929
open fire

36th Div.
detached
to join C.S.10.

Convoy
JW55B

36th Div.
0840

CAUTION
This chart is based on a series of
plan projections. Meridians will
necessarily be distorted, and are
therefore omitted. Bearings,
except between units in immediate
vicinity of one another, will be unreliable.

SCALE-MILES
0   5   10   15

129

Force 1 Shadowing Operations

The *Scharnhorst* had by this time given up all idea of attacking the convoy,[31] and for the next three hours her course was to the south-east and southward. As she was retiring on a course so favourable for interception by Force 2, Vice-Admiral Burnett did not attempt to re-engage, and kept his cruisers concentrated, shadowing by radar from just outside visibility range – about 7½ miles – and slightly to the eastward of the enemy's course. The 36th Destroyer Division, which owing to the heavy sea had been unable to close the enemy sufficiently to attack with torpedoes, was stationed to the westward by the Commander-in-Chief at about 1600, to guard against the *Scharnhorst* breaking back in that direction towards the convoy or Altenfjord.[32]

Despite her damage the *Norfolk* kept up with Force 1 throughout the afternoon, but at 1603 she was obliged to reduce speed to fight a fire in a wing compartment, and a few minutes later (1607) the *Sheffield* dropped back, reporting her port inner shaft out of action and speed reduced to 10 knots. By 1621 she was able to proceed at 23 knots, but the delay and the reduction of speed prevented her from rejoining Force 1 till 2100, and for the rest of the action she remained some 10 miles astern, conforming to the general movement of the battle. The *Norfolk* rejoined the Vice-Admiral 1700.

Movements of the German Destroyers
(Plan 2)

All this time, while the *Scharnhorst* was being gradually hounded to her doom, the German destroyers had played a singularly ineffective part. After losing contact soon after 0800, they continued on the south-westerly course (230°) to which the force had just turned, spread approximately five miles apart. No orders were received from the Flag Officer, Battle-group, until 1009 – just after the close of the first action with Admiral Burnett's cruisers – when a signal arrived directing them to "advance into the immediate vicinity of the convoy." To this Z.29, the Flotilla leader, replied that they were advancing according to plan, course 230°, 12 knots. Twenty minutes later, Admiral Bey had apparently come to the conclusion that the convoy was further to the north than he had previously supposed, and at 1027 he ordered the flotilla to alter course to 070° and to increase speed to 25 knots; an hour later (1135) he ordered a further change of course, to 030°.

At 0945 a report from U.277 had been received in the *Scharnhorst* placing the convoy in Lat. 73° 58' N., Long. 19° 30' E., but this seems to have been disregarded by Admiral Bey and it was not until two-and-a-half hours later (1218) that he ordered the destroyers to operate in this area. Course was accordingly altered to 280° and the flotilla concentrated on the northern ship; but by then it was too late and the convoy was well to the north-eastward of the position reported by the U-boat, though the destroyers must have passed within 10 miles of it at about 1300 on passage to the new area, owing to Captain McCoy's turn to the south-eastward at noon. Of this Admiral Bey was unaware, and at 1418 he ordered the destroyers to break off the operation and make for the Norwegian Coast. With the exception of Z.33, which had become separated in the bad weather, the flotilla – then some 16 miles south-east of Bear Island – at once altered course to 180° and eventually entered Norwegian coastal waters[33] at about 0200/27.

Z.33 made her own way back; at 1810/26, she sighted what was believed to be a straggler from the convoy. At this target she fired four torpedoes, which missed, and continued on her way to her base. This was the sole contribution of the destroyers to the fortunes of the day.

Movements of the Commander–in–Chief, Home Fleet

Meanwhile Force 2, acting on the reports of Vice-Admiral Burnett's cruisers, had been steering throughout the day to intercept.[34] During the first two cruiser engagements the composition of the enemy's force was not clear to the Commander-in-Chief, but on confirmation by the Vice-Admiral that only one heavy unit was present, he decided to engage on similar courses, with the *Jamaica* in support, opening fire at about 13,000 yards and detaching his destroyers to make a torpedo attack. At 1400 he estimated that if the enemy maintained his course and speed, Force 2 would engage him at about 1715, but the *Scharnhorst* altered to the south soon afterwards, and at 1617 the *Duke of York*'s Type 273 radar picked her up at 45,500 yards, bearing 020°.

The range closed rapidly, and soon the *Belfast* was picked up astern of the target. At 1632 – a quarter of an hour after first contact – the *Duke of York*'s Type 284 found the enemy at 29,700 yards, apparently zig-zagging on a mean course of 160°. Five minutes later the destroyers, which had formed sub-divisions on either bow of the flagship shortly after first contact, were ordered to take up the most advantageous position for torpedo attack, but not to attack till ordered to do so.

At 1642 the enemy seemed to alter course slightly to port, and two minutes later Force 2 altered to 080° in order to open "A" arcs. At 1647 the *Belfast* opened fire with starshell, followed at 1648 by the *Duke of York*. Those from the latter illuminated the enemy at 1650;[35] the Commander-in-Chief made his first enemy report and Force 2 opened fire with main armament.

Plan 3

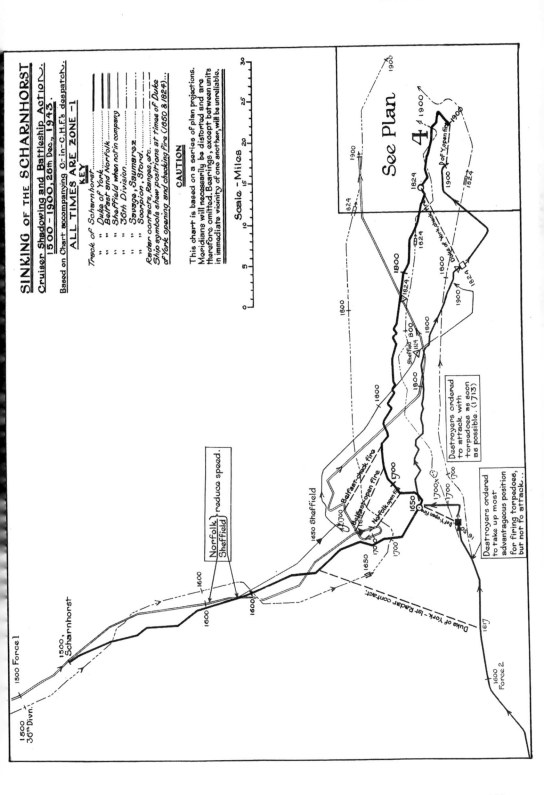

SINKING of the SCHARNHORST

Cruiser Shadowing and Battleship Action
1500 – 1900, 26th Dec., 1943.

Based on Chart accompanying C-in-C.H.F.'s despatch.

ALL TIMES ARE ZONE –1

KEY

Track of Scharnhorst
" " Duke of York
" " Belfast and Norfolk
" " Sheffield when not in company
" " 36th Division
" " Savage, Saumarez
" " Scorpion, Stord.

Radar contacts, Ranges, etc.
Ship symbols show positions at times of Duke
of York opening and checking Fire (1650 & 1824).

CAUTION

This chart is based on a series of plan projections.
Meridians will necessarily be distorted and are
therefore omitted. Bearings, except between units
in immediate vicinity of one another, will be unreliable.

Scale - Miles
0   5   10   15   20   25   30

See Plan 4

Force 2 Engages[36]
(Plan 3)

When the *Duke of York* and *Jamaica* opened fire at 12,000 yards, there was every indication that the *Scharnhorst* was completely unaware of their presence; her turrets were reported trained fore and aft, she did not immediately reply to the fire of Force 2, and when she did so her fire was erratic. Prisoners subsequently confirmed that she made no radar contact during the approach of the battleship; they had been told they would not have to engage anything larger than a cruiser, and were badly shaken when informed that a capital ship to the southward was engaging them.

The enemy altered round at once to the northward, and the *Duke of York* to 360° to follow, and also to avoid torpedoes which the enemy, had he been on the alert, might have fired.[37] On this, the *Belfast* prepared to fire torpedoes, but the *Scharnhorst* altered away to the eastward, probably with the double objective of avoiding Force 1 and of opening "A" arcs; and the *Belfast* and *Norfolk* then engaged her with main armament, steering northerly and north-easterly courses in order to prevent her breaking back to the north-westward, until 1712, when she ran out of range, after firing two ineffective salvoes at the cruisers. Vice-Admiral Burnett continued to the north-north-west till 1720, and as it was then apparent that the enemy meant to escape to the eastward, gradually altered round to follow. Just then orders were received from the Commander-in-Chief to "steer 140°" and join him, and the cruisers steadied on this south-easterly course at about 1727.

The hunt was up, and for the next hour there was a chase to the eastward, the *Duke of York* and *Jamaica* engaging at ranges which gradually increased, as the enemy's superior speed began to tell. "By 1708 the *Scharnhorst* was steady on an easterly course and engaging the *Duke of York* and *Jamaica* with her main armament. Her tactics were to turn to the southward, fire a broadside and then turn end-on away to the east till ready to fire the next, making the *Duke of York*'s gunnery a difficult problem."[38]

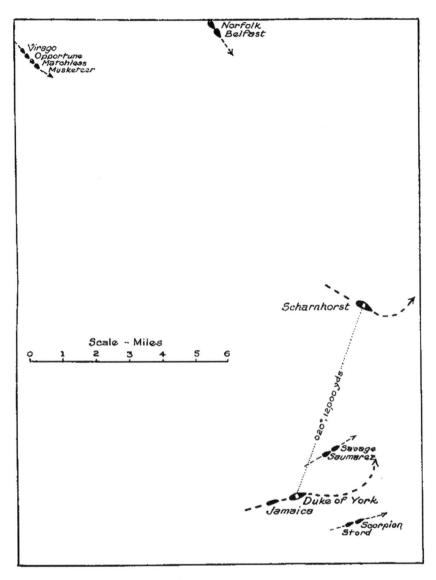

Fig. 5 Duke of York: "Open Fire" 1650, 26 December, 1943
(positions are approximate)

By 1730 the situation was as follows: To the south-west of the enemy, the *Duke of York* and *Jamaica* were engaging him and pursuing similar tactics. Force 2's destroyers – still well astern of him – were endeavouring to gain bearing to attack with torpedoes, taking individual avoiding action when fired on, the *Savage* and *Saumarez* edging over to get on his port side,[39] the *Scorpion* and *Stord* remaining to starboard, while to the north-west the 36th Division, which had turned at 1700, was creeping up on an easterly course roughly parallel to that of the enemy and some miles to the northward.[40] Further to the north-west the *Belfast* and *Norfolk* were steering to the south-eastward to join the Commander-in-Chief, with the *Sheffield* some distance astern, and dropping owing to her reduced speed. What the German Admiral thought of the situation may be judged from his signal to the German War Staff (timed 1724); "Am surrounded by heavy units."

The *Duke of York* probably obtained hits with her first and third salvoes, which, according to prisoners, were on the quarter-deck close to "C" turret, and low down forward. This latter hit may have put "A" turret out of action, as it did not fire again. Little is known about any other hits during the first engagement, but it seems certain that the *Duke of York* obtained at least three – the last of which may have caused underwater damage that eventually reduced the *Scharnhorst*'s speed – and the *Jamaica* claimed one. The hits appeared "as greenish sparks along the water line on two or three occasions, and as vivid red orange flashes when hitting the upper deck level."[41] Once a fairly considerable fire blazed up under the after superstructure and was used as a point of aim till it disappeared – "to the intense disappointment of the layer and trainer"[41] – some broadsides later.

The *Scharnhorst*'s gunfire was erratic to begin with, but improved in speed and accuracy as the range increased, till at 17,000 to 20,000 yards the *Duke of York* was frequently being straddled, and there were many near misses; her hull was not hit, but both masts were shot through by 11-in. shell, which, fortunately, did not explode.[42]

By 1742 the range had opened to 18,000 yards, and the *Jamaica* then ceased fire, her blind fire at this range being considered of doubtful value and liable to confuse the *Duke of York*'s radar spotting. At this time all the cruisers were out of range, and the destroyers had not yet been seriously engaged by the enemy. The gun duel between the *Duke of York* and the *Scharnhorst* continued till 1820, when the enemy ceased firing at 20,000 yards, and reduced speed, though this was not immediately apparent. At the same time, the Commander-in-Chief decided to turn to the south-eastward towards the Norwegian coast, in the hope that she would also lead round and so give his destroyers a chance to attack. Four minutes later (1824) the range having opened to 21,400 yards, the *Duke of York* checked fire.[43] She had then fired 52 broadsides, of which 31 had been reported as straddles and 16 as within 200 yards of the enemy.

Just at this moment the *Scharnhorst* was sending her final signal – a message from Admiral Bey and the Captain to the Führer: "We shall fight to the last shell." This was the last report the German Naval War Staff received from her as to her fate, though no doubt they were able to draw their conclusions three-quarters of an hour later (1919) when they intercepted a British signal, "Finish her off with torpedoes."

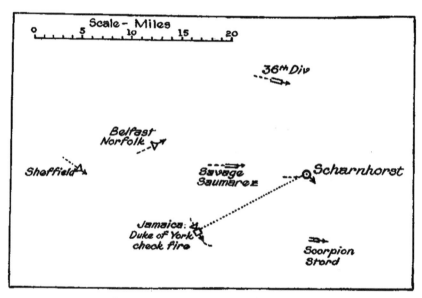

Fig. 6 Duke of York: "Check Fire" 1824, 26 December, 1943
(positions are approximate)

First Destroyer Attack
(Plans 4, 5, Appendix C)

"At this time (1824) it seemed quite probable that *Scharnhorst* would escape, and much depended upon the four 'S' class destroyers."[44] Since 1713, when they had been ordered to attack, they had been gradually gaining bearing on the *Scharnhorst*, but their progress was very slow and their chances of attack depended on a radical alteration of course by their quarry. Then, at 1820, when they closed in to 12,000 yards, they started to forge ahead. The enemy had reduced speed.[45] By 1840 the first subdivision (*Savage* and *Saumarez*), astern of the enemy, and the second subdivision (*Scorpion* and *Stord*), on his starboard beam, had each closed in to about 10,000 yards. Some three minutes earlier the Commander-in-Chief, observing on his radar plot the enemy's reduction in speed, had altered course directly towards her, and was beginning to close in rapidly.

The *Scharnhorst* opened a fairly heavy, though ineffective, fire on the *Savage* and *Saumarez*, which they returned when the range closed to 7,000 yards.[46] As these two approached from the north-westward, drawing the enemy's fire, the *Scorpion* and *Stord* were closing in "apparently unseen, and certainly unengaged," from the south-eastward. At 1849 starshells from the 1st Subdivision (*Savage*) illuminated the enemy, and she was seen to be turning to the southward.[47] The *Scorpion* and *Stord* immediately swung to starboard, each firing eight torpedoes at 2,100 and 1,800 yards respectively. The *Scorpion* claimed one hit, the *Stord* none, probably due to the *Scharnhorst* combing the latter's tracks; both destroyers were engaged by the enemy's secondary and light armament while retiring, but the firing was wild and inflicted no damage; they returned the fire and scored several hits on the superstructure. The *Scharnhorst* continued to alter round to starboard after this attack till on a south-westerly course, thus placing the first subdivion in an excellent position on her starboard bow. Her movements could be followed clearly in the light of their starshell, and the *Savage*, with the *Saumarez* on her starboard quarter, hastily training their tubes to starboard, turned in to attack at 1855, coming under heavy fire from the enemy's entire armament as they did so. The *Savage* fired eight torpedoes at a range of 3,500 yards, but the *Saumarez* received damage which prevented her training one set of tubes, and got off only four torpedoes at a range of 1,800 yards. Subsequent analysis credited these attacks with three hits altogether, though it is doubtful which destroyer fired the successful torpedoes. The destroyers then withdrew to the northward, engaging the *Scharnhorst*, which had by then steadied on a southerly course, as they did so. Fortunately the damage to the *Saumarez* was all above the waterline; shells had passed through her director and under her rangefinders without exploding, but she had suffered considerably from splinters, which reduced her speed to 10 knots on one engine only. One officer and 10 ratings were killed and 11 ratings wounded.

Commenting on these destroyer attacks, the Commander-in-Chief remarked: "This gallant attack was practically unsupported, and carried out, particularly in the case of the first subdivision, in the face of heavy fire from the enemy. Three underwater explosions were heard in the *Duke of York* and six in *Belfast* during this time." Prisoners state that at least three hits were scored, and that the relentless attack had a great effect on the morale of the ship's company. They attributed its success mainly to the bad handling of the *Scharnhorst*'s secondary and A.A. armament. One torpedo appears to have hit in a boiler room and damaged a shaft, which immediately reduced the enemy's speed to 22 knots; another is said to have flooded several compartments aft.

Second Engagement of Force 2

As the destroyers withdrew to the northward, the *Duke of York* and *Jamaica*, coming up from the south-west, re-engaged at a range of 10,400 yards, opening fire at 1901. Hits were immediately scored, while the enemy continued to fire at the retiring destroyers. The *Norfolk*,[48] too, joined in from the northward, but had difficulty in finding the right target, and checked fire after a couple of salvoes. "After five minutes, when *Scharnhorst* had been repeatedly hit and fires and flashes from exploding ammunition were flaring up, she shifted her secondary armament fire to the *Duke of York* at a range of 8,000 yards."[49] During this second action she apparently engaged the *Duke of York* and *Jamaica* with only part of her main armament,[50] and that intermittently.

The battle was then approaching its end. Between 1901 and 1928 the enemy's speed fell drastically from 20 to about 5 knots. At 1915 the *Belfast* opened fire on her at a range of 17,000 yards, and a few minutes later she steadied on a northerly course. About this time (1919) the Commander-in-Chief ordered the *Jamaica* and *Belfast* to close the enemy, who was then almost stationary, and to sink her with torpedoes. The *Duke of York* continued firing – getting off 25 broadsides, of which 21 were straddles – till 1928, when she checked fire to enable the *Belfast* and *Jamaica*, which had altered course towards the enemy, to deliver their torpedo attacks. Little information was forthcoming from prisoners about this part of the action, as they had been "not unnaturally stunned by the success of our destroyer attacks"[51] and the pounding inflicted on their ship. They were, however, able to account for at least 10 of the *Duke of York*'s hits (see Appendix. D).

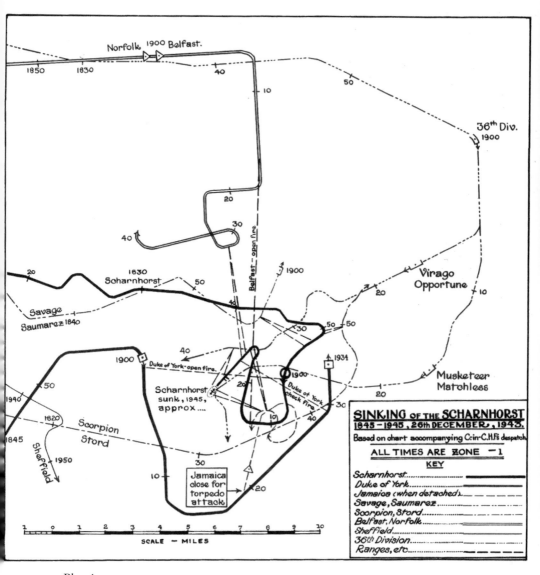

Plan 4

Torpedo Attacks by the *Belfast* and *Jamaica*

(Plans 4, 6, Appendix C)

In the *Scharnhorst* – battered by gunfire and crippled by four torpedoes – resistance was practically at an end as the cruisers closed in from north and south. Prisoners subsequently stated that after sending their final signal to Hitler, assuring him that the *Scharnhorst* would fight to the last shell, the Admiral and Captain had shot themselves on the bridge.[52]

The *Jamaica* fired three torpedoes to port (one of which misfired) at 1925 at a range of 3,500 yards, but claimed no hits.[53] Two minutes later the *Belfast* also fired three torpedoes, one of which may have hit, though this was subsequently considered unlikely. Both cruisers then hauled round to fire their remaining tubes, the *Jamaica* scoring several hits with her main and secondary armament while doing so. The *Scharnhorst* replied with wild fire from her secondary armament and light weapons, which did no damage, and had ceased altogether when at 1937, at a range of 3,750 yards, the *Jamaica* fired three torpedoes to starboard at the enemy, broadside on and almost stopped. The result could not be seen, as the target was completely hidden by smoke, but underwater explosions were heard after the correct time interval, and it is probable that two torpedoes took effect. Two minutes earlier (1935) the *Belfast* had turned to fire her port torpedoes, but by this time the *Musketeer*'s division had arrived on the scene, and there was such a mêlée of ships and fire round the target that she altered round to the southward to await a more favourable opportunity.

Torpedo Attacks by the 36ᵗʰ Division

(Plans 4, 6, Appendix C)

The 36ᵗʰ Division, starting the chase well to the westward of the other forces, had been tracking the enemy by radar and slowly gaining bearing on a parallel course to the northward throughout the action. As previously mentioned, Commander Fisher had endeavoured to synchronise his attack with that of Force 2's destroyers,[54] but was unable to establish wireless touch with the *Savage*; and owing to his unfavourable position at the start and the course taken by the action, only arrived in the target area when the *Belfast* and *Jamaica* were completing their first attacks. The destroyers closed in by subdivisions from the north and astern. The enemy, steering an erratic course, was then staggering round from north-east to south-west, but by the time they fired she was fairly steady on a south-westerly course and almost stopped. At 1930 they made their attack, the *Musketeer* and *Matchless* the port side, and the *Opportune* and *Virago* from starboard. The *Opportune* fired two salvoes of four torpedoes each at 1931 and 1933 at a range of 2,100 and 2,500 yards, and claimed two unobserved hits. The *Virago* followed her in, and at 1934 fired seven torpedoes at a range of 2,800 yards. Two hits were observed, and the subdivision retired to the westward, the *Virago* firing on the enemy as long as visible.

On the port side, the *Musketeer* fired four torpedoes from a range of 1,000 yards at 1933, observing two – possibly three – hits between the funnel and the main mast, and then withdrew to the westward. The *Matchless*, following her in, was less fortunate. Shortly before the attack, the training gear of her torpedo tubes had been strained by a heavy sea; as the attack developed the tubes had to be trained from port to starboard, and just then another sea struck her bridge and broke all communications with the tubes, with the net result that they were not trained in time. The *Matchless* therefore hauled round without firing, and came in to attack again on the enemy's port bow, but by that time the *Scharnhorst* had sunk, and she joined the *Scorpion* in picking up survivors from the wreckage.

"The hits scored by the 36th Division are again difficult to assess, as some were not observed, and as the cruisers were attacking at about the same time; five hits in all is considered the most probable assessment. Little information is available from prisoners, most of whom were engaged in abandoning ship; but *Scharnhorst* seems to have taken a list to starboard, and they therefore consider that most of the hits were on her starboard side. One prisoner has confirmed three hits from the same destroyer, possibly *Musketeer* or *Savage*."[55]

Plan 5

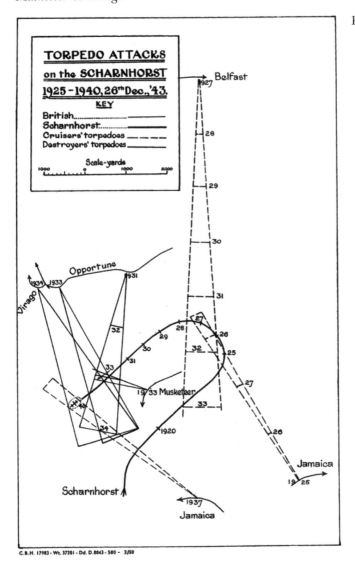

TORPEDO ATTACKS

on the SCHARNHORST

1925 - 1940, 26th Dec., '43.

KEY

British..................................
Scharnhorst.........................
Cruisers' torpedoes _ _ _ _ _
Destroyers' torpedoes _____

Scale-yards

Sinking of the
Scharnhorst

The torpedoes of the 36th Division and the *Jamaica* brought the battle to an end. "Three cruisers and eight destroyers were now in the target area; and the *Duke of York* steered to the northward to avoid the mêlée. All that could be seen of the *Scharnhorst* was a dull glow through a dense cloud of smoke, which the starshell and searchlights of the surrounding ships could not penetrate. No ship therefore saw the enemy sink, but it seems fairly certain that she sank after a heavy underwater explosion which was heard and felt in several ships at about 1945."[55] She was last seen by the *Jamaica*, *Matchless* and *Virago* at about 1938; ten minutes later, when the *Belfast* closed to deliver her second torpedo attack, it was clear from the surrounding wreckage that she had sunk. This occurred in approximately Lat. 72° 16' N., Long. 28° 41' E. She had received at least 13 hits from the *Duke of York*, 10 or 12 from the cruisers, and 11 torpedoes.

Just at this time, Grand Admiral Dönitz was having what was probably a difficult interview. The War Diary of the German Naval War Staff records that "at 1935 the Führer was informed of the position by the Commander-in-Chief of the Navy in person, who expressed the hope that the *Scharnhorst* would complete the action successfully, or in any case inflict severe damage on the British."

For the next hour the *Belfast*, *Norfolk* and most of the destroyers searched the area for survivors, the *Jamaica* rejoining the *Duke of York* to the northward. The darkness, heavy weather and icy water afforded little chance of survival to the luckless crew of the *Scharnhorst*; in all thirty were picked up by the *Scorpion* and six by the *Matchless*. No officer was among them, the most senior of the prisoners being of the equivalent rating of Acting Petty Officer. The *Scorpion* reported subsequently that the Captain and the Commander were seen in the water seriously wounded; the Commander grasped a lifeline, but succumbed before he could be hauled in, and the Captain died before he could be reached.[56]

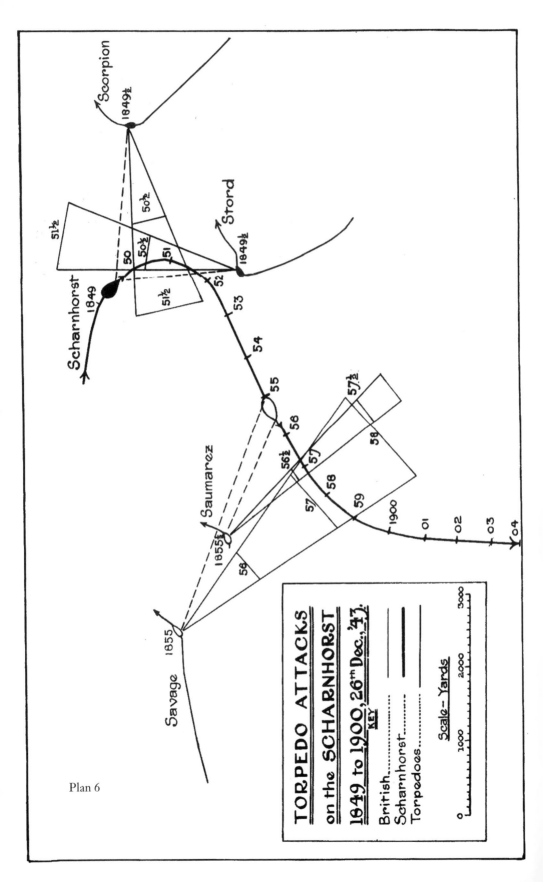

Plan 6

TORPEDO ATTACKS
on the SCHARNHORST
1849 to 1900, 26ᵗʰ Dec., '43.
KEY

British..............
Scharnhorst.............
Torpedoes.............

Scale – Yards

Scorpion

Scharnhorst

Stord

Saumarez

Savage

The Commander-in-Chief's Summing Up

Commenting on the operation, the Commander-in-Chief remarked:–

"The conduct of all officers and men throughout the action was in accordance with the highest traditions of the service. Earlier in the day, the resolute attack by Force 1 to drive off the enemy undoubtedly saved the convoy, and their subsequent shadowing was invaluable to me in my approach.

The *Duke of York* fought hard and well, having drawn for over an hour and a half the whole of the enemy's fire. She was frequently straddled with near misses, ahead, astern and on the beam. Both masts were shot through by 11-in. shell, which fortunately did not explode. That she was not hit was probably due to masterly handling, aided by accurate advice from the plot. There is no doubt that the *Duke of York* was the principal factor in the battle. She fought the *Scharnhorst* at night and she won.

This in no way detracts from the achievements of the 'S' class destroyers, who with great gallantry and dash pressed in unsupported, to the closest ranges, to deliver their attacks, being subjected the while to the whole fire power of the enemy. Their resolution and skill shortened the battle, and ensured the sinking of the ship.

In general the speed of wireless communication and the exceptional performance of radar[57] reflects the greatest credit on the personnel concerned, and in this night battle contributed in great measure to its success.

Plotting arrangements in the Fleet flagship worked well, and were of great assistance both to me and to the ship. I myself alternated between the plot and the Admiral's bridge, the Chief of Staff remaining in the plot. I feel very strongly that the officers in the plot must always be in the closest contact with the Admiral, who should obviously be on the bridge.

Although failings in material and personnel were few during this action, it should, of course, be remembered that the enemy inflicted very little damage on our ships, and they were therefore not extensively tested under adverse conditions.

I should also like to record that the accurate and concise information supplied by the Admiralty in the early stages of this operation was of great assistance."

Conclusion

Little more remains to be told. Soon after 2100 the *Sheffield* rejoined Force 1 and all forces in the area were ordered to proceed independently to Kola Inlet, where they arrived without incident the next day (27 December). Convoy J.W.55B continued its voyage unmolested. Of the destroyers which had accompanied the *Scharnhorst* nothing was seen; save for the statements of prisoners and occasional radar intercepts during the day, it might be doubted that they had ever left harbour. As mentioned previously, no ship had actually seen the *Scharnhorst* sink, and it was not till 2035, 26 December – nearly an hour after the event – that confirmation from prisoners enabled the Commander-in-Chief to inform the Admiralty that she had sunk. The result of the long day of storm, cold, darkness and battle was epitomised in the Admiralty reply:–

"GRAND. WELL DONE."

Appendix A

Warships Employed in Operations

Ship	Main Armament	Commanding Officer
	Force 2	
HMS *Duke of York*	10–14-in., 16–5.25-in. H.A./L.A.	Flag, Admiral Sir Bruce Fraser, K.C.B., K.B.E., Commander-in-Chief, Home Fleet. Capt. Hon. G. H. E. Russell, C.B.E., R.N.
HMS *Jamaica*	12–6-in., 8–4-in. H.A., 2 triple 21-in. torpedo tubes.	Capt. J. Hughes-Hallett, D.S.O., R.N.
HMS *Savage*	4–4.5-in., 2 quadruple 21-in. torpedo tubes.	Com. M. D. G. Meyrick, R.N.
HMS *Scorpion*		Lt.-Com. W. S. Clouston, R.N.
HMS *Saumarez*	4–4.7-in., 2 quadruple 21-in. torpedo tubes.	Lt.-Com. E. W. Walmsley, D.S.C., R.N.
HNorMS *Stord*		Lt.-Com. S. Storeheill, R.Nor. Navy.
	Force 1	
HMS *Belfast*	12–6-in., 12–4-in. H.A., 2 triple 21-in. torpedo tubes.	Flag, V.Adm. R. L. Burnett, C.B., D.S.O., O.B.E. Capt. F. R. Parham, R.N.
HMS *Norfolk*	8–8-in., 8–4-in. H.A., 2 quadruple 21-in. torpedo tubes.	Capt. D. K. Bain, R.N.
HMS *Sheffield*	12–6-in., 8–4-in. H.A., 2 triple 21-in. torpedo tubes.	Capt. C. T. Addis, R.N.

36th Destroyer Division

(Detached from Convoy
R.A.55A to convoy J.W.55B,
25 December and from convoy
J.W.55B to Force 1
26 December.)

HMS *Musketeer*	6–4.7-in., 1–4-in. H.A., 2 quadruple, 21-in. torpedo tubes.	Com. R. L. Fisher, D.S.O., O.B.E., R.N.
HMS *Matchless*		Lt.-Com. W. S. Shaw, R.N.
HMS *Opportune*	4–4.7-in., 2 quadruple 21-in. torpedo tubes.	Com. J. Lee-Barber, D.S.O., R.N.
HMS *Virago*	4–4.7-in., 2 quadruple 21-in. torpedo tubes.	Lt.-Com. A. J. R. White, R.N.

Escort, Convoy J.W.55B
(19 Merchant Ships)

HMS *Onslow*	4–4.7-in., 1–4-in. H.A., 2 quadruple 21-in. torpedo tubes.	Capt. J. A. McCoy, D.S.O., R.N. (Capt. (D)17).
HMS *Onslaught*		Com. W. H. Selby, D.S.C., R.N.
HMCS *Haida*	6–4.7-in., 2–4-in. H.A./L.A., 1 quadruple 21-in. torpedo tube.	Com. H. G. de Wolf, R.C.N.
HMCS *Iroquois*.		Com. J. C. Hibberd, D.S.C., R.C.N.

Escort, Convoy J.W.55B–contd.

HMS *Orwell*	4–4.in. H.A., 2 quadruple 21-in. torpedo tubes.	Lt.-Com. J. A. Hodges, D.S.O., R.N.
HMCS *Huron*	6–4.7.-in, 2–4-in. H.A./L.A., 1 quadruple 21-in. torpedo tube.	Lt.-Com. H. S. Rayner, D.S.C., R.C.N.
HMS *Scourge*	4–4.7-in, 2 quadruple 21-in. tubes.	Lt.-Com. G. L. M. Balfour, R.N.
HMS *Impulsive*	4–4.7-in., 2 quadruple 21-in. tubes.	Lt.-Com. P. Bekenn, R.N.
HMS *Gleaner*	1–4-in.H.A. 2 quadruple 21-in. tubes.	Lt.-Com. F. J. S. Hewitt, D.S.C., R.N.
HMS *Whitehall*[58]	4–4.7-in., 2 triple 21-in. tubes.	Lt.-Com. P. J. Cowell, D.S.C.
HMS *Wrestler*[58]	4–4in, 2 triple 21-in. tubes.	Lt. R. W. B. Lacon, D.S.C.
HMS *Honeysuckle*[58]	1–4-in. 2 triple 21-in. tubes.	Lt. H. H. D. MacKilligan, D.S.C., R.N.R.

HMS *Oxlip*[58]	1–4.in. 2 triple 21-in. tubes.	Lt.-Com. C. W. Leadbetter, R.N.R.

Escort, Convoy R.A.55A
(22 Merchant Ships)

HMS *Milne*	6–4.7-in, 1–4-in. H.A., 2	Capt. I. M. R. Campbell, D.S.O., R.N.
HMS *Meteor*	quadruple 21-in. torpedo tubes.	Lt.-Com. D. J. P. Jewitt, R.N.
HMS *Ashanti*	6–4.7-in., 2–4-in. H.A., 1	Lt.-Com. J. R. Barnes, R.N.
HMCS *Athabaskan*	quadruple 21-in. torpedo tube.	Lt.-Com. J. H. Stubbs, D.S.O., R.C.N.
HMCS *Seagull*	1–4-in. H.A., 1 quadruple 21-in. torpedo tube.	Lt.-Com. R. W. Ellis, D.S.C., R.N.
H.M.C.S *Beagle*[58]	2–4.7-in., 2 quadruple 21-in. torpedo tubes.	Lt.-Com. N. R. Murch, R.N.
HMCS *Westcott*[58]	2–4-in., 2 triple 21-in. torpedo tubes.	Com. H. Lambton, R.N. (Retd.)
HMCS *Dianella*[58]	1–4-in., 2 triple 21-in. torpedo tubes.	Temp. Lt. J. F. Tognola, R.N.R.
HMCS *Poppy*[58]	1–4-in., 2 triple 21-in. torpedo tubes.	
HNorMS *Acanthus*[58]	1–4-in., 2 triple 21-in. torpedo tubes.	Temp. Lt. D. R. C. *Onslow*, R.N.R.

Appendix B

Cruiser Actions – Force 1

Summary of Observed Hits and Salvoes

I – Observed Hits

Time	Ship	Number of Hits	Remarks
0932	*Norfolk*	2	1st Phase.– Certain. Seen in *Belfast*. *Norfolk* only ship firing.
1224	*Norfolk* (?) *Belfast* (?)	1+	2nd Phase.– Certain. Seen in *Belfast* and not seen in *Norfolk*. Probably *Norfolk*'s hit, as *Belfast* saw nothing to coincide with fall of shot hooter.
1225	*Sheffield*	1+	Seen in *Sheffield*.
1239	*Belfast*	4	Certain. Seen in *Belfast* as fall of shot hooter sounded.
1916	*Belfast*	2	Probable. Seen in *Belfast* when in visual fire at 17,000 yards.

Note:– Other unobserved hits may well have been obtained, particularly by *Norfolk*, whose shell were set "delay."

II – Salvoes

Ship	Fired Blind	Fired Visually	Total	Ammunition Expended
Belfast	24	14	38	316
Sheffield.	–	26	26	97
Norfolk	31	–	31	161

Battleship Actions – Force 2

Summary of Broadsides

I – *Duke of York*

Time	14-in. Broadsides	5.5-in Broadsides	Remarks
Phase I (1650-1844)	52	97	Three 14-in. hits observed.
Phase II (1901-1928)	25	42	At least ten 14-in. hits.
Ammunition expended	443	531 S.A.P.	155 5.5-in. starshell.

II – *Jamaica*

Time	6-in. Broadsides	Remarks
Phase I (1652-1742)	19	One hit claimed.
Phase II (1901-1928)	22	–
Phase III (torpedo attack)	4	Several hits.
Ammunition expended	461	

Appendix C

Summary Of Torpedo Attacks

Note:– Radar was fully used by all ships, although the enemy was sighted before firing, in accordance with the current Home Fleet doctrine.

| Ships | Firing | | | | Hits | | |
	Time	Range	Number of Torpedoes	Claimed	Observed or Unobserved	Time	Assessed "Probable Hits"
Scorpion	1849 ½	2,100	8	1	Observed	1851	
Stord	1850	1,800	8	Nil	–	–	
Savage	1855	3,500	8	3	Observed	1859	4
Saumarez	1856	1,800	4	–	–	–	
Jamaica	1925	3,500	2	Nil	–	–	Nil
Belfast	1927	6,200	3	1	Unobserved	1931	Nil
Opportune	1931	2,000	4	1	Unobserved	? 1933[59]	
Musketeer	1933	1,000	4	3	Observed	1934	
Matchless	–	–	0	–	–	–	5
Opportune	1933	2,500	4	1	Unobserved	? 1935[59]	
Virago	1934	2,800	7	2	Observed	1936 ½	
Jamaica	1937	3,750	3	2	Unobserved	1939 ½	2
Totals			55	9	Observed		11[60]
				5	Unobserved	–	

Appendix D

Summary of Intelligence Obtained from Prisoners

The following main points of interest concerning the action were obtained from the 36 prisoners. The most senior survivor was of the equivalent rating of Acting Petty Officer.

(i)   The morale of the prisoners was high. Interrogation was difficult owing to their security consciousness and the fact that all but four were between decks, where they saw little of the action and were unable to distinguish between the explosion of torpedoes, the impact of heavy shells and the concussion of their own guns.

(ii)   *Scharnhorst* had left Langefjord at 1900 on 25 December with the destroyers Z.28, Z.31 and Z.34 in company.

(iii)   *Scharnhorst* flew the flag of Rear-Admiral Bey, Admiral Commanding Destroyers, who was taking the place of Admiral Kummetz, away on leave. The Admiral and his staff of 30 joined just before the ship left Langefjord. He was not well known to the ship's company.

(iv)   *Scharnhorst's* captain was Hintz, formerly captain of the *Leipzig*, who took over command in October from Captain Hoffmeier. This was his first operational sortie in the ship. He seems to have been popular onboard, but was criticised by all survivors for his handling of the ship.

(v)   She carried 40 cadets onboard, who were under training.

(vi)   Her normal complement was 1,903 officers and men.

(vii)   It was stated that she could attain a maximum speed of 33 knots.

(viii)   She carried three above water torpedo tubes each side, but did not fire them during the action.

(ix)   She carried three Arado aircraft on this occasion, two in the hangar abaft the funnel and one on the catapult. None of them was used and all were destroyed when a shell hit the hangar during the second engagement with the *Duke of York*.

(x)   Prisoners state that she was designed to withstand 14 torpedo hits without being sunk. They ascribed her loss to the fact that nearly all the torpedo hits (they believed eight in all) were on the starboard side. (N.B:–The probable hits are assessed as six port side, five starboard side.) They were also emphatic that she was sunk by torpedoes and that *Duke of York* would never have sunk her by gunfire.

(xi) The following ten hits during the second engagement with *Duke of York* were confirmed, although their order is unknown:–

(a) On the forward port 150-mm. twin turret, putting the gun and ammunition hoist out of action.

(b) On the aircraft hangar, destroying both planes and causing a fierce fire, which was apparently put out in 10 minutes.

(c) On the forward 105-mm. mounting on the starboard side.

(d) On the starboard side near the funnel.

(e) In the tween deck on the port side in compartment 10.

(f) In the battery deck on the port side in compartment 9.

(g) On the forward starboard 150-mm. turret, immediately before the final torpedo attack.

(h) On the starboard after single 150-mm. gun.

(i) On one quadruple 20-mm. mounting on the starboard side which flew through the air and crashed on the deck.

(j) A hit somewhere on "B" turret causing the ventilation system to fail and the turret to fill with smoke every time the breeches were opened.

(xii) Survivors insist that no shells penetrated the armoured deck, though a large number penetrated the decks above it and exploded on contact with the armour causing great havoc and many casualties.

(xiii) One prisoner who had been in the fore top stated that a shell hit aft at 1820, and reduced the Scharnhorst's speed, and that he had seen the needle of the speed recorder drop from 29 to 22 knots.

(xiv) Abandon ship drill was apparently rudimentary and none of the survivors seems to have had an abandon ship station. Lifebelts were apparently not worn and were only put on if they could be found at the last moment.

Appendix E

Battleship Actions: Chronology and Important Signals

Time	Event
1600	From C.-in-C. to C.S.10. "Keep your destroyers to westwards in case of a westerly deployment." (T.O.O. 1559. T.O.D. 1600.[61])
1617	*Duke of York*. First Radar contact with enemy, bearing 020°, 45,500 yards.
1632	*Duke of York*. Radar range 29,700 yards; enemy zig-zagging; mean course 160°.
1637	From C.-in-C. to destroyers in company. "Destroyers in company take up most advantageous position for firing torpedoes, but do not attack till ordered." (T.O.O. 1637. T.O.D. 1640.)
1650	*Duke of York* opened fire. Range 12,000 yards.
1705-1712	*Belfast* and *Norfolk* firing on *Scharnhorst* from north-west.
1707[62]	*Savage*, while taking position to the southward of the enemy, illuminated by starshell from both *Scharnhorst* and *Duke of York*. *Scharnhorst* opened fire on her; range 7,400 yards.
1710[62]	*Savage* reduced speed and altered course to starboard, since range was decreasing rapidly and no orders had been received to fire torpedoes.
1713	From C.-in.-C. to destroyers in company. "Destroyers close and attack with torpedoes as soon as possible." (T.O.O. 1713. T.O.D. 1717.)
1716[62]	*Savage* steadied on course 090°; enemy steering mean 110°; range had opened to 19,000 yards.
1722	From C.-in-C. to C.S.10. "Steer south to get between enemy and his base." (T.O.O. 1722. T.O.D. 1723.)
1723	From C.-in-C. to C.S.10. "Steer 140°; join me." (T.O.O. 1723. T.O.D. 1724.)
1727	Vice-Admiral Burnett steadied on 140°.
1732	From C.-in-C. to C.S.10. "My mean course 090°." (T.O.C. 1732. T.O.D. 1733.)
1735	From C.-in-C. to C.S.10. "My 1732. I am to the south-west of the target." (T.O.O. 1735. T.O.D. 1739.)

1755	From C.-in-C. to *Norfolk, Sheffield, Jamaica, Belfast.* "Cruisers remain to the north of the target and engage when possible." (T.O.O. 1755. T.O.D. 1803.)
	Vice-Admiral Burnett, then about 7 miles to the west-ward of the *Duke of York*, altered course to the east-north-eastward.
1820	*Duke of York* altered course to the south-eastward. *Scharnhorst* ceased firing and reduced speed.
1824	*Duke of York* checked fire; range 21,400 yards.
1837	*Duke of York* altered course to 042°, directly towards enemy.
1840	From C.-in-C. to C.S.10. "I see little hope of catching *Scharnhorst*, and am proceeding to support convoy." (T.O.O. 1840. T.O.D. 1847.)
	From C.-in-C. to C.S.10. "My position, course and speed, 024 T V W R 28,[63] 042°, 27 knots." (T.O.O. 1840. T.O.D. 1849.)
1849-1856	*Savage's* division attacked with torpedoes.
1901	*Duke of York* and *Jamaica* re-engaged. Range 10,400 yards.
1906 (?)	From C.-in-C. to *Jamaica*. "Finish her off with torpedoes." (T.O.D. 1906?)
1915-1917	*Belfast* firing on *Scharnhorst* from north.
1918	From C.-in-C. to *Jamaica*. "Attack with torpedoes." (T.O.O. 1918. T.O.D. 1922.)
1925-1927	*Jamaica* and *Belfast* attacked with torpedoes.
1927	From C.-in-C. to Home Fleet in company. "Main target nearly stopped." (T.O.O. 1927. T.O.D. 1929.)
1928	*Duke of York* checked fire.
1929	From C.-in-C. to Admiralty. " . . . *Scharnhorst* bears 295°, 3 ½ miles. On fire and nearly stopped." (T.O.O. 1929. T.O.D. 1950.)
1931-1934	*Musketeer's* (36th) division attacked with torpedoes.
1937	*Jamaica's* second attack with torpedoes.
1945 (?)	*Scharnhorst* sank.
1951	From C.-in-C. to Home Fleet in company. "Clear the area of the target except those ships with torpedoes and one destroyer with searchlight." (T.O.O. 1951. T.O.D. 1952.)
2014	From C.-in-C. to *Scorpion*. "Please confirm *Scharnhorst* is sunk." (T.O.O. 2014. T.O.D. 2015)
2030	From *Scorpion* to C.-in-C. "Survivors state *Scharnhorst* has sunk." (T.O.O. 2030.)
2035	From C.-in-C. Scapa. "*Scharnhorst* sunk." (T.O.O. 2035.)
2136	From Admiralty to C.-in-C., repeated C.S.10. "Grand: well done."

Endnotes

1. *Scharnhorst*, built 1934–39; 32,000 tons, 29 (?) knots; 9–11-in., 12–5.9-in. H.A./L.A., 14–4.1-in., H.A., 16–1.46-in. A.A. guns.

2. The battleship *Tirpitz* was out of action as the result of damage inflicted by midget submarines on 22 September, 1943. The *Scharnhorst*'s sister ship, *Gneisenau*, was in Home waters, dismantled.

3. Admiral Sir Bruce Fraser, K.C.B., K.B.E.

4. Vice-Admiral R. L. Burnett, C.B., D.S.O., O.B.E.

5. See Battle Summary No. 22, Russian Convoys, 1942.

6.

	FORCE 1
HMS *Belfast*	Flag, Vice-Admiral R. L. Burnett, C.B., D.S.O., O.B.E. (Flag Officer Commanding, 10th Cruiser Squadron). Captain F. R. Parham, R.N.
HMS *Norfolk*	Capt. D. K. Bain, R.N.
HMS *Sheffield*	Capt. C. T. Addis, R.N.

7.

	FORCE 2
HMS *Duke of York*	Flag, Admiral Sir Bruce Fraser, K.C.B., K.B.E. (Commander-in-Chief, Home Fleet). Captain the Hon. G. H. E. Russell, C.B.E., R.N.
HMS *Jamaica*	Capt. J. Hughes-Hallett, D.S.O., R.N.
HMS *Savage*	Commander M. D. G. Meyrick, R.N.
HMS *Scorpion*	Lieut.-Commander W. S. Clouston, R.N.
HMS *Saumarez*	Lieut.-Commander E. W. Walmsley, D.S.C., R.N.
HNorMS *Stord*	Lieut.-Commander S. Storeheill, R.Nor.N.

8. Commander-in-Chief's Despatch. Admiral Fraser added that "such a reminder would hardly seem necessary, except that within the Home Fleet there are frequent changes of officers and men, and, with constant escort requirements, adequate training is not easy to achieve."

   Fortunately, Force 2 had then been in company for nearly a fortnight, and they knew each other and had practised night encounter tactics together. A final practice was carried out after leaving harbour in the early morning of 24 December, using the *Jamaica* as target.

9. All times are Zone I.

10. Actually, the convoy had been sighted the day before (1045/22) by a German Meteorological aircraft, which had reported it as consisting of "40 troop transports, with an escort of cruisers and presumably an aircraft carrier". This gave rise to the belief that a raid on the Norwegian coast was imminent and the U-boats were ordered to

concentrate off Vest Fjord: after further consideration, the force sighted was assumed to be an ordinary convoy and the U-boats were concentrated in the Bear Island Strait.

11. This step would have had little effect in bringing the convoy closer to Force 2, but if enemy surface forces had been searching to the westward, it would have prevented the convoy being located by them before dark.

12. Rear-Admiral I. G. Glennie, C.B., Senior Naval Officer Afloat, Scapa Flow.

13. Admiralty Message 260319.

14. 4th Destroyer Flotilla: Z.29, Z.30, Z.33, Z.34, Z.38.

15. Rear-Admiral Bey, the Admiral Commanding Destroyers, was taking the place of Admiral Kunmetz, Commanding-in-Chief of the "North Group", who was on leave. The Commanding Officer of the *Scharnhorst*, Captain Hintz, had only taken over the command in October, 1943, and this was his first operational cruise. In addition to her normal complement of 1,903 officers and men, 40 cadets were embarked for training, bringing the total to about 1,970.

16. This reasoning is of interest, as in fact the exact opposite was the case; it was the safe arrival of the two convoys which convinced Admiral Fraser of something being attempted against the third.

17. U.716 later signalled that she had attacked one of the destroyer escorts at 1503/25, but her 5 torpedoes missed ahead.

18. Group Command, North, considered that such an attack would involve the *Scharnhorst* in very serious risks, and a signal was sent to the Naval War Staff stressing this view.

19. Subsequent information confirms that the enemy was unaware of the existence of convoy R.A.55A until it was well to the west of Bear Island and out of danger; it was never sighted by German forces and its presence in the Arctic was only suspected late on 26 December after several British signals referring to it had been intercepted. Convoy R.A.55A was scattered by a gale on 26 December, but reformed and arrived safely at Loch Ewe on 1 January, 1944.

20.

LATITUDE	NAUTICAL (Sun 12° below Horizon)		CIVIL (Sun 6° below Horizon)	
	From	To	From	To
71° N'.	0817	1545	1020	1342
72° N'.	0827	1534	1056	1306
73° N'.	0839	1523	No civil twilight.	

Twilight, 26 December

21. U.716 having been attacked by British escort vessels in approximately 73° N., 17° 25' E.

22. No visual contact with the enemy destroyers was reported by any of our forces throughout the whole operation, though many unidentified destroyer radar echoes persisted during the day. Prisoners of war stated that the destroyers made contact with the convoy, and signalled with the Verey lights that they had done so before Force 1 engaged; but this is not borne out by post-war information from German sources, nor was anything seen of them by the convoy escort.

23. The Vice-Admiral made his enemy report at 0922, but is failed to get through to Scapa W/T station, and when this became clear a little later the Commander-in-Chief broke

wireless silence to inform the Admiralty.

24. The cruisers had been formed on a line of bearing 180°, roughly at right angles to the initial radar contact; the subsequent adjustment to 160° at 0915 proved insufficient to allow for the high rate of change of bearing, resulting from the enemy's alteration of course to the eastward at about the same time.

25. This hit was subsequently confirmed by prisoners of war.

26.
Musketeer	Commander R. L. Fisher, D.S.O., O.B.E., R.N.
Opportune	Commander J. Lee-Barber, D.S.O., R.N.
Virago	Lieut.-Commander A. J. R. White, R.N.
Matchless	Lieut. W. D. Shaw, R.N.

27. Commander-in-Chief's Despatch.

28. One of these aircraft was heard making reports and was in radar contact for nearly three hours, after which it was heard intermittently till about 1400, when it either lost touch or returned to base. It is now known that the reconnaissance aircraft reported several ships in Lat. 72° 7' N. Long. 21° 5' E. at 1012; but it was their radar gear which had picked up the ships and they were unable to identity them or give their number. It is not possible to know what construction Admiral Bey put on this report, but senior German naval officers have expressed the opinion that the subsequent appearance of the *Duke of York* and her consorts proved a surprise to him.

29. The *Musketeer* opened fire on the enemy at a range of 7,000 yards at 1222 and continued firing till 1236. During this time the range was never less than 4,000 yards and the *Scharnhorst*, retiring at high speed, was not considered to be a possible torpedo target.

30. Commander-in-Chief's Despatch.

31. Prisoners of war report. But the German Admiral seems still to have hoped his destroyers might do something. It was not till 1418 that he ordered them to return to harbour.

32. Had this happened neither the *Duke of York* nor the destroyers with her could have kept up against the head sea.

33. At 1911, the Admiral, Group Command, North, ordered the flotilla to proceed at full speed to the scene of the *Scharnhorst's* action, but an hour later it had become clear that there was no hope for the battlecruiser, and at 2013 these orders were countermanded. All submarines had been ordered to make for the action at full speed about an hour earlier (1815) by the Flag Officer, U-boats.

34. "The exemplary fashion in which C.S. 10 with Force 1 shadowed the enemy until Force 2 made contact had given me all the information I required. At one time I feared that our respective positions might be in error, but D/F bearings indicated that the approach was being made on a steady bearing." – Commander-in-Chief's Despatch.

35. "At first impression *Scharnhorst* appeared of enormous length and silver grey in colour."- "*Duke of York*," Gunnery Narrative.

36. See Appemdix E., Chronology and Important Signals.

37. The *Scharnhorst* carried three above water tubes each side, but did not fire them during the action. (*Prisoners of War*.)

38. Commander-in-Chief's Despatch.

39. The *Savage* had reached a position to the southward of the enemy when she was

illuminated by starshell from both the *Duke of York* and the *Scharnhorst*, and came under fire at about 7,400 yards range. The destroyers were still under orders not to attack till ordered to do so; as the range was closing rapidly, Commander Meyrick therefore reduced speed, and altered course away from the enemy, gradually turning through 360°. At 1713 the Commander-in-Chief ordered the destroyers to "close and attack with torpedoes as soon as possible," but by the time the *Savage* had again turned to the eastward the range had increased to about 9 miles.

40. Commander Fisher hoped to synchronise the attacks of the 36th Division and Force 2's screen, but owing to a technical failure in the *Musketeer*'s wireless, was unable to get in touch with the *Savage*; and Force 2's screen delivered their attack nearly 40 minutes before the 36th Division reached the target area.

41. The *Duke of York*: gunnery narrative.

42. "The reported improvement in accuracy of the enemy's fire in the later stages was probably due to some or all of the following:–

    use of full flash cordite by the *Duke of York*'s secondary armament, thus providing a point of aim;

    cessation of radar jamming when *Duke of York*'s mainmast was hit, and the jamming set put out of action;

    Scharnhorst settling down after her initial surprise." – Commander-in-Chief's Despatch.

43. "A distinct atmosphere of gloom and disappointment was felt at the order to check fire when it appeared that, despite undoubted hits, the enemy would escape with her superior speed." – HMS *Duke of York*, Gunnery Narrative.

44. Commander-in-Chief's Despatch.

45. The Commander-in-Chief states that this reduction of speed must have been due to a hit from the *Duke of York*, which – according to one survivor – occurred at 1820. (See Appendix D.)

46. That both subdivisions were not engaged by even heavier fire and considerably earlier appears, from prisoners' statements, to have been due to muddled handing of the *Scharnhorst*'s A.A. and secondary armament. When the *Duke of York* first engaged, the *Scharnhorst*'s A.A. armament (4.1-in. and below) guns' crews were ordered to take cover, leaving only a skeleton crew at the guns, and this order seems never to have been countermanded. The secondary armament apparently suffered from considerable disagreement between the ship's gunnery officers, resulting in a series of contradictory orders.

47. This alteration may have been to avoid torpedoes from the *Stord*, which at this moment was turning to fire.

48. The *Belfast* and *Norfolk* had reached a position some 7 miles to the westward of the *Duke of York* in compliance with the order to join the C.-in-C. when at 1755 they received orders to "remain to the northward of the target and engage when possible." Vice-Admiral Burnett accordingly altered to the east-north-eastward, and by 1900 was well to the northward of the *Scharnhorst*.

49. Commander-in-Chief's Despatch.

50. Of the enemy's main armament "A" turret does not appear to have fired at all, probably

on account of damage sustained earlier; "B" turret, though damaged and full of smoke, seems to have functioned intermittently till shortly before the ship sank; "C" turret was believed by prisoners to have fired right up to the end. Most of the crews of the secondary and A.A. armament are thought to have been killed during the second engagement with the *Duke of York*.

51. Commander-in-Chief's Despatch.

52. This does not seem a particularly helpful proceeding, and in the case of the Captain is not borne out by the *Scorpion*'s evidence. (See postea.)

53. Probably due to underestimation of the enemy's speed.

54. The Commander-in-Chief remarked: "Although *Musketeer*'s action in attempting to synchronise attacks was correct, *Savage* would have been justified in proceeding with his attack as it was essential that *Scharnhorst*'s speed should be reduced at the earliest possible moment."

55. Commander-in-Chief's Despatch.

56. The more interesting points brought out by the interrogation of the prisoners are summarised in Appendix. D.

57. "There is no doubt that despite its shortcomings British radar is still far superior to any yet encountered in German ships, and that this technical superiority and the correct employment of the gear enabled the Home Fleet to find, fix, fight and finish off *Scharnhorst*." – Commander-in-Chief's Despatch.

58. Western Approaches Command.

59. Times not recorded.

60. The only unobserved claims assessed as "probable hits" were the two by the *Jamaica*. These torpedoes were fired after all others should have crossed the line, and underwater explosions were felt after the correct time interval.

61. T.O.O.: Time of Origin. T.O.D.: Time of Despatch.

62. The times given in the *Savage*'s report cannot be reconciled with the *Duke of York*'s, and are unreliable.

63. Lat. 72° 25' N., Long. 28° 35' E.

Part III

B.R. 1736 (5)

NAVAL STAFF HISTORY
SECOND WORLD WAR

BATTLE SUMMARY No. 13

ACTIONS WITH ENEMY DISGUISED RAIDERS
1940 – 1942

T.S.D. 965/42
Training and Staff Duties Division (Historical Section), Naval Staff, Admiralty S.W.1.

CONTENTS

Overview

This Battle Summary deals with eight actions fought with enemy merchant ship raiders up to the end of 1941. During this period of 28 months Axis merchant ship raiders sank one British cruiser, one armed merchant cruiser, and 618,108 tons of merchant shipping.[1] Their own losses were three out of the seven identified during that period, and two other ships, which were probably supply ships.

These figures may be compared with those of the last war. In 1914–18, 51 months, ten armed merchant raiders sank 427,433 tons out of a total of 12,741,781 tons, or 3.3 per cent. Of the ten raiders, four were sunk, three were interned, one was wrecked, and two got back to Germany.

The action between the *Sydney* and *Kormoran* off the west coast of Australia on 19 November, 1941,[2] may be compared with that between the *Alcantara* and *Greif* on 28 February, 1916, in the North Sea. The *Alcantara*, approaching within torpedo range, was torpedoed, but before she sank she opened a heavy fire on the *Greif* and sent her to the bottom.

The principal lesson to be drawn from the *Alcantara*'s action was the necessity of keeping well out of torpedo range. After the armed boarding steamer *Ramsey* had been torpedoed by the disguised minelayer *Meteor* in the Moray Firth on 8 August, 1915, the Commander-in-Chief, Admiral Jellicoe, issued an order warning ships to approach suspected vessels on the quarter and to avoid bearings on which torpedoes could be fired; also that the Master of the suspected ship should be required to bring his papers onboard in his own boat.[3]

The *Alcantara*'s Action

On 15 July, 1940, HMS *Hawkins*, flying the flag of Rear-Admiral Sir Henry Harwood, K.C.B., O.B.E., Rear-Admiral, South America Division, entered Montevideo for a 24-hour visit. Next day she sailed to patrol the Plate area. There had been recent indications that an enemy raider was in the North Atlantic, and on 17 July a report reached the Admiral that D/F bearings had placed a German vessel to the westward of the Cape Verde Islands on 15 July. This information, coupled with earlier reports of unidentified vessels off the coast of Ireland, indicated that a possible raider was bound for the South Atlantic. Admiral Harwood therefore ordered the armed merchant cruiser *Alcantara*,[4] Captain J. G. P. Ingham, R.N., which was patrolling the Rio de Janeiro–Santos area, to patrol off Pernambuco, while the *Hawkins* moved up to the Rio–Santos area. To protect the important focal area of the Plate against a raid the Admiral intended to move both ships back to their original patrol areas by the time that the anticipated raider would be well to the southward of Pernambuco on the assumption that she was proceeding direct to the Plate at economical speed.

Next day, 18 July, the Admiral received news of the sinking by a raider in the West Indies area, on or about 13 July, of two British ships, the *Davisian* and *King John*,[5] and of the sailing of the German tanker *Rekum* from Tenerife on 17 July. It seemed very probable that the oiler intended to refuel the raider, and from 19-21 July the *Hawkins* patrolled off Rio. By 22 July Admiral Harwood estimated that if the raider had come south from the position given by the D/F bearing on 15 July she would be south of the latitude of Pernambuco, and shortly after 1630[6] he ordered the *Alcantara*, which had reached the Pernambuco area on 20 July, to proceed south to examine Trinidad[7] Island, as this island had occasionally been used by German raiders in the last war. She was subsequently to patrol an area south-west of Trinidad at a distance of over 250 miles from the South American coast.

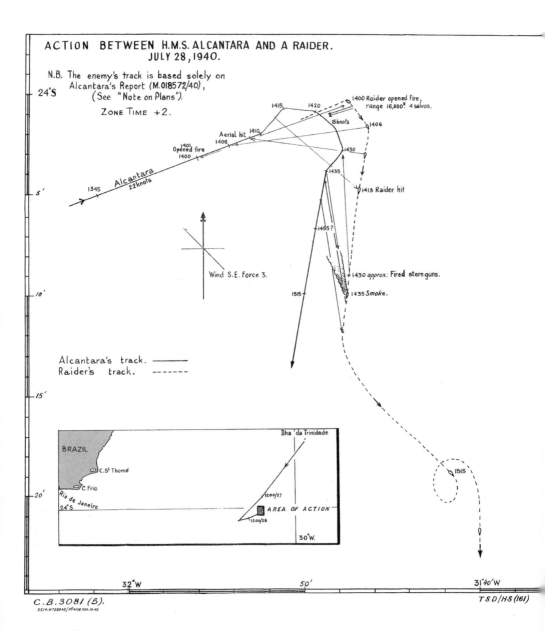

ACTION BETWEEN H.M.S. ALCANTARA AND A RAIDER.
JULY 28, 1940.

N.B. The enemy's track is based solely on
Alcantara's Report (M.018572/40),
(See "Note on Plans").

ZONE TIME +2.

Plan 1

On 23 July the *Hawkins* fuelled from the *Arndale* north-east of Sao Sebastiao Island,[8] and then patrolled the British shipping routes off the South American coast between Rio de Janeiro and the Plate.

On 25 July Admiral Harwood learned that a German submarine had sunk a Norwegian tanker near the Cape Verde Islands on 18 July. Clearly it was this submarine, and not a raider, that had been located by D/F on 15 July. Further reports from the West Indies, however, and the fact that three ships were overdue at Freetown, indicated the probability of there being one raider in the West Indies and another in the South Atlantic. During 26/27 July, therefore, the *Hawkins* continued patrolling the British shipping routes between Rio and the Plate.

During the forenoon of 26 July the *Alcantara* inspected the Island of Trinidad, and at noon next day was in 23° 25' S., 31° 47' W. At 1000 on 28 July she was in 24° 39' S., 33° 7' W.,[9] steering N. 75° E. at 11 ½ knots, when the tops of two masts were sighted from her crow's nest; due east, fine on the starboard bow. She altered course to intercept, but when the range had closed to 23,000 yards the unknown ship turned momentarily towards her and then turned away. The *Alcantara* followed, and, as the range was opening, increased to 15 knots and then to full speed. By noon she was doing 20 knots and by 1300 nearly 22. The day was fine and clear with a light breeze from the south-east. At 1400, when the *Alcantara* was in 24° 3' S., 31° 56' W., the unknown vessel altered course to starboard, and, hoisting the German ensign, opened fire with a two-gun salvo at 16,000 yards, 2,000 yards beyond the extreme range of the *Alcantara*'s eight 6-in. guns, followed a few seconds later by two four-gun salvoes.

One shell of the two-gun salvo fell 100 yards over, on the port quarter: one of the second salvo struck the *Alcantara* just abaft her dummy funnel, and another, bursting over her quarterdeck by P 4 gun, killed its trainer, severed a number of fire control leads and put its range and deflection instruments out of action. It was probably this salvo that brought down her main aerial, which was shot away between 1406 and 1409. A shell of the third salvo hit the *Alcantara* abreast the stokers' mess deck, and another, bursting on her quarterdeck, killed the Officer of Quarters. At 1408 a hit on the water line abreast the engine room resulted in an inrush of water, which gradually reduced her speed.

Meanwhile the *Alcantara* had opened fire at extreme range at 1401, her first salvo falling short to the right. A hail of fragments flying around her fire control prevented the fall of her second salvo from being observed. The enemy, who was keeping up a very high rate of fire, was straddling constantly, and a number of shells bursting close overhead sent steel shards whistling uncomfortably near. These explosions and the noise of the *Alcantara*'s guns made it difficult for the sight-setters to hear, and the sights were soon out of step. Several times the *Alcantara* had to check fire to correct them for range and deflection. In spite of these delays she straddled the raider with a number of salvoes, and at 1413 observed a bright flash abreast her foremast. The enemy's foremost starboard gun fired no more, her salvoes became ragged, and her rate of fire decreased.

By 1420 the *Alcantara*'s speed had dropped to 15 knots, and at 1430 the raider turned away, dropping smoke floats and firing two stern guns. The *Alcantara* continued to reply, but the range, which had previously closed to 9,800 yards, was opening. At 1435 the *Alcantara* turning to starboard opened fire with her port battery obtaining a hit on the enemy's stern. The raider replied with three of her port guns, and dropped another smoke float. By this time the *Alcantara*'s speed had dropped to 10 knots, and the enemy, steaming at something between 12 and 15 knots, drew rapidly away till only her topmasts were visible. The *Alcantara* continued to fire at extreme elevation, but the target was obscured by smoke. When the enemy emerged from it the *Alcantara* fired a few more rounds from her port battery at extreme range, and the raider replied with a few ragged three-gun salvoes. At 1515 the *Alcantara* was in 24° 10' S., 31° 51' W. Firing had ceased except for a few desultory rounds which fell short.

For some time the *Alcantara* had been almost stopped: the raider, after altering course as though to close her, turned round and steamed away at 15 knots with a slight list to port. When last seen at 1530 she was steering south, 29,000 yards away. Thus ended a sharp but inconclusive action, during which the *Alcantara* had fired 152 rounds.

A close examination of the effects of the enemy's fire showed that she had used only shrapnel or similar "anti-personnel" shell throughout. Some had burst in the air and eight others instantaneously on impact. Their fragmentation was very great and as many as 500 perforations and dents were found near one burst. The danger to personnel was obvious, and the *Alcantara*'s reports[10] contain the following recommendations:–

(1) Gun shields to be fitted to all guns, not only as protection, but also to shield the sight-setters from blast.

(2) Fire control circuits to be run below decks and given greater protection.

(3) Steel helmets to be provided for all whose duty may require them to be in an exposed place.

(4) Telemotor leads to be further protected.

(5) Protection for ammunition bollard and operator.

(6) Further supply of protective mattresses for bridge, fore control and elsewhere.

(7) The 6-in., Mark VII guns with their 14,000 yards range, which had been outranged by the enemy raider, to be replaced by 6-in., Mark XII, or other suitable long range guns.[11]

Everything possible was done by the *Alcantara* to force the action, and it can only be ascribed to the fortune of war that an unlucky hit in the engine room reduced her speed and enabled the raider to escape.[12]

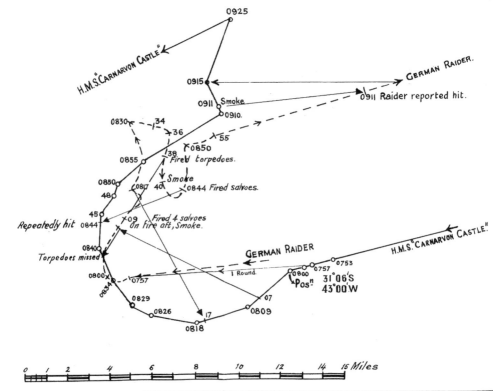

H.M.S. CARNARVON CASTLE'S ACTION
WITH A GERMAN RAIDER,
DECR 5TH 1940.

This plan is based on a diagram, (Plan 3),
in M.02910/41, (See "Notes on Plans").

Zone Time + 2.

Wind N.E. Force 3.

Plan 2

The *Carnarvon Castle*'s Action

On 5 December, 1940, the armed merchant cruiser *Carnarvon Castle*,[13] Captain H. W. M. Hardy, R.N., fought an action with an enemy raider in the South Atlantic very similar to the *Alcantara*'s action of 28 July, 1940. These actions emphasised the heavy handicap under which both vessels laboured owing to their large silhouettes, short range guns, and primitive fire control opposed to smaller adversaries equipped with long range guns and modern fire control systems. While the *Alcantara*'s 6-in. guns were outranged by 2,000 yards the *Carnarvon Castle*'s guns were outranged by 3,000 yards, which gave her opponent 20 minutes of uninterrupted firing at a large target before she could get within range.

The following summary of the action is based largely on the *Carnarvon Castle*'s narrative.[14] At 0642 on the morning of 5 December, 1940, HMS *Carnarvon Castle* was in 30° 52' S., 42° 53' W., off the east coast of South America,[15] steering S.35° W. at 18.3 knots, with orders to arrive at Montevideo on 9 December, when she sighted a suspicious vessel at a range of 19,000 yards, the extreme limit of visibility. The stranger was steaming directly away, and the *Carnarvon Castle*, increasing speed, signalled her to stop. She did not do so, and at 0757 the *Carnarvon Castle* fired one round: which fell short. She replied within 30 seconds at a range of approximately 17,000 yards, with a four- or five-gun salvo. As this was 3,000 yards outside the maximum range of the *Carnarvon Castle*'s eight 6-in. guns, Captain Hardy turned to port to close the range and to bring all his starboard battery to bear. The enemy also altered course to port, but soon turned back to starboard.

These changes reduced the range, after 20 minutes, to 14,000 yards, and the *Carnarvon Castle*, opening fire, claims to have hit the enemy several times, setting her on fire aft and apparently reducing her port battery temporarily to one effective gun, with which she continued the action for some time. The enemy then turned to starboard behind a smoke screen, and on reappearing reopened fire with his starboard battery in four-gun salvoes.

At 0838 the *Carnarvon Castle* sighted two torpedo tracks approaching on slightly diverging courses, but, turning under full helm to starboard, was able to steer between them, and, they passed harmlessly 50 yards away on either side.

By 0844 the range was down to 8,000 yards when the enemy, bringing his port battery once more to bear, hit the *Carnarvon Castle* repeatedly, setting her on fire in several places. At 0911, therefore, Captain Hardy decided to open the range and get the fires under control behind a smoke screen. All the *Carnarvon Castle's* fire control communications were disabled and her guns in individual control. The haze had increased, and as the enemy was continually turning smoke on and off, spotting through the splashes of her shorts became extremely difficult and hitting a matter of luck. The *Carnarvon Castle*, however, claimed a last hit at her extreme range of 14,000 yards, the shell bursting under the enemy's bridge. The raider continued firing until the range had opened to 18,000 yards, and although the *Carnarvon Castle* altered course in an attempt to keep in touch, the enemy finally disappeared behind a smoke screen in the increasing haze, steaming at 18 knots in a north-easterly direction.

It was 1115 before the *Carnarvon Castle* was able to extinguish all her fires, and in view of her extensive damage Captain Hardy steered for Montevideo, which he reached safely at 1900 July December. The ship was too damaged to be of any further service, though there was no immediate need to dock her.

The enemy ship was a long, low vessel of about 10,000 tons displacement, painted a very dark grey or black, with two masts, one funnel, straight stem and cruiser stern. As in the *Alcantara's* action the enemy shell showed very high fragmentation, but in this action no shrapnel was used. The *Carnarvon Castle* had received no less than 27 direct hits: all her electrical and voicepipe communications were shot away, her engine-room telegraphs and telephones cut, her wireless aerial destroyed, all her boats, except one, were riddled, her galley completely wrecked, the main exhaust pipe from her engines extensively cut, and her fore peak was flooded. Commodore F. H. Pegram, the Commodore Commanding the South America Division, who visited her the following day, considered that she had put up a gallant and spirited action against a superior enemy.[16]

The *Leander* Sinks the R.A.M.B.1

On 27 February, 1941, HMS *Leander*,[17] New Zealand Division, Captain R. H. Bevan, R.N., fought a successful action in the Indian Ocean with the Italian raider R.A.M.B.1.

At 1037[18] on the morning of 27 February, the *Leander* was patrolling northward off the Maldive Islands in about 1° N., 68° 30' E., at 20 knots, when she sighted a vessel steering eastward on a steady course at a comparatively high speed right ahead: she increased to 23 knots to close, and as she gradually approached, her suspicions were aroused by the stranger's resemblance to the *R.A.M.B.* class of Italian banana freighters and by a gun on her forecastle. She therefore went to action stations at 1115 when the range was 11,000 yards, keeping her turrets trained fore and aft. At 1125, when the range was down to 10,000 yards, she ordered[19] the stranger to hoist her colours. Four minutes later the stranger hoisted the red ensign. The *Leander* then ordered her to hoist her signal letters, and after a delay of 5 minutes she hoisted GJYD. It was then 1134. As these letters did not appear in the "Signal Letters of British Ships" nor in the "Signal Letter Index", the *Leander* , at 1141, made the secret challenge, to which there was no reply.

Captain Bevan therefore decided to board, and at 1145 ordered the stranger by lamp and flags to stop instantly. She did not reply, but at 1150, just as the *Leander* was about to fire across her bows, she hoisted the Italian mercantile ensign[20] and started training her guns.

The *Leander* at once trained her own turrets. She was just before the stranger's beam with the stranger bearing Red 95. At 1153, without further warning, the stranger suddenly opened fire, and the *Leander* replied immediately with a broadside at 3,000 yards. The enemy's fire was short and erratic. When the *Leander* had fired five rapid salvoes Captain Bevan ceased fire and signalled to the enemy "Do you surrender?". The enemy, who had not fired more than three rounds a gun, was already on fire and abandoning ship. No crews remained at her guns, and she had struck her ensign. She had turned to starboard, and the *Leander* , stopping on her starboard quarter, lowered a boarding boat with orders to save the burning ship if possible. Two lifeboats were leaving the ship, stragglers were jumping overboard and climbing down her sides. An Italian officer in the water warned the boarding boat not to approach the burning ship as it was loaded with ammunition. The boat therefore lay off and watched the fire spread slowly aft until a heavy explosion before the bridge sent flames and smoke shooting high overhead. The raider was lying head to wind, and the fire continued to spread aft until at 1243 a very heavy explosion, evidently of the after magazine, sent the stern hurtling into the air. Five minutes later[21] the raider disappeared in 1° N., 68° 30' E., leaving only a patch of oil burning on the surface of the sea.

Meanwhile the *Leander* had picked up her boarding boat and 103 Italian survivors,[22] including the captain of the R.A.M.B.1, who stated emphatically that he had not scuttled his ship. Steaming away from the scene of action the *Leander* passed through the floating wreckage. The Commander-in-Chief, East Indies, Vice-Admiral R. Leatham, C.B., considered that the R.A.M.B.1 might well have become a serious menace to shipping and that the *Leander* was to be commended for ridding the seas of a potential raider before it had time to do any harm.[23] At a range of only 3,000 yards, however, she was perhaps fortunate to escape the fate which befell the Australian cruiser *Sydney* less than nine months later.[24]

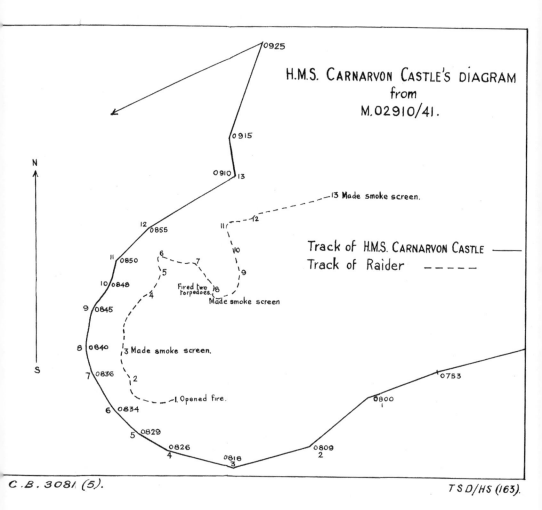

H.M.S. CARNARVON CASTLE'S DIAGRAM
from
M.02910/41.

13 Made smoke screen.

Track of H.M.S. CARNARVON CASTLE ————
Track of Raider — — — — —

Fired two torpedoes.
Made smoke screen

3 Made smoke screen.

1. Opened fire.

C.B. 3081 (5).

T S D/HS (163).

Plan 3

The *Voltaire*

Early in April, 1941, the British armed merchant cruiser *Voltaire*,[25] Captain J. A. P. Blackburn, D.S.C., R.N., left Trinidad for Freetown with orders to pass through two areas west of the Cape Verde Islands on the way.

On 5 April the Commander-in-Chief, America and West Indies, Vice–Admiral Sir Charles Kennedy-Purvis, K.C.B., informed the Commander-in-Chief, South Atlantic, Vice-Admiral Sir Robert Raikes, K.C.B., C.V.O., D.S.O., that according to a German communique the *Voltaire* had been sunk by a German cruiser and that he had ordered the Canadian armed merchant cruiser *Prince David* to proceed along her track at her best possible speed., On 11 April Admiral Raikes informed the Admiralty that nothing had been heard of the *Voltaire* though she had been due at Freetown on 9 April.

Late on 15 April the Commander-in-Chief, America and West Indies, informed the Admiralty that the *Prince David* had sighted a patch of very heavy oil covering an area of 3 square miles, together with charred wood, clothes and newspapers in 14° 31' N., 40° 32' W., half-way between the West Indies and the Cape Verde Islands, at 1430 July April. This was the *Voltaire*'s estimated position on 4 April, and the Admiralty considered that it was probably her wreckage that the *Prince David* had sighted. As there were no survivors no details are available of the *Voltaire*'s encounter, but it seems possible that like the *Alcantara* and *Carnarvon Castle* she was outranged and, in view of her slow speed, out-manoeuvred also. Nothing is definitely known about her end, nor of the identity of the vessel which destroyed her, though Admiral Raikes states that it was probably the German armed merchant ship raider *Santa Cruz*.[26]

Opposite, Plan 4

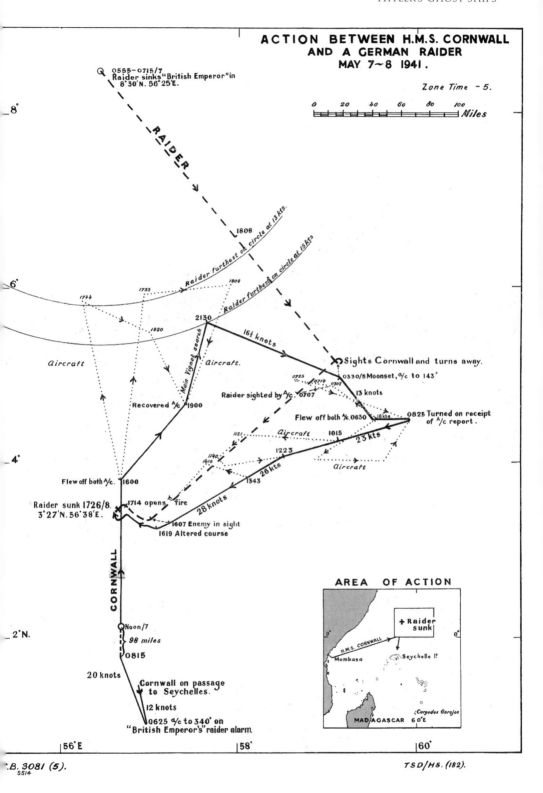

ACTION BETWEEN H.M.S. CORNWALL
AND A GERMAN RAIDER
MAY 7~8 1941.

Zone Time −5.

0   20   40   60   80   100
Miles

0555-0715/7
Raider sinks "British Emperor" in
8°30'N. 56°25'E.

RAIDER

8°

1808

Raider furthest on circle at 13 kts.

6°

1733   1808

Raider furthest on circle at 15 kts

1744

2130

1820   16½ knots

Aircraft.   Aircraft

Main Vignot search

Sights Cornwall and turns away.

0725   0714 0701   0330/8 Moonset, a/c to 143°
Raider sighted by A/c 0707   13 knots

Recovered A/c. 1900

Flew off both A/c. 0630   18 kts   0825 Turned on receipt
of A/c report.

1121   Aircraft   1015   23 kts

4°   1140/   1223   26 knots   Aircraft
                          0410

Flew off both A/c. 1600   1343   26 knots

Raider sunk 1726/8.   1714 opens fire   28 knots
3°27'N. 56°38'E.

1607 Enemy in sight
1619 Altered course

CORNWALL

Noon/7

2°N.   98 miles
        0815

20 knots

Cornwall on passage
to Seychelles.

12 knots

0625 a/c to 340° on
"British Emperor's" raider alarm.

AREA OF ACTION

+ Raider
sunk

H.M.S. CORNWALL

Mombasa   Seychelle I.

Cargodes Garajos

MADAGASCAR 60°E

56°E   58°   60°

The *Cornwall* Sinks Raider No. 33

On 8 May, 1941, HMS *Cornwall* fought an action with an enemy raider in the Indian Ocean.

On 7 May at 0555[27] the *Cornwall* was near the equator in 0° 2' 5., 56° 55' E.,[28] steering 160° at 12 knots with orders to refuel at the Seychelles when a raider report reached her from the SS *British Emperor*. Altering course to 340° at 0625 she increased to 20 knots to close the enemy's position without an unduly heavy consumption of fuel. As this position was 500 miles away, in 8° 30' N., 56° 25' E., she anticipated a prolonged search.

A scheme for the search with the aid of aircraft was worked out on the principle of closing the enemy's "furthest on" line and then starting a Vignot search to cover before dark the largest possible variation of the enemy in speed and course. At 0756 the *Cornwall* increased to 24 knots, but at 0815, on receipt of a signal[29] from the Commander-in-Chief, East Indies, Vice-Admiral R. Leatham, turned north at 25 ½ knots to cover the gap between the Seychelles and the islands of the Chagos Archipelago to the eastward.

As Admiral Leatham was unaware of her exact position, the *Cornwall* decided to regard his signal as an instruction and to proceed with her own original scheme of search as the most practical manner of complying with it.

The scheme and the *Cornwall's* movements can best be followed by referring to Plan 4,[30] and to the record of the courses she steered.[31] The search before dark was designed to cover the raider's courses between 144° and 190° and speeds between 13.4 and 16.6 knots.

Between 1600 and 1615 the *Cornwall* launched both her aircraft, recovering them shortly after 1900. At 1900 she altered course N. 15° E. to get on to the line of the main Vignot search. This was made out for a mean speed of 13 knots from one hour after the time of the raider report, on the assumption that the raider would require an hour to deal with the *British Emperor* and would then steam at high speed until dark, when she would ease down. At 2130 the *Cornwall* altered course to 113° and reduced to 16 ½ knots to search on this line while the moon was up.

The direction of search was correct, but the search was unsuccessful for, though by 0330 August May, the *Cornwall* was close to the enemy, who claims to have sighted[32] her as she turned against the setting moon, several hours were to pass before she herself sighted the raider. From 0330 until dawn the *Cornwall* steered 143° at 13 knots. At dawn, between 0630 and 0700, she launched both aircraft to cover a variation of 3 knots on either side of the enemy's estimated speed; and at 0635 increased to 18 knots.

At 0707 one of the aircraft sighted a merchant ship of the suspected type steaming about 13 knots, 228°, some 65 miles westward of the *Cornwall*, but made no report before returning about 0800. At 0825 the *Cornwall* altered course to 255° to close the suspect and increased speed, at first to 20 knots and then, at 0834, to 23 knots. It was about 0930 when she recovered her aircraft. Though she hoped that it had not been sighted, later information proved that it had been detected, probably by R.D.F. On this as on all other occasions the aircraft approached and left the suspicious ship in the direction away from the cruiser, a ruse apparently successful in hiding the cruiser's actual position.

At 1015 the *Cornwall* catapulted her second aircraft with instructions to close the still unidentified ship and discover, if possible, whether she were a raider or not. When the aircraft returned at 1223 it reported that the unknown vessel was steaming at least 15 knots and had hoisted signal letters. These were identified as those of the Norwegian SS *Tamerlane*, which she closely resembled, though the *Tamerlane* was not in the *Cornwall's* list of expected ships.

It was then past noon and it was clear that the *Cornwall* must increase speed to get within striking distance of the suspect with plenty of daylight in hand. She accordingly increased to 26 knots and at 1300 to 28 knots. At 1345 she catapulted an aircraft with orders to keep her informed of the bearing, course, and speed of the still unidentified vessel. She estimated the suspect to be within 32 miles unless he had altered course. When the aircraft returned it was able to give an accurate bearing of the unknown ship which was in sight from the air, and a few minutes later, at 1607, was sighted from the bridge of the *Cornwall*, bearing 282°, Green 50.

At 1612 the *Cornwall* altered course to close, but the stranger turned away, stern on, steering 300°. At 1619, therefore, the *Cornwall* altered course to bring her fine on the starboard bow in order to close as quickly as possible to 12,000 yards without crossing her track. At 1630 the stranger began making "Raider reports", stating that she was the Norwegian SS *Tamerlane*. The plane in the air was therefore told to inform her that the ship chasing her was a British cruiser and that she should stop engines. The *Cornwall* turned at the same time to give her a good broadside view, and then resumed the chase.

At 1656, when the range was down to 19,000 yards, the *Cornwall* signalled three times "Heave to or I fire", and backed this up with one warning round of 8-in. over and to the left, but though the stranger disobeyed the order the *Cornwall* refrained from opening direct fire, still thinking that she might be a normal merchant ship whose master was gallantly determined not to stop.

An order was therefore given for the second aircraft to take off and drop a 250-lb bomb close to the suspect, and, if that did not stop her, to drop the other on her forecastle. It was some time, however, before this order reached the aircraft.

At 1710 the *Cornwall* again signalled "Heave to or I fire", and followed this with another round of 8-in. As the range was then inside 12,000 yards she turned to port to open it. This apparently convinced the stranger that the *Cornwall* was about to open fire in earnest, for when the 8-in. shell fell near her she turned to starboard, and then, making a large alteration to port, opened fire with five guns just before 1715.[33]

The enemy could hardly have chosen a better moment for starting the action. Just as the *Cornwall* turned after firing her second warning shot, her training circuit failed. Realising that she was dangerously close to the raider, she immediately turned away to port to the limit of "A" arcs to avoid danger from torpedoes and to open the range, which had closed to 10,500 yards. It opened quickly, but for a time the *Cornwall* was in grave danger. She was frequently straddled by rapid and fairly accurate gunfire while her own main armament was pointing anywhere but at the enemy. In these circumstances she turned further away, and an officer was sent from the bridge with a message to "B" turret to train on the enemy and, if necessary, to take over control of "A" turret. The necessary orders had, however, already been passed from the fore control, and as the turrets trained, the *Cornwall* turned back to starboard to open "A" arcs. As soon as they would bear, "A" and "B" turrets fired two salvoes, but a 5.9-in. hit then put her fore steering gear out of action, and she swung away, closing her "A" arcs once again for a short time. The breakdown was fortunately only temporary. The after steering gear was rapidly brought into use and the ship was out of control for a matter of seconds only. Meanwhile, unfortunately, communication between the bridge and the catapult had failed, with the result that, before the order to launch the second aircraft was received, the aircraft was put out of action by a shell splinter.

By 1718 all the *Cornwall's* turrets were firing[34] and her salvoes straddling the enemy. The range was again outside 12,000 yards and she was reasonably safe from torpedo attack. The enemy's fire was falling off in accuracy and volume. At 1719 it was nearly 1,000 yards short, and the *Cornwall* turned to bring the ships on to roughly parallel courses. By this time she had received two direct hits, but although a minute or two later the raider managed to straddle her she was not hit again. The action was virtually at an end. At 1726 a salvo hit the enemy and she blew up,[35] disappearing in a cloud of white vapour which rose vertically some 2,000 ft. and hung over the scene for many minutes. As she sank she fired an ineffective salvo which straddled the *Cornwall* 20 seconds after she herself had finally disappeared.

Although the *Cornwall* had destroyed the enemy her own troubles were not yet at an end. With one of her two aircraft out of action she was naturally anxious to recover the other before dark. She therefore decided to hoist it in before searching for survivors among the debris, which covered a wide area and which would have been dangerous to the aircraft. As she turned to recover it, however, it was suddenly realised that although an order had been given for speed to be reduced to 12 knots the *Cornwall* was still steaming very fast.[36] She therefore turned to pass to windward of the wreckage, ordering the aircraft to land as best it could. The *Cornwall* gradually stopped and picked it up, but, as the plane was being hoisted in, electric power failed. This breakdown brought all the fans to a standstill, the engine-room temperature rose to 200°, and for a time the engine room had to be abandoned.[37]

About this time the *Cornwall's* starboard engines suddenly went half speed astern, presumably in accordance with an order given some time before. This brought her into the middle of the wreckage, and before darkness fell she was able to pick up a number of British and German survivors clinging to it in the water.[38] She remained without electric power from 1815 until 1850.

At 1850 power was restored, but she lay stopped in the wreckage until 2140, when, after making temporary repairs, she went ahead and steered once again for the Seychelles.

Although the *Cornwall* had found and sunk the enemy the Admiralty considered that the conduct of the operation left much to be desired. They regarded the scheme of search as well designed, but when, at 0707, her aircraft sighted a merchant ship of the type for which it was searching, it should have reported the fact at once instead of waiting until its return to the ship at 0800. As a result of this failure to make an immediate report the *Cornwall* continued to steam away from the enemy for nearly an hour, which might have been vital, while her other aircraft was kept unnecessarily in the air.

It was considered, too, that the *Cornwall* should have kept the Commander-in-Chief, East Indies, informed of events and of her intentions. With the information at his disposal he could then have informed her that no friendly merchant ship was anywhere near. She appears, however, to have been unduly concerned with the possibility of her wireless being intercepted by the raider's direction finder.

The *Cornwall* was engaged on a definite raider hunt and employing, quite correctly, both aircraft for the search. When the suspicious ship was sighted by one of them it could have shadowed her while the other was recalled and refuelled in readiness to relieve the shadower, thus ensuring that the suspect would be almost constantly under observation. As it was the advantage of having two aircraft was lost[39] and the enemy was left unwatched from 0725 until 1125, and again from 1150 until 1410. If he had made a big alteration of course, or if the visibility had drastically decreased, the chance of finding him again would have been slender.

The Admiralty considered that during this phase the rigid adherence to wireless silence resulted in essential reports not being made from the aircraft to the *Cornwall* when the signal letters were hoisted by the suspect, and from the *Cornwall* to the Commander-in-Chief when these had been identified as the *Tamerlane*'s. In view of the nature of the operation and the obvious importance of making contact with the suspicious ship as quickly as possible, the Admiralty considered, too, that the *Cornwall* should have brought all her boilers to immediate notice at 0800, the time of the aircraft's first report, instead of waiting until 1250 when the report of the second sighting reached her.

Throughout the period between the surface sighting of the raider and the time when she opened fire the *Cornwall* held on to the idea that the suspect might still prove to be a friendly neutral although in view of her suspicious behaviour all the evidence was very much against it. The Admiralty considered that the *Cornwall*, by allowing herself to close to a range of under 12,000 yards contrary to her expressed intentions, showed a lack of attention to the changing situation. It is quite clear from her report[40] that this was fully appreciated at the time. The error of closing a very suspicious ship was intensified by her temporary inability to open fire, which left no alternative but to turn away and close "A" arcs at a critical moment, which might easily have resulted in the raider's escape and in much more serious damage to herself than she actually suffered.[41]

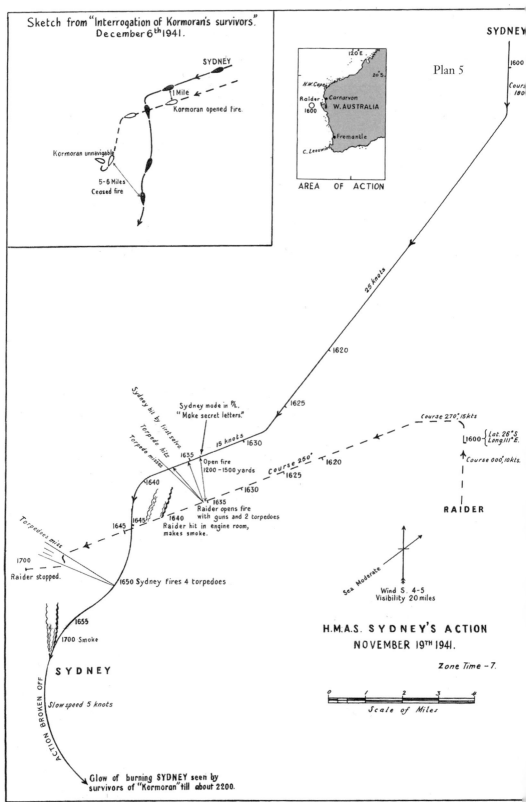

Sketch from "Interrogation of Kormoran's survivors."
December 6th 1941.

SYDNEY

1 Mile

Kormoran opened fire.

Kormoran unnavigable

5-6 Miles
Ceased fire

AREA OF ACTION

120°E

N.W.Cape

20°S

Raider
1600

Carnarvon

W. AUSTRALIA

Fremantle

C. Leeuwin

Plan 5

SYDNEY

1600

Course
180

25 knots

1620

1625

1630

15 knots

Sydney made in P/L.
"Make secret letters."

Sydney hit by first salvo

Torpedo hits

Torpedo misses

1635

Open fire
1200-1500 yards

1640

1645

1640

1635
Raider opens fire
with guns and 2 torpedoes

1640
Raider hit in engine room,
makes smoke.

Course 250°

1625

1630

1620

Course 270° 15kts

1600 { Lat. 26°S
       { Long 111°E.

Course 000°, 10kts.

RAIDER

Torpedoes miss

1700
Raider stopped.

1645

1650 Sydney fires 4 torpedoes

1655

1700 Smoke

SYDNEY

ACTION BROKEN OFF

Slow speed 5 knots

Glow of burning SYDNEY seen by
survivors of "Kormoran" till about 2200.

Sea Moderate

Wind S. 4-5
Visibility 20 miles

H.M.A.S. SYDNEY'S ACTION
NOVEMBER 19TH 1941.

Zone Time -7.

0   1   2   3   4
Scale of Miles

C.B. 3081 (5).
5514

TSD/HS (184)

The *Sydney*'s Action

On 19 November, 1941, HMAS *Sydney*, [42] Captain Joseph Burnett, R.A.N., sank the enemy raider *Kormoran* off the west coast of Australia. As the *Sydney* was herself destroyed with all hands in the encounter, this account is based on the only available report of the action, that of the German survivors.[43]

On 11 November, 1941, the *Sydney* left Fremantle, escorting the SS *Zealandia*, and handed her over to HMS *Durban* in 7° 56' S., 104° 40' E., on 17 November. She signalled that she expected to arrive back at Fremantle on 20 November, but early on 21 November the District Naval Officer, Western Australia, reported that she had not arrived, and followed this on 23 November with a signal that no further word had been received from her. At 1054/23 the Australian Naval Board instructed her to report her expected time of arrival at Fremantle, and an hour later all high power wireless stations were ordered to call her continuously. There was no reply, and an air search on 24 November gave an equally negative result.

At 0816 on 24 November, however, a report came in by wireless from the tanker *Trocas* that she had picked up 25 Germans from a raft in 26° 6' S., 111° 40' E. Eventually 103 survivors from the *Kormoran* came ashore in two boats at Carnarvon, Western Australia,[44] the SS *Koolinda* picked up a boat with 31 more, the *Aquitania* rescued 26, and HMAS *Yandra* picked up two Chinese who had been captured from the SS *Eurylochus* when the *Kormoran* sank her in 8° 15' N., 25° 14' W., on 29 January,[45] and 70 Germans, a total of 315 Germans and two Chinese.

The story of the action between the *Sydney* and the *Kormoran* was told by the *Kormoran*'s Captain, Fregatten-Kapitän A.G.T. Detmers and other prisoners, and bears all the marks of a bonafide account. They could not explain why the *Sydney* came so close before opening fire or attempting to launch her aircraft, but it will be recalled that on 27 February, 1941, the *Leander* closed to within 3,000 yards of the R.A.M.B.1 before either ship opened fire.[46]

About 1600[47] on 19 November the *Kormoran* was in 26° S., 111° E., steaming northwards at 10 knots[48] when she sighted what appeared to be a sail fine on the starboard bow. Commander Detmers soon identified it as a cruiser and immediately turned west into the sun and increased to full speed, which he estimated at 15 knots. The cruiser, which proved to be the *Sydney*, at once turned and came up on the *Kormoran*'s starboard quarter at high speed. For half an hour, as she approached, she repeatedly signalled NNJ, but Commander Detmers had no idea what NNJ meant and did not reply.[49] Meanwhile the *Kormoran* was busily making the "Disguised raider in sight" signal, "QQQQ 26 S, 111 E, STRAAT MALAKKA," and it may be noted that about 1000[50] G.M.T. on 19 November the tug *Uco* picked up a QQ message, but was unable to read the position and ship's name.

When the range had closed to 7 miles the *Sydney* ordered the *Kormoran* in plain language to hoist her signal letters and the raider hoisted PKQJ, the letters of the SS *Straat Malakka*, on her triatic stay between the funnel and foremast where the cruiser could not see them. It is reasonable to suppose that this was a *ruse de guerre* to induce the *Sydney* to close and investigate, for her signal to the *Kormoran* to hoist the letters clear was repeated continuously before the raider complied with it.

The *Sydney* had all guns and tubes trained when she came up with the *Kormoran*. In reply to her signal "Where bound?" the *Kormoran* replied "Batavia." The *Sydney* then apparently hoisted the letters IK, which the raider was unable to understand as in the International Code they mean "You should prepare for a cyclone, hurricane or typhoon." They were, in fact, the second and third letters of the *Straat Malakka*'s secret call sign IIKP. The *Sydney* then ordered the *Kormoran* to show her secret letters, and Captain Detmers, not knowing how to reply, decided reluctantly to fight. The two ships were steaming in a westerly direction at 15 knots on parallel courses, the *Sydney* on the *Kormoran*'s starboard beam. Only a mile[51] separated them when the *Kormoran* suddenly dropped her gun screens and, hoisting the German ensign, opened fire with four of her six 6-in. guns. Her first salvo hit the cruiser's bridge. The *Sydney* immediately replied with a salvo which went over,[52] but her second set the raider's fuel tanks on fire. In the meantime the *Kormoran* had hit the *Sydney* with a torpedo which apparently put her forward turrets out of action, and with a salvo which shot her aircraft to pieces at a range so close that the men round it could be plainly seen.[53]

About 1640 the *Sydney* turned to port and passed so close astern of the *Kormoran* that some of the raider's crew thought that she would ram her. Although an uncontrollable fire was raging in the *Kormoran* all her guns were still in action. The *Sydney's* after turrets, too, were firing, and at 1650 she fired four torpedoes which missed the raider ahead and astern. The *Kormoran* replied with a torpedo which also missed its mark. Both ships were now burning fiercely and the *Sydney* was 6 feet down by the bows.

Barely half an hour had passed since the *Kormoran* opened fire, but the action was virtually over. The *Kormoran*, which had fired 450 rounds and three torpedoes, was lying stopped with a fierce fire in her engine-room. The *Sydney*, with all her superstructure smashed and her boats destroyed, was steaming slowly[54] away in a south-easterly direction under a dense cloud of smoke. At 2300 Commander Detmers decided to abandon the *Kormoran*, and shortly after midnight an explosion hastened her end. By this time all trace of the *Sydney* had disappeared and she was never seen or heard again.[55]

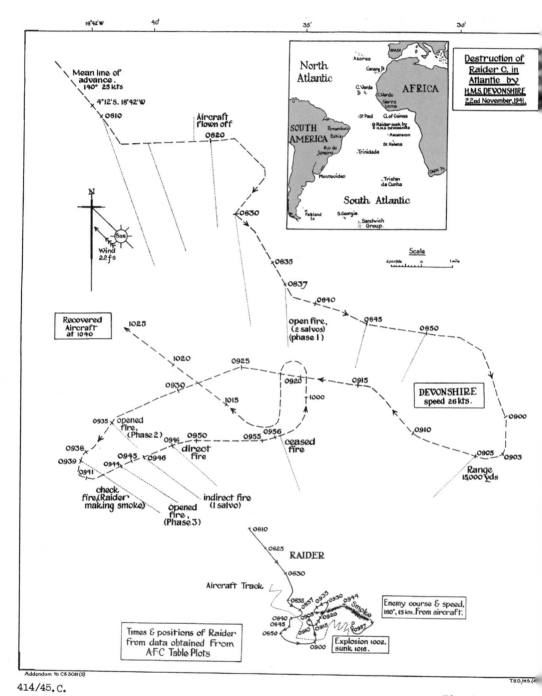

Destruction of
Raider C. in
Atlantic by
H.M.S. DEVONSHIRE
22nd November, 1941.

Plan 6

The *Devonshire*'s Action

On 22 November, 1941, HMS *Devonshire*,[56] Captain R. D. Oliver, D.S.C., R.N., sank an enemy vessel in the South Atlantic.

At 0520 that morning Captain Oliver despatched his Walrus aircraft to carry out an anti-submarine patrol and long range search ahead of the ship. When the Walrus returned at 0710 it reported sighting a merchant ship in 4° 20' S., 18° 50' W. From the aircraft's description Captain Oliver suspected that the reported vessel might well be an enemy raider and he immediately altered course to close her at 25 knots.

An hour later, at 0809, the masts of a ship came into sight bearing 160° in 4° 12' S., 18° 42' W. There was a moderate breeze[57] from the south-east and a slight sea with a short slow swell. The visibility was 10 miles. The *Devonshire* at once turned east to fly off her aircraft, which was catapulted at 0820 with orders to identify the unknown vessel if possible. By this time Captain Oliver's suspicions were thoroughly aroused by the manoeuvres and appearance of the ship, which closely resembled Raider No. 16, with the exception of moveable fittings such as ventilators and samson posts. He therefore manoeuvred the *Devonshire* at 26 knots, and kept her at a range of between 12,000 and 18,000 yards from the unknown ship to frustrate possible torpedo attack.

Immediately after the Walrus had taken off, the stranger turned a complete circle to starboard and, ignoring the *Devonshire*'s signals, made off in a south-easterly direction. At 0837 the *Devonshire* fired two salvoes spread right and left, intended to provoke a return fire and establish the stranger's identity as a raider beyond doubt, or to induce her to abandon ship and avoid unnecessary bloodshed, especially as she probably had a number of British prisoners onboard.

The stranger at once stopped and, turning round, transmitted by wireless at 0840 the warship raider report; "RRR RRR RRR de *Polyphemus* 4° 20' S., 18° 35' W. 0940 G.M.T." It was significant that the "R's" were in groups of threes and not of fours and that no signal letters were included. Captain Oliver could not ignore the possibility that the ship might be the genuine

Polyphemus, which was a vessel of similar appearance with a counter stern, and having been reported at Bilbao on 21 September was within reach of his position. To remove all doubts he made a signal to the Commander-in-Chief, South Atlantic, Vice-Admiral A. U. Willis, C.B., D.S.O., at 0950, asking if this were the real *Polyphemus*. The aircraft was also asked what type of stern the stranger had and replied at 0931 that she had a cruiser stern and a hull similar to the *Atlantis*. All doubts, however, were removed at 0934 when the Commander-in-Chief signalled "No, repetition No." One minute later, at 0935, the *Devonshire* opened fire at 17,500 yards. Her fourth salvo hit and started a fire which, she reports, eventually spread to the enemy's magazine and blew her up. The enemy put up an efficient smoke screen, but made no attempt to return the *Devonshire's* fire.[58] By 0939 the *Devonshire* had fired 30 salvoes, and Captain Oliver checked fire and turned eastward to clear the enemy's smoke screen. He then tried indirect firing by R.D.F. range, but gun blast put the R.D.F. transmitter out of action. At 0943 the enemy was visible once more, and according to the aircraft was maintaining a steady 15 knots. The *Devonshire* therefore reopened fire until 0956, when the enemy was seen to be heavily on fire and down by the stern. Captain Oliver thought that she had consistently attempted to draw him to the south-eastward, and was determined to steam no further in that direction than he could help. At 1002, however, there was a heavy explosion onboard her. It was followed by another at 1014, and two minutes later she sank.

Captain Oliver's next anxiety was to recover his aircraft, which had a damaged propeller, and he successfully picked it up at 1040. It reported that almost certainly an enemy submarine was present. He was therefore unable to stop and rescue survivors, as he could not have done so without running a grave risk of being torpedoed.[59]

Captain Oliver had been assisted in identifying the ship by the description of Raider No. 16 given in a supplement of Weekly Intelligence Report, No. 65, and by a photograph in the American periodical 'Life' of 23 June, 1941, of a Raider called *Tamesis* or *Atlantis*. This was the Hansa ship *Goldenfels* (Captain Bernhard Rogge), 7,862 tons, which left Kiel in March, 1940, armed with seven 5.9-in. guns. Under various names she had sunk 21 ships. She was acting as a submarine supply ship and was apparently about to fuel a submarine when the *Devonshire's* aircraft came in sight, obliging the submarine to cast off and dive. After being sunk, her boats laden with survivors were met by submarines and later by the supply ship *Python* which took a number of them onboard.

The *Dorsetshire*'s Action

On 1 December, 1941, HMS *Dorsetshire*,[60] Captain A. W. S. Agar. V.C., D.S.O., R.N., encountered, in the South Atlantic, an enemy vessel which scuttled herself without opening fire.

The *Dorsetshire* had left Freetown on 26 November to search for enemy ships in the relatively calm area 720 miles south and west of St. Helena. At 0700[61] on 1 December she flew off her Walrus aircraft in 26° 45' S., 6° 25' W., to reconnoitre to the south-east, but it returned without sighting anything. At 11 a.m. the *Dorsetshire* altered course to 111° and increased to 18 ½ knots. At 1515 the Walrus set out again on a similar patrol with orders to search to the southward for an hour and then at right angles to the *Dorsetshire*'s mean line of advance for another hour before rejoining the ship.

At 1633[62] the *Dorsetshire* sighted the masts of a ship bearing 032°, about 18 miles away at the extreme limit of visibility.[63] The sea was calm with a slight swell. Although the Walrus was still out of sight to the southward, Captain Agar decided to close the unknown vessel at once and if necessary to recall the aircraft. He therefore turned to 031° and increased to 25 knots. The stranger soon began making smoke, but remained hull down. She had apparently increased to full speed on sighting the *Dorsetshire*, and was steering away from her. Captain Agar therefore increased to 30 knots and made a recall, which failed to reach the Walrus.

At 1708 the *Dorsetshire* sighted several small patches of oil on the water, and Captain Agar, suspecting the presence of an enemy submarine, turned away to starboard. About this time he sighted an object resembling a submarine's conning tower 6 miles away on the port bow, but at 1720 identified it as a power-boat with four or five other boats in tow. Although he could not entirely reject the possibility that the vessel he was chasing was a British ship which had mistaken the *Dorsetshire* for an enemy cruiser he assumed that she was an enemy raider or supply ship. To reduce the risk of attack by a submarine he kept the *Dorsetshire* moving at high speed outside a range of 16,000 yards. In these circumstances he could neither prevent the enemy from scuttling herself nor could he capture her. At 1731 he fired two warning shots at 24,000 yards,[64] one right and one left of the target. By this time the enemy had stopped and was lowering boats.[65] He therefore withheld his fire in case she had any captured British merchant seamen onboard, and continued zig-zagging outside her range, but inside his own.

By 1744 the *Dorsetshire* had crossed the enemy's bows,[66] and although the range was 17,000 yards, Captain Agar was able to see the boats moving away from her side. At 1751 he observed that the enemy, who had a definite list to port, was on fire. The fire spread rapidly until 1805, when a large explosion forward settled her fate. It was evident that the enemy's self destruction was certain and Captain Agar at once turned away to clear the area as quickly as possible. At 1821 the enemy sank in 27° 50' S., 3° 55' W.,[67] leaving only a trail of smoke and a number of survivors in boats. At 1910 the *Dorsetshire* recovered her Walrus aircraft, and Captain Agar despatched it again at 1935 to reconnoitre the area of the boats.

In the failing light observation was difficult, but as the aircraft circled round at a height of 400 ft. it was able to establish that there were fourteen boats and two large rafts in the position where the ship had gone down. It estimated that each boat contained at least 25 survivors and that the total number of survivors was 500. The Walrus then examined the boats which the *Dorsetshire* had sighted at 1708. They were still 4 or 5 miles from the survivors' boats and were fully loaded with packages and crates. It appears possible that they were actually transferring these stores to a submarine when the *Dorsetshire* arrived, but if so the aircraft saw nothing of it.

The ship sunk by the *Dorsetshire* was the submarine supply ship *Python*, a motor vessel of 3,664 tons, which after meeting U 126 on 23 November, had taken onboard some of the crew of Raider C[68] and then proceeded south-eastward to refuel another submarine. It has been stated by a survivor that two submarines were in the vicinity when the *Dorsetshire* engaged her and that one of them fired a torpedo which missed.

The sinking of the *Goldenfels* and *Python* by the *Devonshire* and *Dorsetshire* had an important result, perhaps not fully realized at the time. It brought to a sudden stop a submarine campaign which was developing in the South Atlantic and postponed any renewal of it in that area for nearly a year.

Opposite, Plan 7

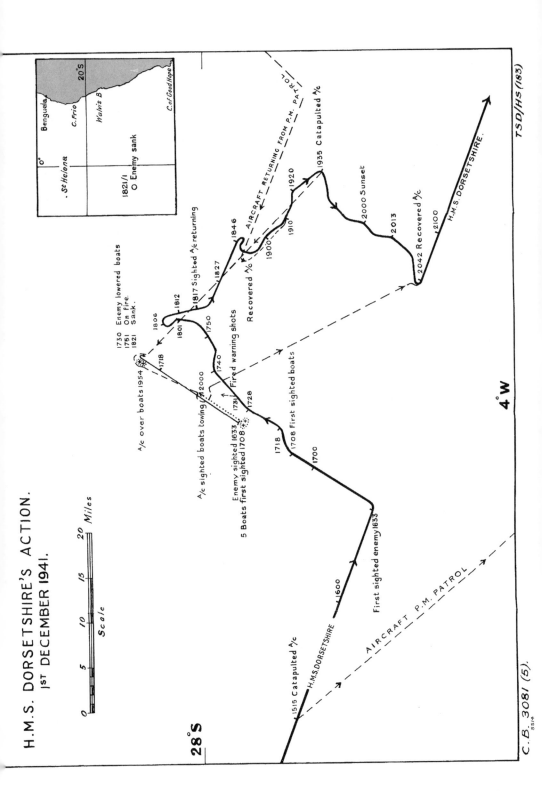

H.M.S. DORSETSHIRE'S ACTION.
1ST DECEMBER 1941.

Scale
0 5 10 15 20 Miles

28°S

4°W

Benguela
C. Frio
Walvis B
C. of Good Hope
St. Helena
20°S
0°
1821/1 O Enemy sank

1730 Enemy lowered boats
1751 On fire.
1821 Sank.

A/c over boats 1954
1718
1806
1801
1812
1818 Sighted A/c returning
1827
1846
AIRCRAFT RETURNING FROM P.M. PATROL
Recovered A/c
1900
1910
1920
1935 Catapulted A/c
2000 Sunset
2013
2042 Recovered A/c
2100
H.M.S. DORSETSHIRE.

1750
Fired warning shots
1740
A/c sighted boats towing 2000
1751
Enemy sighted 1633
5 Boats first sighted 1708
1728
1708 First sighted boats
1718
1700

First sighted enemy 1633
1600
H.M.S. DORSETSHIRE
1515 Catapulted A/c
AIRCRAFT P.M. PATROL

Raider Hunt

In addition to the eight actions against enemy raiders and suspected raiders, fought during 1940 and 1941, there have been a number of cases in 1942 when enemy vessels were encountered but not identified as such. There was also at least one instance in 1941 of a raider report leading to a protracted search when no enemy armed raider was present.

On 4 November, 1941, the RFA oiler *Olwen* reported a surface raider attack at 0530 G.M.T. in 3° 4' N., 22° 42' W.[68] The *Dorsetshire* was at sea, and the Commander-in-Chief, South Atlantic, Vice-Admiral A. U. Willis, after ordering her to investigate, instructed the cruiser *Dunedin* to leave Freetown with the special service vessels *Queen Emma* and *Princess Beatrix* and join in the search.

When the *Dorsetshire*, Captain A. W. S. Agar, intercepted the *Olwen's* raider distress signal at 0600 she turned east immediately to close the position, which was 600 miles away, and at 0645 increased to 20 knots, the maximum speed of the armed merchant cruiser *Canton* which was with her. Captain Agar knew that the U.S. cruiser *Omaha* and U.S. destroyer *Somers*, being well to the north-west of the enemy's reported position, would be able to support the *Canton*, and ordered her at 0745 to make for a position in 5° N., 27° 30' W., to intercept the raider should she steer a north-westerly course, while the *Dorsetshire* steamed south-east at 24 knots to intercept her to the southward. He was unaware that the U.S. cruiser *Memphis* was near the position given by the *Olwen*.

Admiral Willis, not knowing that the *Dorsetshire* and *Canton* had parted company, ordered them at 0931 to search a sector to the southward of the enemy's reported position[70] and the *Dunedin*, *Queen Emma* and *Princess Beatrix* to search a sector to the south-eastward of it.

At 1500/5 November Admiral Willis informed the British ships that the U.S. cruiser *Memphis* and the U.S. destroyers *Davis* and *Jouett* had searched the position of the attack without result until 1900 April. He added that the U.S. cruiser *Omaha* and the U.S. destroyer *Somers* were searching for survivors before proceeding to a position in 5° S., 34° W. That evening, at 1800, he signalled that if nothing further were heard of the raider by dusk on 6 November the *Dorsetshire* and *Canton* were to search on a northerly course between 26° 30' W. and 30° W. to 2° N. The *Dorsetshire* would then return to Freetown, but the *Canton* would continue on patrol. The *Dunedin*, *Queen Emma* and *Princess Beatrix* were to search on a northerly course to 5° N. before returning to Freetown.

Next morning, 6 November, a new light was shed upon the situation. At 1030 the *Olwen* reported that the raider signal had been made when an unseen enemy, probably a submarine on the surface, had fired on her in the dawn light. At 1133 Admiral Willis informed the *Dorsetshire*, *Canton* and *Dunedin* that as the attack had certainly not been made by a raider they were to act forthwith on his signal of 1800/5 November. No fewer than ten British and American warships had searched for two days for a raider with no actual existence. The search, however, was not fruitless, for at 0845/6 November the *Omaha* and *Somers* captured the German supply ship *Odenwald* in 0° 35' N., 27° 45' W., and took her into an American port.[71]

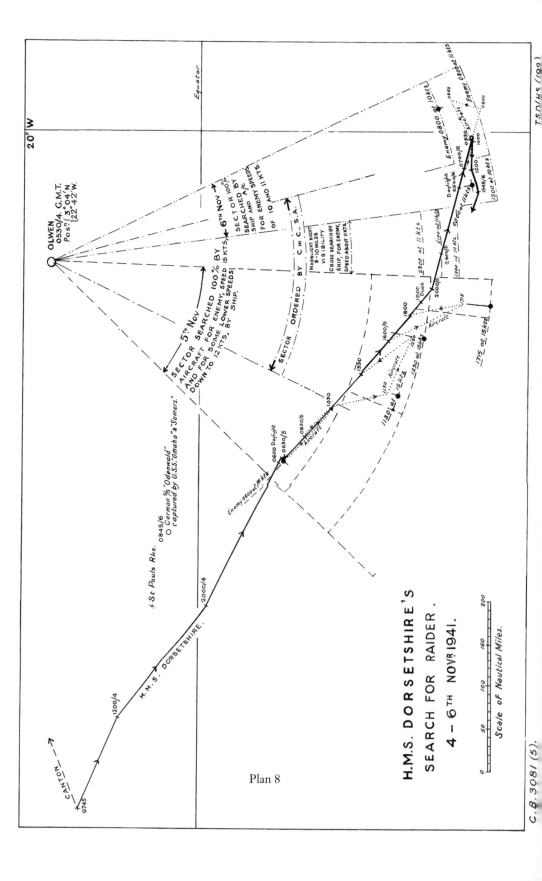

Plan 8

H.M.S. DORSETSHIRE'S
SEARCH FOR RAIDER.
4 - 6TH NOVR 1941.

Scale of Nautical Miles.

OLWEN
0530/4. G.M.T.
Posn 3°04'N.
(22°42'W.

Equator

20°W

CANTON

0745

1200/4

H.M.S. DORSETSHIRE.

1200/4

2000/4

⁑ St Pauls Rks. 0845/6
○ German S/S "Odenwald"
  captured by U.S.S. "Omaha" & "Somers".

5TH NOV
SECTOR SEARCHED 100% BY
AIRCRAFT FOR ENEMY, SPEED 15 KTS,
AND FOR SOME LOWER SPEEDS
DOWN TO 12 KTS, BY SHIP.

6TH NOV
SECTOR 100%
SEARCHED BY
SHIP AND A/C
FOR ENEMY SPEEDS
OF 10 AND 11 KTS.

SECTOR ORDERED BY C IN C.S.A.

Moonlight night
8-10 MILES
VISIBILITY
CROSS SEARCH BY
SHIP FOR ENEMY,
SPEED ABOUT 11 KTS.

0600 Daylight
0630/5
Enemy 0600 at 15 kts
Aircraft
0630/5
0750
1350
1150 Aircraft
1200/5 at 15 kts
1230 at 15 kts
Aircraft
1600/5
1800
1900 Dusk
2000/5
2300 at 11 kts
1200 at 10 kts
0400/6
0200 at 11 kts
1200 at 10 kts
Daylight
0530/6
0550/6
0700/6
0950 Aircraft
1000
1200
1545/6 at 11 kts
55-60 at 10 kts
1200 at 10 kts
Enemy 0800 at 10 kts
0800
0840
Enemy 0800 at 11 kts

1715
1715 at 15 kts

C.B. 3081 (5).

CB3081 (200)

Enemy Vessels Sighted But Not Engaged

On 13 March, 1942, at 1925,[72] HMS *Durban*, steaming 257°, on passage from Durban to Simonstown, at 13 knots with one engine broken down, sighted a ship in 33° 53' S., 20° E., steering east at 10 knots, 11 miles ahead, As the stranger would pass fairly close the cruiser maintained her own course and speed, and at a distance of 6 miles signalled NNJ[73], using a red Aldis lamp in the failing light. The absence of any reply being not unusual[74] the *Durban* then asked "What ship?" using a white Aldis lamp. The stranger replied that she was the *Levernbank*, bound from New York to Durban, and wished the cruiser good-night. Her silhouette corresponded to that of a Bank Line ship.

The weather was too rough for boarding, and the *Durban*, facing the familiar difficulty of identifying a ship in poor light without closing to a dangerously short range, allowed the stranger to proceed. There can be little doubt, however, that the unknown ship was the ex-British ship *Speybank*, captured by the Germans in January, 1941, and probably acting as an enemy minelaying raider.[75]

At 1130 the next day, 14 March, 1942, a bare sixteen hours after the *Durban* had allowed the spurious *Levernbank* to proceed unmolested, the armed merchant cruiser *Cheshire* was in 38° 11' S., 20° 10' E., 258 miles away to the southward, when she sighted an unknown vessel hull down. At 1150 she turned to intercept, and the stranger after momentarily altering course towards her turned away. This, being contrary to recognition procedure, was a suspicious manoeuvre. Half an hour later, however, the stranger passed the *Cheshire* on an opposite course only 3 miles away. To the *Cheshire*'s signal "What ship?" she replied that she was the *Inverbank*, bound from Montevideo to Melbourne, and convinced, from her appearance, that she was a genuine Bank Line vessel, the *Cheshire* allowed her to proceed without further question.

The real *Inverbank*, however, was on passage from Montevideo to Freetown. Though there is no proof that the vessel which falsely assumed her identity was an enemy raider, it seems possible that she was the false *Levernbank* which had deceived the *Durban* 258 miles away on the previous evening.[76] The Commander-in-Chief, South Atlantic, Vice-Admiral E. C. Tait, C.B., M.V.O., thought that it may have been providential that the *Cheshire* did not make the secret recognition signal. With a possible enemy raider within 7,000 yards, and with her own ship's company quite unprepared and not even at action stations, the result might easily have been the mysterious and regrettable disappearance with all hands of one of His Majesty's valuable armed merchant cruisers.[77]

Six weeks later, at 0843/26 April, 1942, a Seafox aircraft, patrolling from the armed merchant cruiser *Pretoria Castle*, sighted an unknown vessel in 1° 17' N., 24° 34' W., steering about 287° at 8 knots.

The Seafox had left the *Pretoria Castle* at 0645 to carry out a routine reconnaissance with orders to return at 0915. The observer was told that so far as was known no ships were in the area, but that he was to return immediately and report any suspicious vessel sighted.

When therefore the unknown steamer came into sight at 0843 he ordered the pilot to approach within half a mile and, circling round before coming down for a closer view, called her up on his Aldis lamp. She replied with identification flags GSLD, but he had no means of decoding them nor of discovering her identity. The Seafox made a thorough inspection at close range but saw nothing suspicious. The vessel was of about 5,000 tons, with one funnel, two slightly raked masts, samson posts on fore side of mainmast, one derrick hoisted aft, but no structure on the well decks. She had normal defensive armament, but apparently no A.A. guns. The only unusual features were roundels painted on the hatch covers. At 0910 the Seafox turned to rejoin the *Pretoria Castle*, 40 miles away.

When the *Pretoria Castle* failed to sight the aircraft by 0905 she called it up and learned that it expected to be back at 0940; but at that hour it was still out of sight. Ten minutes later, however, just as it sighted the ship, the aircraft, running out of petrol, was forced to alight, signalling as it came down "S.O.S. 270°. 5 miles." The *Pretoria Castle* closed, but the distance proved to be 12 and not 5 miles. The sea was choppy with a heavy swell. All attempts to pick the aircraft up failed, and it was not until 1210 that the observer could report the unknown ship which had hoisted identification letters GSLD. These belonged to the SS *Anglo-Canadian*, but this name was not on the *Pretoria Castle*'s shipping plot, and she decided to make a further inspection. The suspect's estimated mean line of advance was roughly parallel to her own course, and to get well ahead she held on at 16 knots until 1315 before turning to intercept. Though she anticipated that the suspect would be in sight by 1700, it had not been sighted half an hour later when she turned to 107° to cross the stranger's probable track. At 1745 she asked if the *Anglo-Canadian* were in the area only to be told that this ship had arrived at Bombay on 19 April. Further air reconnaissance was impossible as *Pretoria Castle*'s second aircraft was unserviceable, and although she continued to search till well after dark she saw nothing of the suspicious vessel.[78]

Appendix A[79]

HMS Alcantara – W/T Messages[80] Sent in Action on 28 July, 1940

IMPORTANT:– Commander-in-Chief, S.A., R.A.S.A.D., from *Alcantara*.

> HAVE SIGHTED SUSPICIOUS MERCHANT SHIP IN POSITION 024° 23' S., 032° 31' W., STEERING 040°. I AM CHASING AT MAXIMUM SPEED BUT NOT GAINING. 1328z/28.

(This message was broadcast at 1410 in Naval Cypher using reserved Block Call Sign.)

IMMEDIATE:– Commander-in-Chief, S.A., R.A.S.A.D., from *Alcantara*.

> MY 1328z. AM ENGAGING ENEMY ARMED MERCHANT SHIP. MY POSITION IS NOW 024° 03' S, 03 1° 58' W. 1500z/28.

(Broadcast at 1506z when main aerial was shot away during repetition. Message was then broadcast on auxiliary W/T at 1551z and at 1608z. Fleet Code.)

IMMEDIATE:– Commander-in-Chief, S.A., R.A.S.A.D., from *Alcantara*.

> MY 1500z. COURSE AND SPEED OF ENEMY 180°, 15 KNOTS. MY SPEED REDUCED TO 10 KNOTS, HOLED IN ENGINE ROOM. MY POSITION NOW 024° 10' S., 031° 50' W. 1555z/28. .

(Broadcast on auxiliary W/T 500 kcs., at 1642z and again at 1657z on main W/T using small broadcast aerial. Fleet Code.)

Appendix B[81]

Record of Courses Steered by HMS *Cornwall*

Time	Altered course to	Speed
7 May, 1941		
0625	340°	20 knots.
0756		24 knots.
0815	000°	25 knots.
1600	040°	23 knots.
1900	015°	23 knots.
2130	113°	16½ knots.
8 May 1941		
0330	143°	13 knots.
0600	090°	
0635		18 knots.
0820	258°	
0825	255°	20 knots.
0834		23 knots.
0838	252°	
1230	240°	
1245		26 knots.
1302		28 knots.
1609	250°	
1612	262°	
1619	295°	

1635		29 knots.
1637	240°	
1642	290°	
1651	285°	
1701	320°	
1713	290°	
1716	240°	
1717	260°	
1719	240°	
1722	220°	
1725	250°	
1727	Altered course towards wreckage.	

Appendix C[82]

Brief Description of the *Kormoran* and Her Cruise[83]

According to her survivors the German raider *Kormoran* was the German SS *Steiermark*, a vessel of 9,400 tons, with a maximum speed of 18 knots, reduced, at the time of her action with the *Sydney*, to 15 or 16 knots by a foul bottom. At this time she was disguised as the *Straat Malakka* with a black hull, black funnel, and buff superstructure, and was flying the Dutch flag. She had sailed as Raider No. 41 and received the name *Kormoran* at sea.

Her armament was not positively established but it appears to have been six 6-in. guns, six torpedo tubes, four on deck and two submerged, and two 3.7-cm. A.A. guns. She also carried a number of mines, probably about 200, and one aircraft which, being difficult to hoist out, was not often used. She carried a number of disguises such as a second funnel and additional masts but as she was built on Dutch lines and flew a Dutch flag which for general purposes provided sufficient disguise these, too, were not used.

She left Germany on 4 December, 1940, and steered along the Norwegian coast before passing between Iceland and Greenland and down the Atlantic where she sank the following ships:–

	Tons		1941
Antonis (Gr.)	3,729	3° S., 30° W.	13 January
British Union (Br.)	6,987	26° 36' N., 30° 15' W.	18 January
Afric Star (Br.)	11,900	8° N., 15° W.	28 January
Eurylochus (Br.)	5,723	8° 15' N., 25° 14' W.	29 January
Agnita (Br.)	3,552	4° N., 23° W.	23 March
Craftsman (Br.)	8,022	3° S., 21° W.	9 April
Nicolaos, D.L. (Gr.)	5,486	20° S., 22° W.	12 April

On 27 March she captured the tanker *Canadolite*, 11,309 tons, in 15° N., 33° W., and sent her into Bordeaux. She entered the Indian Ocean in May and proceeded to the Bay of Bengal where she sank two vessels on 26 June, 1941, the Yugo-Slav ship *Velebit*, 4,153 tons, and the British ship *Mareeba*, 3,472 tons, in 8° N., 88° E. Her last victim was the Greek SS *Stamatios G. Embirikos*, 3,941 tons, which she sank near the Maldive Islands. Including the *Canadolite* she accounted for 68,274 tons of shipping.

Appendix D[84]

Most Secret   **Message**   **1618A/16 December**

Date: 16 December, 1941.

From Admiralty.

Analysis of encounters with enemy merchant raiders by HMS *Cornwall* on 8 May, 1941, in the Indian Ocean; H.M.A.S *Sydney* off the West Australian coast on 19 November, 1941; and HMS *Devonshire* in the South Atlantic on 22 November, 1941, brings out following points:–

(A) Recognition:

(1) *Cornwall*'s raider reported herself as SS *Tamerlane*, who was not on the station.

(2) *Sydney*'s raider replied to a challenge that she was SS *Straat Malakka*, who had that day left Beira.

(3) *Devonshire*'s raider reported herself as SS *Polyphemus* then in New York.

Comment–

(4) Enemy raiders will always disguise themselves and use the appropriate name in any signal whether by an RRRR message on 500 k/cs or the reply to a challenge.

(5) In no case so far has the disguise adopted been such as should have deceived commanding officers had they trusted the negative intelligence that information of the ship's movements had not been reported to them.

(6) Positive information of British, Allied and U.S. merchantmen from Admiralty or Shipping Intelligence Officers is sufficiently

accurate, and positive information of neutral vessels by local War Trade Reporting Officers should be sufficiently accurate to enable commanding officers to be kept informed of the position of all non-enemy ships they may meet. Commanders-in-Chief should ensure that their information and plotting organisations can achieve this.

(B) Challenge procedure:

Merchant ship recognition procedure laid down in Recognition Manual and N.C.S.I. 371 does not appear to have been used. This is now only applicable to red ensign and some Dutch ships, but arrangements are in hand for its extension to U.S. and all Allied shipping.

(C) Tactics:

There is a possibility that commanding officers underestimate the offensive power of raiders. They should be warned that enemy raiders are often powerfully armed with guns and torpedoes and if fitted with modern R.D.F. may be able to open fire even at long range with great accuracy.

(D) U-Boats:

Commanding officers should be warned that all enemy vessels throughout the world may be accompanied by U-boats and that the merchant vessel's tactics will be designed to lead the British ship towards the U-Boat.

Notes on Plans

Plan 1

The *Alcantara*'s Action. 28 July, 1940

The diagram in the *Alcantara*'s report (M.018572/40) shows the *Alcantara*'s track, but not that of the raider. The report gives only the initial bearing of the enemy from the *Alcantara* and it has not been possible to produce a reliable track of his course. The raider's track in Plan 1, while conforming with all the available data, must therefore be regarded merely as a diagram of the enemy's probable movements.

Plans 2 and 3

The *Carnarvon Castle*'s Actions. 5 December 1940

M.02910/41. "HMS *Carnarvon Castle*, Report of Action with German Raider on 5 December, 1940," contains a diagram of tracks of the *Carnarvon Castle* and the raider. The diagram is not to scale and the enemy's track differs in many respects from the data in the text of the report. The raider's track has therefore been redrawn in Plan 2 to conform as far as possible with the available data, but as in Plan 1, it must be regarded merely as a diagram of the enemy's probable movements. The *Carnarvon Castle*'s diagram is reproduced in Plan 3.

Endnotes

1. Or about 7.3 per cent of the total shipping sunk.
2. 4s 195-197.
3. Grand Fleet Order, 24 August, 1915.
4. The *Alcantara*, 22,209 gross tons, 19 knots. Guns, eight 6-in., 14,000 yards range.
5. SS *Davisian*, 6,433 tons, sunk on 10 July in lat. 18° 20' N., long. 54° W., '447 miles N.E. of Barbado'; and M.V. *King John*, 5,228 tons, sunk on 13 July in about lat. 20° 45 N., long. 59° 43' W., "250 miles E.N.E. of Sombrero Channel." These are very approximate positions.
6. 1632 on 22 July.
7. Formerly Trinidada.
8. Between Rio de Janeiro and Santos.
9. About 600 miles east of Rio de Janeiro. See Plan 1.
10. M.018572/40. A full list of recommendations is in M.021171/40.
11. The *Alcantara* was subsequently rearmed with two 6-in. guns, range 18,500 yards, and six 6-in. guns, range 17,700 yards.
12. For signals sent by *Alcantara* during the action see Appendix A.
13. The *Carnarvon Castle*, 20,063 gross tons, 18 knots, guns, eight 6-in., 14,000 yards range.
14. It is not easy to follow the course of the action from the report, as few times are registered and the track chart attached to it is not to scale. See Plan 3 and Notes on Plans, page 211.
15. See Plan 2.
16. M.02910/41 and T.S.D.6133/41. It is now known that the enemy was Raider E (*Santa Cruz*).
17. The *Leander*, cruiser, 7,270 tons, 32.5 knots, guns, eight 6-in., eight 4-in. H.A.
18. Times are Z-5 ½.
19. By lamp and flags.
20. According to Captain Bevan's report in M.07842/41 she hoisted the Italian mercantile ensign, but according to C.-in-C., East Indies, in T.S.D.5459/41, page 10, she hoisted the Italian naval ensign.
21. That is at 1248Z-5 ½ 0718 G.M.T.
22. One died subsequently.
23. M.07842/41, the report of the destruction of the R.A.M.B.1, does not include a track chart and there are no data available for the construction of a plan.
24. See pages 197-199.
25. The *Voltaire* , 13,300 tons, 14.5 knots, guns, eight 6-in., 14,000 yards range.
26. T.S.D. 6136, War Diary, C.-in-C., South Atlantic, April, 1941. It is now known that HMS

Voltaire was sunk by Raider E (*Santa Cruz*), the raider engaged by the *Carnarvon Castle* on 5 December, 1940. According to repatriated prisoners of war, the enemy, which was small and very fast, opened fire at very long range. Her first salvo crippled the *Voltaire*, which sank after three hours' continuous shelling. A number of survivors were picked up by the raider. See W.I.R., Raider Supplements Nos 2 and 3 and N.I.D. 09133 April3.

27. The *Cornwall*, cruiser, 10,000 tons, 31.5 knots, guns, eight 8-in., eight 4-in. H.A.
28. Times are Zone-5.
29. According to *Cornwall*'s report (M.012944/41) "on receipt of the C.-in-C., East Indies, 0546Z July May." Note that 0546Z in C.-in-C.'s signal (Greenwich time) is 1046 in *Cornwall*'s time (Z-5), but according to *Cornwall*'s deck log the *Cornwall* increased to 24 knots at 0756 and to 25½ knots at 0815, more than two hours before the C.-in-C. made the signal. Time of receipt and text of signal are not given in M.012944/41 nor in T.S.D. 5465/41.
30. Plan 4.
31. In Appendix B.
32. Or possibly detected her by R.D.F. See Plan 4.
33. According to the *Cornwall*'s deck log the *Cornwall* opened fire at 1715. This does not agree with her reports in M.012944/41.
34. "A" and "B" turrets in quarters and "X" and "Y" in group control.
35. In 3° 27' N., 56° 38' E.
36. At 25 knots at least.
37. One engineer officer was fatally overcome by the heat. The failures in the engine-room were the subject of a board of enquiry.
38. 9 British, 15 Indian and 60 German survivors were rescued.
39. Owing to the shortage of Fleet Air Arm personnel the *Cornwall* had no qualified observer for her second aircraft.
40. In M.012944/41.
41. An Admiralty message re *Cornwall*'s action, dated 16 December, 1941, is in Appendix D.
42. The *Sydney*, Australian cruiser, 6,830 tons, 32½ knots, guns, eight 6-in., four 4-in. H.A.
43. In M.05540/42.
44. See Plan 5.
45. See Appendix C.
46. See pages 186-187.
47. This and all the times following are Z-7.
48. At 14 knots according to Sub-Lieutenant Bunjes.
49. NNJ means "You should make your signal letters."
50. 1700. Z-7.
51. See Plan 5. According to some of the witnesses the range was only 1,200 metres.
52. According to one witness the *Sydney*'s first salvo hit the *Kormoran* amidships.
53. The aircraft was warming up when the engagement began.
54. At about 5 knots.
55. For a brief description of the *Kormoran* and her cruiser, see Appendix C. An Admiralty message re *Sydney*'s action dated 16 December, 1941, is in Appendix D.

56. *Devonshire*, cruiser, 9,850 tons, 32 ¼ knots, guns, eight 8-in., eight 4-in. H.A.

57. Force 4.

58. According to *Devonshire*'s report the enemy abandoned ship, but she was subsequently reported to be proceeding at 15 knots. It is possible she may have been carrying ammunition supplies for submarines.

59. See Plan 6.

60. The *Dorsetshire*, cruiser, 9,975 tons, 32¼ knots, guns, eight 8-in. and eight 4-in. H.A.

61. Times are Z-1.

62. From *Dorsetshire*'s deck log.

63. See Plan 8.

64. From "B" turret.

65. At 1730. The order to fire was given at 1728.

66. The enemy had turned to starboard before stopping.

67. Approximate position, from track chart in M.0799/42.

68. Sunk by the *Devonshire*. See pages 201-203.

69. See Plan 8.

70. See Plan 8.

71. T.S.D. 6145/42, War Diary, C.-in.-C, South Atlantic, November, 1941, and M.019371/41 *Dorsetshire* and *Canton* R. of P., 2-9 November, 1941.

72. 1725 G.M.T.

73. "You should make your secret letters."

74. According to the *Durban* only 25 per cent. of merchant ships answer the NNJ signal correctly.

75. For details see N.L.11382/42.

76. If so she must have covered the distance at an average of 16 knots.

77. For details see N.L.9560/42.

78. For details see N.L.9557/42.

79. See pages 178-181.

80. None of these signals was received by the *Hawkins* which was a thousand miles away at the time.

81. See pages 190-196.

82. See pages 197-199.

83. M.05540/42.

84. See pages 190-202.

Admiral Sir Jonathon Band

Jonathon Band was appointed a GCB in the 2008 Queen's Birthday Honours and retired in July 2009, after an illustrious naval career and a prominent presence in world media.

His training began in 1967 at Britannia Royal Naval College, Dartmouth, with sea training in the Far East, before attending university in England. He served in junior officer appointments in the minesweeper HMS *Lewiston* and the Type 12 frigate HMS *Rothesay*. In the 1970s, during an exchange programme with the United States Navy, he served in the guided missile cruiser USS *Belknap*. Following warfare training, he served for two years as Principal Warfare Officer and Operations Officer onboard the Tribal class frigate HMS *Eskimo*.

In the early 1980s Band commanded the minesweeper HMS *Soberton* in the Fishery Protection Squadron and also served as Flag Lieutenant to Commander-in-Chief Fleet. Promoted to Commander, he commanded the *Leander* class frigate HMS *Phoebe* until 1985, when he attended the Joint Services Defence College and was then appointed to the MoD in the Directorate of Defence Policy. Promoted to Captain in 1988, he took command of the Type 23 (*Duke* class) frigate HMS *Norfolk*.

During the 1990s, he was Assistant Director Navy Plans and Programmes in the MoD, during the implementation of the Options for Change Review; then a member of the Defence Costs Study (Front Line First) Secretariat. His last sea command was of the aircraft carrier HMS *Illustrious* (1995–1997), which included two operational deployments to the Adriatic, where *Illustrious* supported intervention operations in Bosnia.

As Rear-Admiral, he returned to the MoD as Assistant Chief of Naval Staff during the period of the Strategic Defence Review. In 1999, he became Team Leader of the Defence Education and Training Study and in 2000 he was promoted to Vice-Admiral.

After a tour as Deputy Commander-in-Chief Fleet from May 2001, he served as Commander-in-Chief Fleet, August 2002 – November 2005, and was appointed a KCB in the 2002 New Year's Honours List.

Band became First Sea Lord and Chief of Naval Staff in 2006, leading the Royal Navy's involvement in planning the Iraq War. In early 2007, he threatened to resign if the British Government failed to finance two new aircraft carriers it had previously promised. By May, the Government had agreed.

In retirement, he is one of the Patrons of the International Scott Centenary Expedition (2012), commemorating Captain Scott's expedition to Antarctica in 1912 .

Dr G. H. Bennett

Dr G. H. Bennett is the author of over a dozen books covering military, diplomatic and maritime history. His works include: *Destination Normandy: Three American Regiments on D-Day; Hitler's Admirals; Survivors; British Merchant Seamen in the Second World War;* and *The RAF's French Foreign Legion: De Gaulle, the British and the Rebirth of French Airpower 1940–1945.* He has worked at Plymouth University since 1992, where he is an Associate Professor of History. Dr Bennett is a Trustee of The Britannia Museum, Britannia Royal Naval College, Dartmouth.